The patience of a S

St Helens Rugby League 1978 to

Kevin Ward battling forward for St Helens at Warrington

Mike Critchley

London League Publications Ltd

The patience of a Saint
St Helens Rugby League 1978 to 1996

A CIP catalogue record for this book is available from the British Library.

First published in Great Britain in May 2007 by:
London League Publications Ltd, P.O. Box 10441, London E14 8WR

ISBN: 978-1903659-32-8

Cover design by: Stephen McCarthy Graphic Design
                          46, Clarence Road, London N15 5BB

Layout: Peter Lush

Printed and bound by: Biddles Ltd
                          King's Lynn, Great Britain

Preface

The last 11 years of summer rugby league and full time professionalism have been good for St Helens. So much so that Saints fans of a certain age sometimes feel the need to pinch themselves to make sure what is happening is real and not a dream.

At the time of writing the Knowsley Road sideboard has all four available trophies – the Challenge Cup, Super League, League Leaders' Shield and the World Club Challenge trophy. Added to that players and coach won all the individual honours and the club was voted team of the year in BBC's Sports Personality of the Year awards. The Saints class of 2006-07 have won the lot.

How the times change. For a 20 year spell the club with one of the richest heritages in the XIII man code seemed to have lost their touch forever. Although the town could still produce talented rugby league footballers by the dozen in the 1980s, when it came down to it the team could not win trophies. Although they were never among the game's basket cases, Saints seemed destined to be the perennial bridesmaids as other clubs overtook them. Despite living in the shadows of the Hull FC and Hull KR, Widnes and then latterly and painfully Wigan, Saints supporters stayed patiently loyal, waiting for the tide to turn. This book is about that wait, littered with false dawns and heartache, which made us appreciate the good times when they arrived.

Introduction

It is impossible to grow up in St Helens without hearing about the rugby league greats of the 1950s and 1960s. The names Tom van Vollenhoven, Vinty Karalius, Alan Prescott and Alex Murphy have been etched permanently into the glass town's sporting folklore. Talk of Voll in particular was drummed into me as a child – how he would swerve, fend and race away down the wing leaving all and sundry clutching at thin air. I had heard it so many times off my mam and dad that I felt like sticking my fingers in my ears and shouting *'Jackanory, Jackanory!*

My mam showed me a tatty old black and white picture of the flying Springbok and it was hard to imagine that this thin faced, shaven headed bloke was the subject of such respect and adulation. Every winger the club has since had – no matter how good – has had to contend with 'He's no Vollenhoven,' from those lucky enough to see him play.

Rugby league went over my head and like the rest of my junior school classmates I was transfixed with the more simple game of football. Colour posters of Peter Lorimer and Allan 'Sniffer' Clarke ripped from *Shoot* adorned my bedroom wall.

Images of soccer were everywhere. My early years were spent collecting the miniature cards from packets of toffee cigarettes, loose tea and chewing gum. Soccer heroes like Geoff Hurst, Bobby Moore and Bobby Charlton were even displayed on the lids of Hartley's jam jars. For a month of Thursdays in 1973 I had my mam rooting though trays in *Krazy Kuts* to see if she could swap George Best and strawberry jam for Billy Bremner and damson.

The round ball game also seemed easier to play as all you needed was a ball, or something that resembled one, and a couple of jumpers or two old house bricks and then you could play anywhere. Rugby league was something you matured into, like listening to jazz and taking snuff, and was something old people talked about in Wilf Young's newsagents in Dentons Green.

Maybe all this is just an attempt to justify why it took me 11 years to make my way to the Knowsley Road home of the Saints, missing out on the chance to see the side win Championships, Premierships and the Challenge Cup as I hesitated.

Mike Critchley
St Helens, April 2007

About the author

Mike Critchley has been a Saints fan since 1978 – spending his early days in the paddock before moving to the Popular Side on a free transfer.

His current job as *St Helens Star* sports editor means he now watches most games from the press box, although he can still be seen sneaking up onto the 'Scaff' for the odd game, especially when Wigan are in town.

Mike spent 12 years exiled in Birmingham, where he worked as a reporter on the *MetroNews* and the *Evening Mail* before heading 'home' in 2001.

This is his second book, having assisted in the writing of Chris Joynt's autobiography *The Quiet Man*. He used to write and edit a retro fanzine *Off the Ball*, which took a nostalgic look at Saints of yesteryear.

Mike is 40 and was born and brought up in Dentons Green, St Helens. He lives with his wife Kate (the best thing to come out of Widnes) and beautiful daughter Rosa.

Acknowledgements

The bulk of this book has been hanging around on floppy discs and bits of paper for over ten years so I am grateful to Peter Lush and Dave Farrar at London League Publications Ltd for letting it see the light of day. When it was first written it was done largely from memory, assisted by my scrawl in old programmes and cuttings from the *Post and Chronicle*, *St Helens Star* and the *St Helens Reporter*. Facts have subsequently been checked by logging onto to the fabulous Saints Heritage website – www.org.saints.uk or through additional research in the local history section of St Helens Central library.

I would like to thank everyone who has assisted in writing this book – especially Paul Pritchard, for reading it before anyone else, Michael O'Hare for his subediting, Steve McCarthy for designing the cover, Paul Devanney, Dave Davies, Ant Morgan, Andrew Quirke, Kev and Mick Gill, Andy Colquitt, George Hotel licensee Alan Turner and the staff of Biddles Ltd for printing it.

I am especially grateful to photographers Bernard Platt and Brian Peers for the many outstanding pictures they have kindly allowed me to use in this book.

I would also like to thank my wife Kate for her constant support throughout this project and over the past 13 years and also pay tribute to my mam, who passed away in March 2006. When I was a kid my mam always came up with the 'spend' to pay for my coach fare to away games, usually packing me away with the words – 'don't let any big lads lay on you'. Even though she had not set foot in Knowsley Road since the early 1960s, she still wrote the Saints score in her diary every week without fail.

The opinions expressed in this book are entirely my own and do not in any way reflect the views of the club, my current employers or anyone else who has assisted with the production if this title.

Mike Critchley
St Helens, April 2007

Photo credits: Unless otherwise stated, the photographs are by Bernard Platt and Brian Peers and are credited Platt and Peers respectively. Any photographs without a photographer's credit are courtesy the *St Helens Star*, and we would like to thank them for their support.

Contents

Paul Newlove scoring against Halifax. (Platt)

Chris Joynt in action against London in 1996. (Platt)

1. 1978 Thank you, Derek Noonan

St Helens 12 Leeds 14, 13 May 1978
Challenge Cup Final, Wembley

My school class had spent the week prior to the big game making red and white rosettes. In those days Cup final day was a more inclusive affair and shops all over town decked out their windows in red and white. Even if they hated rugby the store owners knew which side their bread was buttered. Many more armchair fans from the competing finalists made the trek to London in the 1970s and 1980s than today, with shops, factories, clubs and pubs organising coaches for the big day.

In an era before replica shirts and heavy club merchandising became the order of the day, women's clothes shops would do a roaring trade in white and red clobber - dresses, hats and headscarves. There was more DIY involved with Wembley banners and day out garb. A gang of lads from Dentons Green took the red and white theme to the limit of taste that year by going all the way to the capital dressed in bloodied butchers' aprons.

Anybody from St Helens not in London was sitting in front of the telly that afternoon. I did not watch the first half, opting to mow my nan's overgrown back lawn instead. But the cheers and screams coming from the armchair fans inside told me things were going well for the Saints.

Hooker Graham Liptrot had touched down Harry Pinner's up-and-under to grab the opener and then Bill Francis side-stepped through for the second to give Saints a ten-point lead after only 12 minutes.

I came in to watch the rest of the game after the siren had gone. This was not the half-time hooter, but the wailing sound that used to go off inside the grounds of Rainhill Hospital - one of Europe's biggest psychiatric hospitals at the time. Rainhill bordered my nan's house and rightly or wrongly I had heard a thousand and one horror stories about the place, which always made me pass by t' sylum wall to Nutgrove with trepidation. As a toddler I was told that haunting sound meant "a patient has escaped!" It was nonsense, but it still quickly sent me inside my nan's home.

For the second half I parked myself in the worst seat in the house and pretended to look annoyingly disinterested. Leeds had edged their way back into the match with a try midway through the first half. Their opening score came from John Atkinson via a Les Dyl pass that the entire room had balled "for-ward" at. A David Ward drop-goal and tries from winger David Smith and barnstorming Phil Cookson levelled it eight minutes from time. That was when the nerves set in among those people of all ages sitting in that living room – and probably every lounge across the borough from Blackbrook to Billinge, and Rainford Road to Ramford Street. I didn't understand rugby – but everyone in the room was calling for fresh legs because the Yorkshire side were now running rampant. Despite the advice of countless armchair coaches, both Saints substitutes stayed on the bench. Two well-executed drop-goals – one by John Holmes and another by their young, balding captain Ward put Leeds ahead for the first time.

But there was to be one final twist and a split second moment that would be added to the Saints folklore forever. As the game entered the closing stages Saints pounded the Leeds line and Peter Glynn squeezed a pass out to lanky centre Derek Noonan.

It was Saints' last chance, but with the try line only a yard or two away the ball flapped off the hands of the unfortunate Noonan and hit the deck. The loud groans from the 35,000 fans packed into the Saints end of the Empire Stadium were echoed by those emanating from living rooms across St Helens.

Although the hapless three-quarter did not drop the ball on purpose - and was not even guaranteed to get past the two robust defenders on the line had he taken the pass – it didn't stop him being referred to as "that bloody Noonan" for the rest of the summer by exasperated fans.

Despite there being no cup to parade, townsfolk still turned out in their thousands to welcome the players on their open top bus journey which went from town up Dentons Green Lane and then back down Greenfield Road. There was a really good-natured feeling of solidarity among the fans which I had not witnessed through the years of bragging when Saints were bringing home the silverware. Perhaps that is what made me want to dip my toe in and try the halo for size.

Wales 13 England 60, 28 May 1978
European Championship, Knowsley Road

St Helens was still buzzing from the aftermath of the Wembley final and this international gave fans one last chance of rugby before the long summer kicked in.

The European Championship was an odd little competition – on a par with football's Home Internationals and this game had been carried over from earlier in the year when snow had forced the original game at Swansea to be called off.

It was a fine Spring Bank Holiday weekend and a large shirt-sleeved crowd swarmed over the Black Bull car park, past the hot dog, rosette and programme sellers. The last shop before the ground at the foot of the brew on Dunriding Lane was doing a roaring trade with toffees and sweets already bagged up in quarters – dolly mixtures and midget gems for the kids whose eyes were bigger than their bellies, and mint imperials and Uncle Joe's Mintballs for their dads and granddads.

A God botherer at the front entrance of the training ground brandished a bold black and white placard declaring: "Be sure your sins will find you out!" He was not a fire and brimstone preacher, just an innocuous old bloke with thin silvery hair and thick-rimmed glasses, the kind of man you would imagine having a bit part in Coronation Street as Emily Bishop's platonic acquaintance. He would be there every week, denouncing all passing fans as sinners for watching sport on the Lord's Day.

I knew little about the game, the positions and rules, but was told "the forwards are fat and the backs are quick and skinny." That was my first lesson on positional play!

Although Wales contained plenty of old heads in their ranks, and had beaten France earlier on in the competition, they were simply too slow and were run off the park with England rattling in 60 points. In the Welsh side you couldn't mistake the hulking figure of Jim Mills – a bloke who filled his red jersey to bursting point naturally without needing to be pumped up by daily weights sessions like the modern players. Everybody had heard of Big Jim, primarily for his reputation as a tough guy and he had notoriously been banned from playing in New Zealand three years previously for trampling over Kiwi forward John Greengrass in a World Championship game.

These rugby players like Mick Harrison, George Nicholls and Paul Rose seemed a different breed to the soccer stars I had been idolising for years. It sounds stupid but they looked older, rougher, and bigger and made Scottish centre-half Gordon McQueen, with his Harmony Hair sprayed blond mop, and his Leeds United team-mates look like a bunch of Mary Ellens.

I took the programme home with me – spending time studying it, learning the positions, the numbers and the players who played there. That one little booklet became my study manual for the summer – but I still kept half an eye on the football World Cup in Argentina. England had failed to qualify for the second successive time, so Scotland – who were, in the words of the song, "on the march with Ally's army" - carried the hopes of the home nations. They returned home with their tails between their legs after humiliation at the hands of minnows Peru and Iran.

Like most kids I still preferred playing sport to watching it, and most of summer was spent playing cricket, soccer and rugby in Ruskin Drive with my mates, invariably getting chased off by Sam the parky. It is not all sport – bung-off, ball tick, hunter and sardines were still the games to play in a summer that had the music from *Grease* as its mainstream soundtrack and punk and new wave as the undertone.

Ruskin Drive was also the venue for the annual Pilkington Brothers' gala, which attracted thousands of people from all over the country. There were floats, marquees, sports events and the crowning of the Gala queen. The big tents were great for sliding down at night – but once again we had to avoid Sam's clutches.

Geoff Pimblett, Graham Liptrot, Harry Pinner and Mick Hope in action in 1978

Wembley 1978: Bill Francis celebrates scoring Saints' second try

2. 1978-79 Trying the halo for size

St Helens 16 Leeds 11, 23 September 1978
John Player Trophy, Round One

Even though I was told I would "see more on telly", I had already got it into my head that the Challenge Cup Final rematch would be my first ever Saints game. BBC TV's *Grandstand* showed the second half live and televised games traditionally attracted lower crowds. But for kids, the game being on telly was another reason for going because there was always that chance you could get your mug broadcast to the nation.

And anyway it was less a view of the action that I wanted – more the event, the atmosphere and the laugh with my mates. After seeing just one match live you soon realise that televised sport is like watching the game with a box on your head. The other bonus was you didn't have to put up with the inane warbling of commentator Eddie Waring.

Although Waring was a likeable and knowledgeable bloke, his portrayal of the sport kept rugby league's image in the dark ages. It suited the Beeb's old school tie brigade down to the ground to have him as the game's jocular figurehead, especially as he also co-hosted *It's a Knockout*. An in addition every Saturday night 18 million viewers would watch impressionist Mike Yarwood lampoon Waring's "early bath" and "oop and unda-rr" catchphrases and contorted vowels – with our game mocked by association.

It was a good match to pick and Leeds' pack, fronted by Steve Pitchford and Phil 'Blond Bomber' Cookson, meted out plenty of punishment. But Saints's forwards, brilliantly led by George Nicholls, were able to deal with that and we won 16-11.

It was hard to believe that a bloke shaped like Pitchford was capable of walking 100 yards, let alone run around for 80 minutes. He looked like an old-school darts player, or a professional wrestler, but he was hard to get hold of and had a fitness level that defied his appearance. Even the Australians, who had dubbed him the 'Bionic Barrel', found him almost impossible to stop during the previous year's World Championship. He was like that old toy – a Weeble that wobbled but wouldn't fall down.

The following week we thrashed Castleford 48-14, with our new signing John Knighton from Salford being given the man-of-the-match award despite only playing half a game. Saints were an ageing side and still contained many of the 'Dad's Army' cup winning side of 1976. Recruiting Knighton, who already had a few greying hairs, hardly represented an injection of youth. I was not that bothered though – the Saints bug had bitten me, and that was it.

St Helens 27 Leigh 20, 3 November 1978
Division 1

Friday night games were a rarity and this one had been switched because Great Britain were playing the Australians in the second Ashes test that Sunday. Although evening kick-offs usually knocked a few hundred off the crowd, there was something strangely appealing about them. They were petty, little things like seeing the brightness radiating from the Knowsley Road floodlight pylons illuminating the night sky and indicating to those within a mile radius that there was a game on. Walking up Rivington Road and seeing the crowd flock to the lights in the distance was like witnessing the townsfolk being called to prayer.

There were other little atmospheric things. On cold, damp nights you could see the contrast as the body heat of the players clashed with the cold night air. The steam that billowed out of the scrums when the sweaty bodies met gave rise to the old nickname of 'steam pigs' as it resembled the way iron ingots or 'pigs' reacted as they were sprayed down after coming out of the furnace. And the Wintergreen and Ralgex odours that escaped from the dressing room seem to hang that much heavier in the tunnel area on cold, damp, winter nights, almost catching the back of your throat if you inhaled sharply.

Saints beat a mediocre Leigh team 27-20 in a match that saw young Chris Arkwright score his first points in senior rugby and Les Jones, who was at the other end of the age spectrum, cross for a hat trick. The latter, known as 'Jonah' was another unlikely looking character – bald with clumps of curly red hair he looked a little bit like a circus clown. There was nothing comical about his playing ability though, the veteran wingman was a lethal finisher and regularly found his way to the top end of the try-scoring charts year-on-year throughout the 1970s.

The biggest talking point of the game was a fight in which a Saints player retaliated by booting Leigh's prop Jimmy Fiddler right up the arse. The game was rough enough in the 1970s without the benefit of cameras and video referees in the stand - and you had the lot flying in - fists, elbows, stiff arms and head butts. Kicking, however, was really frowned upon because in the hard-knocks code of honour it was almost like cheating at being tough. The old blokes around me were appalled.

There were already enough tough guys in town as it was and you used to see plenty of them knocking about when taking short cuts home from Saints through St Teresa's cemetery and past Queen's Park. That was the down side of an evening game – getting home without coming across a group of 'big kids' that might be lurking down an alleyway – punks, skins, glueys or members of the Reccy Park Boot Boys. The graffiti on the side of Boundary Road baths told us that this is where the RPBB hung out. Did the infamous gang really exist? As a young kid it was hard to distinguish between fact and urban myth – people also talked back then about the Galosher Man, Rainford Liz and Gonk, just in the same way they will no doubt talk about other characters in the future. Gonk – to use the derogatory name – was a young man afflicted with learning difficulties who looked different because of his ill-fitting clothes and long neck. Unfortunately when he regularly waited for his bus at Greenfield Road, hysterical kids would scream at him and make up stories of the night he chased them. It was sad for the poor lad, who the authorities tried to keep in society rather than plonk into Rainhill.

With hindsight there was nothing wrong with punks – and had I been born six years earlier I would have been there, po-going, if not gobbing, with the best of them. In 1978 the punk rock movement was probably dying off in London, but it was still going strong in St Helens. They had daubed some fascinating graffiti over the walls at the back of Krazy Kuts and down by the disused railway cutting that ran from the side of Saints' ground through to Boundary Road. The 'artwork' there was so much more interesting than our 1970s versions of tag artists Jedder and Mick & Boo, who penned, painted and plastered their names all over town.

Although the punks were harmless enough, the sight of them sitting round in a circle among the old gravestones in the then overgrown St Teresa's cemetery, sniffing glue, used to petrify me.

My RE teacher - an armchair sociologist, St Vincent de Paul helper and *Play for Today* watcher - told me that St Helens' glue-sniffing problem was second worst in the country after Glasgow. The evidence came in the discarded, shrivelled-up bags and empty tins of glue you would find in the bushes of any park you cared to go in. One lad I knew got hooked on glue to the extent that getting high was his only motivation and led him to spend his days lurking in the bushes at Ruskin. It was a sorry, sad demise from there and he ended up living in the toilets at the bottom of Kiln Lane. Older people in the town tried to make sense of the 'glueys' and the punks with their baggy ripped jumpers, tartan kecks, safety pins and razor blades.

Increasingly you would hear the old folks imploring the authorities to "get a grip" and "bring back national service!" as the answer to all the country's ills. They applied the same prescription to the denim wearing, long-haired lads or 'gimps' who were into heavy rock bands like Led Zeppelin, Yes and Black Sabbath and knocked about around rockers club Geraldo's in town.

St Helens 4 Australia 26, 12 November 1978
Tour match

There was one thing our game had that soccer didn't – tour matches. Saints tackling the Australians was the equivalent of Liverpool playing Brazil at Anfield. Unfortunately my first sight of the Green and Gold machine was disappointing. I hadn't even gone to marvel at the Australians – because Saints had a good record against the tourists I naively thought we were going to beat them.

The rain lashed down, and was so bad at one stage that referee Mick Naughton considered calling it off. It would have been a blessing because the rampant Australians coasted to a 26-4 triumph. This was a shock, particularly as the match programme made a big thing of Saints' magnificent post-war record against the tourists, winning seven of the previous 11 matches. The Kangaroos took no prisoners, possibly because they were a bit sore about the previous week's loss to Great Britain which had levelled the test series at one each.

Even then you could see the Australians did things that were different – such as when their bulky full-back Graham Eadie kicked for goal, deliberately floating it well wide to allow half back Alan Thompson to leap like a salmon to pluck the ball out of thin air to score. Now our Bill Francis was a very skilful player – but he could never 'leap like a salmon'.

Two Geoff Pimblett goals were Saints' only scores, which meant the 16,531 crowd trudged home to bad Sunday evening television, wet and disappointed.

The tourists rampaged through Britain that year with only Widnes and Warrington getting in their way. The deciding test was embarrassing, with the tourists triumphing over a British side whose front row line up of Jim Mills, Tony Fisher and Vince Farrar totted up a century in years and was so long in the tooth it was dubbed Dad's Army.

Things were to get worse for Saints too, with unthinkable defeats against Rochdale Hornets and Huddersfield who were two quite ordinary sides that were in the relegation zone.

Sundays were bad enough without having to put up with these sorts of debacles. It was traditionally the dullest day of the week, probably for religious reasons. Sunday television was dire – especially if you were aged under 40. With *Sing Something Simple* on the radio, *Stars on Sunday*, *The Golden Shot* and *Sunday Night at the London*

Palladium on the box, it seemed to be part a conspiracy by the bosses and teachers to make going to school or work the next day more palatable. Even the first few bars of the theme tune from *The Onedin Line* was enough to send me into fits of depression as it invariably meant I had to go for a bath and then let my mam squeeze my blackheads ready for school the next day.

St Helens 7 Widnes 13, 12 December 1978
BBC2 Floodlit Trophy Final

The BBC2 Floodlit Trophy was an odd little competition tucked away on a Tuesday night in the first three months of the season. It was open to all clubs with floodlights and televised games were shown on BBC2 with the second half basis until it changed to a highlights package for its last couple of seasons.

Despite home advantage, Saints lost the final – my first - to a classy Widnes side. It had been a tight game and we were in with a shout until a late try by Chemics winger Stuart Wright put it beyond doubt. It was probably a better game than I appreciated at the time – only the daft things stick out for me, like jumping off the wall to celebrate Roy Mathias's try. I did not realise that the referee had already blown for a forward pass because I was not au fait with the man in the middle's signals in those early days.

I spent half the game distracted by the small pockets of crowd trouble at the Eddington End where the rival gangs of teenagers were doing their best to replicate Manchester United's Stretford End on the terraces. There was very little in the way of actual fighting, more the Saints kids chasing a bunch of ragged-looking bomber-jacket wearing Widnesians out of 'their' section. It was amazing how much noise three or four lads in their bovver boots kicking the corrugated sheets at the back of the Eddington End could make.

It was quite comical really – especially seeing one rather fat special copper trying to restore some sort of order by taking out his wooden nightstick, his big red cheeks huffing and puffing.

The BBC had erected a makeshift podium in the paddock for Widnes skipper Reg Bowden to climb and collect the rugby-ball shaped cup – but I left the ground as soon as the hooter went. There was nothing much to stick around for really in those days, only winners did laps of honour then and the Chemics did them regularly.

Widnes were the top dogs at the time – they had already won the Lancashire Cup that year and their pack combined the strength of Jim Mills, Brian Hogan and Glyn Shaw with the guile of Mick Adams and player-coach Doug Laughton. In the middle the diminutive Keith Elwell, who looked more like a jockey than a rugby player, was at the heart of everything.

The back line boasted bags of talent - Mick George, Mal Aspey, Stuart Wright and Eric Hughes were now joined by Mick Burke, already turning into a points machine since his signing from Waterloo RUFC. His success at Widnes galled many in St Helens, as they felt that Saints should have offered this former Cowley School lad a decent contract. He scored a try in the final to underline that point. Saints were once the club players wanted to play for – now they went elsewhere. Times had changed – Widnes had well and truly displaced us as the force on the west side of the Pennines. The Chemics went on to make it a four-trophy haul, adding the Challenge Cup and the John Player Trophy to their cabinet to earn the nickname of 'Cup Kings.'

St Helens 7 Wakefield 9, 7 April 1979
Challenge Cup Semi-Final, Headingley

Much of the December to February programme had been decimated by bad weather, leading to a massive fixture backlog that would only be resolved in May. That spell is now famed in political history as 'The Winter of Discontent' on account of the strikes by low-paid public-sector workers, unhappy with further attempts at pay restraint by Jim Callaghan's Labour government. The television news and papers painted a lurid picture of rats feeding off the uncollected rubbish that was piling up on the streets and told of schools being closed due to lack of heating. It had all been brewing for a while, and that too, for good or ill, would only be resolved in May's General Election.

It seemed that even staunch Labour folk were muttering it was time for a change – but at the time I didn't really understand it.

Understandably I couldn't figure out the politics, but nor did I understand the discontent in the Saints' ranks where long serving full-back and club captain Geoff Pimblett retired when he was dropped for the cup semi-final with Wakefield. Pimblett, who was the first player to win both the Lance Todd and Harry Sunderland award, had been a constant presence during the 1970s – then suddenly he was no longer there.

Despite a dismal post-war record of seven successive defeats in the spring, Saints were only 80 minutes away from a return to Wembley, which would have been that season's salvation. After narrowly beating Rochdale and Castleford on their travels in the early rounds, Saints' passage to the Cup Final seemed as good as booked after leading Wakefield 7-6 with only a few minutes left.

All Saints had to do was 'stick the ball up their jumpers' and we were walking down Wembley Way. We had possession deep in Trinity's half when Eric Chisnall went for broke, but his pass wide was intercepted by nippy half-back David Topliss and the next minute mop-headed Andrew Fletcher was racing to the line to dash our hopes.

Our season petered out with a series of quite pointless games – with the backlog caused by the weather and our cup run meaning Saints' fixtures stretched out until the middle of May. Hull Kingston Rovers had won the Championship, which was another indication that Humberside was emerging as the new power base in rugby league. If further evidence was needed both they and Second Division champions Hull were attracting massive crowds which were at least double all other club averages.

Saints actually beat the champions-elect Rovers 14-5 that May despite having prop Dave Chisnall sent off in the first half for giving veteran winger Clive Sullivan a knuckle butty. Chissy and Sully were chalk and cheese really. Sullivan was highly respected in the game having been awarded an MBE after captaining Great Britain to the World Cup in 1972. Chissy, on the other hand, played the rogue and you just couldn't picture him having tea with the Queen. Yet he remained a real character and was an excellent scrummager in an era when a prop forward's ability to pull and push his opposite number about was essential to getting a good supply of ball. And, as everyone is aware, you can't play without the ball. Chissy was also deceptively quick for a big man and startled many a defence with his turn of pace. However, he was still loathed by some for his job as a spoiler and niggler. If a skirmish started, you could always see Big Dave in the middle of it once the dust settled, wagging his finger like wrestler Mick McManus as the referee and touch judges pulled the players apart.

Our victory was remarkable not simply because of our numerical disadvantage, but because we were also playing with two trialists or 'A. N. Others', as they were listed in the match programme. They had to use that moniker, because had their identity become known they would have been automatically barred from 'amateur' rugby union for playing rugby league aged over 18. The fact that they were not paid because it was merely a trial on their part was immaterial; playing alongside league men was a sufficient crime for rugby union's hierarchy. One of the trialists was a winger, the other turned out to be Welsh second-row Chris Seldon who signed professional forms a week later for the Saints.

By bringing in Seldon, Saints were trying to alter the age profile of their pack by sticking to a successful formula. In Wales we had mined a rich seam in the past with Kel Coslett, Roy Mathias, John Mantle and Mel James all proving their worth in the red V since heading north. Although Seldon could be bit of a rough handful – and had been told to spice it up on the pitch - he did not really settle and after about a season he returned to South Wales.

Four days before the Rovers game, Britain elected a new Prime Minister in Margaret Thatcher. She had been booed mercilessly when Leader of the Opposition she had been announced as guest of honour at the 1976 Challenge Cup final.

3. 1979-80 Not as bad as Wigan

St Helens 16 Widnes 28, 19 August 1979
Lancashire Cup, Round 1

The highlight of an otherwise eventless summer was buying a season ticket for the first time. Apart from that I spent three days at Sherdley Show when it 'used to be good.' I suppose it is a matter of opinion, but there always seemed to be a lot more than just a fairground at the big, free show. We spent most of our time in front of the Radio City stand, which was by far and away the most popular radio station in town at the time. One of its most popular presenters was Norman Thomas, a Saints fan, who was living in Dentons Green at the time. He would always give Saints some encouragement over the airwaves, although it was probably lost on the football-loving Liverpudlians who made up most of his audience.

At the stand you could get up and make a request – and one lad, boldly predicted that Saints were going to smash Widnes in the Lancashire Cup – the game that would end the summer rugby drought. It was easier said than done for a side that was in transition.

Filling the boots of popular full-back and skipper Geoff Pimblett was always going to be a difficult task for Saints' board. Once again they looked to rugby union, signing the relatively unknown Llanelli full-back Clive Griffiths who was pitched in at the deep end for the first game of the season.

Matches did not get much tougher than a cup game against Widnes and a big derby crowd had turned up to see our new star signing, who we expected to be a young JPR Williams.

It was a real baptism of fire for the quiet Welshman – who was out of his depth in the most exposed position on the park and was turned inside out on the way to the line by a procession of Widnes backs. It was not Griffiths' fault because there were plenty of holes appearing in the middle before they got to the last line of defence.

St Helens 17 Warrington 23, 2 September 1979
Division 1

Warrington fans had a bad reputation and the violence that took place on the opening day of the league season was horrendous. 'Wires die!' had been daubed on the wall outside the ground and fighting erupted just as the minutes silence got underway for Lord Mountbatten, who had been killed by the IRA earlier that week. The hush of the crowd was shattered after only 10 seconds with a yell of "F... off, granddad" then all you could hear were more chants, running and the sound of boots impacting on bony backsides. It was awful, those who did not want to get caught up in it got out of the way. I stayed to watch, keeping one eye on the game and the other on this army of yobs who had invaded our comfortable world.

The running battles continued for a while and the police eventually put a column between the two warring factions and bundled the worst culprits down the overgrown steps at the back of the Eddington End. It was shocking to see it first hand – it was like something you would read about in the papers. Football hooliganism was quite bad in Britain at the time. The violence seemed a million miles away from the gang chants like

11

'A-G, A-G-R, A-G-R-O, AGGRO!' that you would hear on television's *Match of the Day* in the mid-1970s and then imitate in the school playground.

The fighting must have been contagious – on the field Warrington's stand-off Ken Kelly was sent off following a punch-up. Despite having only 12 men Warrington won with Welsh wing John Bevan storming over for four tries, each one greeted with his famous outstretched fist-in-the-air salute.

It was a miserable day to mark my first game as a season ticket holder. And to cap it all for Saints, our much-heralded new signing Griffiths broke his arm early in the second half. Things got worse before they got any better with Saints losing their opening four league games. The newspapers were full of crisis talk, and it was obvious the club needed to spend some cash on proven talent rather than gambling on union players because our star-studded team of the mid 1970s was ageing as one. Although talented young backs like Chris Arkwright, Neil Holding and Brian Parkes were establishing themselves in the first team, the squad lacked quality forwards on the right side of 30. We had made the mistake of selling big, aggressive prop Neil Courtney, who seemed to be one for the future, to Warrington.

Looking at those who remained, it was sad to see players who had given their all for Saints now being played into the ground, their best days long behind them. We could have coped with one or two – but Saints had half a dozen. It was exactly how Leeds United had declined in the latter part of the 1970s. It was difficult to know what was stopping Saints from moving on – perhaps it was loyalty, lack of money to bring in better players or the thought that each of those older players still had some 'big games' in them.

Coach Eric Ashton pleaded for time and there was movement on the transfer front. Out went 'stay away' centre Eddie Cunningham to Leeds for a record fee of £30,000 and in came tall Cumbrian second row forward Peter Gorley from Workington Town for £22,500.

The 'stay away' syndrome was prevalent in rugby league at the time. Generally speaking it seemed to work like this: If a player wished to leave or wanted more money, or a backhander, he would first request a transfer. If the club wanted to keep him they would put a prohibitively high asking price on the player. If he really wanted out and could not be cajoled back, he would stop training and playing, and threaten retirement in an attempt to force his club to release him. It became a battle of wills between the player and the club, who wanted the maximum price if they were forced to part.

St Helens 51 Workington Town 0, 23 December 1979
Division 1

Big Welsh winger Roy Mathias was my first idol because of the way he aggressively hit the ball and bashed his way over the try line. Being on the flank meant he was also the closest player to the pitch wall.

Mathias was more than just a phenomenal try scorer, he did the physical stuff as well and seemed afraid of nothing. His nose had been broken many times, usually after taking a switch crash ball into thick defence, and it was plastered across his face. Slasher, as he was known, was another product of that oval-ball hotbed of Llanelli. A former Welsh rugby union international flanker he switched to the wings when he turned professional in 1973, immediately becoming a prolific scorer.

Slasher was going well again in 1979 and two days before Christmas, he gave fans an early present of an incredible five tries against an abnormally subdued Workington Town side. Workington were one of those sides that was always there or thereabouts, an underrated constant, just like the toffee pennies that you find left over in a tin of Quality Street chocolates at Christmas. But they were off their game against us and Saints rattled in 51 points without reply, with Clive Griffiths slotting over a touchline conversion to take us past the half-century mark late in the game.

I giddily ran home to tell my dad about Mathias's scoring feat, only to be told that "Voll had twice scored six tries!" So too had Steve Llewellyn, but I had probably already stopped listening before Frank Myler's name was mentioned.

Pacy back Peter Glynn, who had an uncanny ability to ghost into space, also grabbed a hat trick. He was another favourite, even if he did look like one of the blokes from Cockney singing duo Chas 'n' Dave.

Three days later Saints beat Wigan at Central Park, which seemed to be only a minor detail in that season. Wigan were dormant as a rugby league power and were a side that had been well and truly on the slide for a decade. For newer fans, lacking a proper historical perspective, beating them didn't really mean that much then.

It was good to see Griffiths finding some form with the boot. He had been getting quite a hard time since his switch north. One of the sources of aggravation in town was his reported fee of £26,000 – what his deal was potentially worth – which caused envy and a degree of resentment in the eyes of some supporters in a town that was beginning to feel the full force of the recession. As we crept into the 1980s, unemployment was rocketing across the country with industrial towns like St Helens being hit badly.

It was utterly grim for those souls being chucked onto the dole queue, but also for those who were left nervously looking over their shoulders. Early on, the lengthening dole queue was seen as a blip by those cushioned from it – and one television comedian at the time joked "everyone wears jeans now, but nobody wants to work!"

I didn't take anything about economics on board - and like most kids I just expected food on the table, presents at Christmas and 50p to spend on a weekend to see Saints. The first few weeks back at school after Christmas would always see giddy kids setting the stop watches on the new-fangled-red-lighted digital watches and punching rude words into their Japanese calculators. Others made do with dismembering Rubik cubes, putting them back together to pretend we had done them.

Music wise the kids swapped their punk gear very briefly for fishtail parkas, which had become trendy since Mod film *Quadrophenia* had been shown at the Savoy. And as the year rolled out Ska music came into vogue, as teenagers got into Madness, The Specials and The Beat and used it as an excuse to get a skinhead haircut. The Mod phenomenon was a little mixed up in town and kids at our school used to have 2Tone patches stitched to the back of their parkas. Still it was better than listening to mod groups Secret Affair or The Lambrettas. In the 1970s and 1980s you bought your records from Rumbelows, Preedy's and Ames. One shop in Bridge Street used to sell singles that had been discarded from jukeboxes – the only problem with them was that they had the middle panel missing. Unfortunately, Rothery's in Ormskirk Street, which had listening booths to let you have a blast before you bought, had been turned into a clothes shop.

St Helens 10 Bradford Northern 11, 23 February 1980
Challenge Cup Round 2

Of the six trophies rugby league had available, the Challenge Cup was the one supporters and players wanted to win. The allure of Wembley was the one thing that would lift the fair weather fans out of their armchairs. The fact that many of the 40,000 'fans' who had headed down to Wembley in 1978 hadn't set foot inside Knowsley Road since was a source of aggravation to the regulars.

After beating Workington we were drawn at home to Bradford Northern in the televised second round. Northern were a tough side coached by the wily Peter Fox, whose record spoke for itself. Fox built his teams around a big, dour pack that did the basics very well. And Jimmy Thompson, Colin Forsyth, Geoff Clarkson and Jeff Grayshon were streetwise forwards who could knock the opposition down all day.

Bradford were dull in every sense of the word – their name, kit and style of play could send a glass eye to sleep. Although half-back Nigel Stephenson could throw a fine pass, they lacked real flair or panache in the back line. But their soporific, no frills and fewer thrills style of rugby paid dividends and they went on to win the Championship that year.

Despite Saints' home advantage, Bradford took a commanding 11-0 lead and our Wembley hopes seemed dashed for another year. At this point a handful of St Helens yobs, who hadn't set foot in the ground since the early battle against Warrington, taunted the visiting fans with a few renditions of, 'We hope the Ripper gets your mam!', a reference to mass murderer Peter Sutcliffe who had been brutally killing women in Leeds, Bradford and Huddersfield. He was caught in Sheffield a year later – but not before his murder tally had reached 13.

The yobs left the ground chanting "you're gonna get your f...ing heads kicked in!" and then set about throwing bricks at a couple of the Bradford coaches that had been parked outside. They were idiots, not simply for the obvious reasons, but they also missed a brilliant comeback by the Saints. It was a "Grandstand finish" as Eddie Waring was no doubt telling the television viewers sitting at home. Peter Glynn swept in for two converted tries, but at 11-10 we simply ran out of time.

It was bitterly disappointing, and I would not have been the only lad who traipsed back home that evening to play with my tea instead of eating it.

St Helens 20 Wigan 17, 4 April 1980
Division 1

The Jam's classic political anthem *Going Underground* was number one at Easter – and how appropriate it was for Wigan. They suffered the indignity of going down into Division 2 with three of the sides that had been promoted the preceding year – Hunslet, York and Blackpool.

Saints had played their part in Wigan's demise, doing the double – winning the Good Friday clash 20-17 after tries from Neil Holding with two, Peter Glynn and Peter Gorley. Although there was some gloating in St Helens, there was nowhere near as much as there would have been had the result occurred post-1985. Others were probably thinking "if the once mighty Wigan could go down, reputation alone was not going to be enough to save us in years to come."

Some Saints fans were genuinely quite sad to see Wigan go down because tradition counts for something in rugby league. Boxing Day and Good Friday would not be the same without them.

The rivalry between the two clubs was strong enough to bring out the best crowd of the season – 8,456. The late 1970s saw Saints and Wigan as a pair of faded giants living on past glories and still having the old arguments about whether Tom van Vollenhoven was a better winger than Billy Boston. The rugby league balance of power had shifted towards Humberside, who in 1980 provided both finalists at Wembley's Cup Final, with Rovers coming out on top. Both clubs had bought in the best players money could buy, bankrolled by five-figure crowds the rest of the clubs could only dream of. In a short space of time Hull had become the undisputed capital of rugby league.

West of the Pennines, Widnes were still the force to be reckoned with and had mastered a way of evolving and rejuvenating their side without breaking the bank.

The season had petered out for Saints and we finished as mid-table also-rans, losing our last five games, including being nilled twice. Injuries had taken their toll and lads like Dennis Nulty, Tony Bolton, Keiron Pickavance and John Canning had been drafted in from the 'A' team. It ended with an inevitable 30-0 thrashing at champions Bradford in the opening round of the Premiership. There was no such thing as mid-table respectability for a club of Saints' tradition. The expectations of the fans were as high as they had been in the 1960s and 1970s and yet the actions of the board remained limited. Coach Eric Ashton handed in his resignation. On the wall of the Popular side, daubed in paint in big letters, was the inscription "Eric Ashton's red and white army". It meant little – the army was in retreat, and those die-hard supporters of 1978 were deserting by the day.

So that was another season over and done with – and even though it was a pretty mediocre one I didn't really want it to end.

There was one opportunity for those wanting a glimpse of Knowsley Road in the summer – although wrestling was the sport, with Big Daddy taking on Canadian Mighty John Quinn in a tag match. The ring was in front of the main stand and the crowd got really carried away. We mocked wrestling, but rugby league has since borrowed some techniques from the television sport such as having music introducing the fighters to the ring. Big Daddy always came out to the sound of The Seekers' *We shall not be moved*.

One old woman in front of me swore like a trooper and kept shouting "Yanks go home" and her big, daft son was three sheets to t' wind and got so agitated he lobbed an apple core into the ring.

The script for tag wrestling always seemed the same when Big Daddy was fighting a couple of baddies like Kojak Kirk, Rollerball Rocco, Giant Haystacks and Bully Boy Muir. They would invariably knock seven bells out of Daddy's weakling partner and take the first fall. But ultimately Big Daddy would somehow manage to get into the ring and bounce both villains with his big fat belly.

Top: Eric Chisnall, left: Eddie Cunningham right: Les Jones

16

4. 1980-81 Just kidding ourselves

St Helens 11 New Zealand 6, 12 October 1980
Tour match

The new season offered a new beginning and fresh start, with former Knowsley Road points machine Kel Coslett becoming coach and Eric Chisnall taking the skipper's armband from fellow second rower George Nicholls.

There were teething problems with first Nicholls being dropped for one week after refusing to move up to prop and then later put on the transfer list. It was a topsy-turvy start to the year and Saints had a tendency to lose daft games by the odd couple of points, with home defeats by Wakefield, Castleford and Leeds being particularly irritating. Widnes had knocked us out of the Lancashire Cup by two points and Warrington did likewise in the John Player Trophy by a similar margin.

The worst one of these was the Wakefield defeat. Trailing 16-14, Saints were awarded a penalty in front of the posts giving them a glorious chance to grab a share of the points. Unfortunately, Griffiths screwed the ball wide allowing the handful of Trinity fans to celebrate wildly. "'You couldn't kick my arse if I bent over, Griffiths!" bawled one irate home fan. Further bad news came in the loss of prolific scorer Peter Glynn, who was carried off on a stretcher after breaking his leg.

Although our league form was patchy, we beat the touring Kiwis 11-6 in a game which saw robust prop Kevin Tamati aggravate the crowd with his tough, uncompromising, no-prisoners style of play. I was hoarse from shouting at him, but really it was like booing the pantomime villain. Players like Tamati add that crackle to proceedings – and he would return to England with Widnes three years later.

New Zealand had always been the minnows of international rugby league, with the XIII-man code very much in the shadow of the union All Blacks in the land of the long white cloud. The Kiwis meant business, drawing the first test at Central Park before winning the second test. It became clear that Britain had fallen still further behind on the international scene. Eventually it took superb two-try effort by explosive young winger Des Drummond in the final test to save Britain's blushes and level the series.

The international transfer ban had been introduced in 1977 to stop British talent haemorrhaging over to Sydney, but it blocked Australians coming in the opposite direction too. However, the ban didn't apply to Kiwis and many of the 1980 tour squad ended up playing in England. Hull led the way signing full-back Gary Kemble, winger Dane O'Hara, quality centre James Leuluai and later Fred Ah Kuoi.

None of the 1980 Kiwis found their way to Knowsley Road - we made do with a staple diet of homespun stars... and Roger Owen. The gruff looking, barrel-chested prop only played 37 games in just under two years at Saints, but he left plenty of tales which are part of the club's folklore. He signed from Welsh club New Dock Stars, who were hardly Cardiff or Swansea, but we initially liked the cut of him. He was a big, bearded, fierce looking unit, with broad shoulders and a massive scar under his eye.

When he signed he is reputed to have said "I love to knock them down". Owen was introduced to the crowd and club president Lady Mavis Pilkington before the Wakefield defeat.

Widnes 11 St Helens 8, New Year's Day 1981
Division 1

It had been an odd Christmas with St Winifred's school choir taking the number one slot in the music charts with a dreadful song called *No one quite like Grandma*. It temporarily displaced John Lennon, who had recently been shot dead in New York.

Also, with Wigan being in the second division, we had to play Oldham on Boxing Day. The match was the non-event of the year, so much so that a lot of fans refused to be dragged away from their leftover turkey and the *Pam Ayres Christmas Special* and stayed at home. None of my mates fancied it so I went on my own and watched the game from the main stand for the first time, with just a piece of Christmas cake wrapped in tin foil as company to remind me what day it was. With a feeble crowd of fewer than 4,500, it felt like Christmas had been cancelled.

The game itself was dull, desperate stuff and Saints only just scraped home 11-10, after an injury time up-and-under hoisted by Harry Pinner resulted in chaos behind the Roughyeds' line and a try under the posts.

Playing Widnes on New Year's Day allowed the continuation of some tradition. Built on the banks of the Mersey, Widnes was famous for its chemical industry and smell. Obnoxious odours hung over the town – especially near West Bank where one unit rendered down animal carcasses. The old joke had it that the birds woke you up with their coughing. Its other claim to fame is that Paul Simon wrote *Homeward Bound* while waiting for a train out of there in the 1960s. A brass plaque on Widnes station now marks where and when he penned those famous lyrics.

Widnes was my first away game, but being only on the other side of Sutton Manor, it was not that much of a trek. Naughton Park was a disappointment with a couple of cow sheds covering both ends, a pokey little main stand and a pitch surrounded by a low perimeter wall. The terraces on either side of the pitch started off below ground level, so you were looking up at the action. With Widnes having enjoyed so much success and appearing at Wembley almost every year since 1975 I expected more. But it was obvious that any money they had made had been used for maintaining the team. The game itself was keenly contested, but we still lost 11-8. On a brighter note, Peter Glynn made a try-scoring comeback after being out with a broken leg since September.

Hull KR 10 St Helens 12, 11 January 1981
Division 1

Rovers' fans always taunted us when they came to our ground with cries of "Where were you at Hull KR?" I only really understood why when I went to Craven Park because we took only one coach and a handful of cars – no more than 100 people.

It looked fewer because once our fans entered the ground we blended into the surroundings like the Mudmen in an episode of *Flash Gordon*. There was a genuine fear of going to Hull KR, which one of the most hostile grounds on the circuit. There was also a lot of singing, which was unusual given that there was none of that at Saints games in those days and was probably worth a few points start.

Theirs was an odd looking stadium with a dog track around the pitch and a massive greyhound scoreboard occupying one end of the ground.

My mam had let me go on the condition I went with 'sensible Niall', who was a mate of my brother. He was older, played chess and both his parents were teachers so he was a good person to have in loco parentis.

Most Saints fans travelled in hope rather than expectation but the scores were level going into the closing stages, which would have been a good result for us. But then a Rovers player infringed in the tackle 30 yards out by the touchline.

Clive Griffiths, who had so often been a let down with the boot, stepped up and neatly stroked the ball between the posts to grab both points. After the hooter sounded, a rush of excitement, combined with the fear of getting a portion of shoe pie from the burly Robins fans standing next to us, spurred us to leg it a mile down the Holderness Road to the park where our solitary Supporters Club coach was parked. It felt better for being witnessed by only a handful of us – and I was probably thinking, "I am proper hardcore now!"

The Supporters Club was invaluable then to fans like me who had no other means of getting to away games. The committee, including stalwarts Jenny Linker, Enid Parsons, John Powell and Gerry Moore, took it in turns manning the shop in front of the training pitch between 6 and 9pm every evening. I was a fanatical programme collector then, which some people consider to be on a par with trainspotting. I was in there most Tuesday and Thursday training nights, rifling through the 15p specials and 10p ordinary programmes in between watching the players do their laps and tick rugby. I probably learned a lot of history from old programmes – this at a time when there were precious few books on rugby league. My collection never remotely matched that of Bill Bates, who would be seen at every game with a neat carrier bag to preserve that day's programme. Even back then he boasted a selection of pre-war Saints programmes and was always destined to have closer links than myself with the club he worshipped.

It was good to get to away matches instead of having to put up with local radio – which did not really cater for Saints fans fully in the early 1980s. Radio Merseyside didn't extensively cover live rugby league on a Sunday then and Radio Manchester tended to concentrate on their patch of Wigan, Swinton, Rochdale, Salford and Leigh. If Saints were playing in Yorkshire, the highly partisan Radio Leeds would always drop in on the game at various stages. They were often quite fleeting visits because they covered the full span of West Yorkshire. The later it got in the day the more there would be interference from German and French channels. No matter how many wire coat hangers were added to the radio aerial, we had to cope with commentator Jack Wainwright's excitable tones, interspersed with an opera singer doing impersonations of the Muppets' Swedish Chef.

St Helens 9 Leigh 10, 8 February 1981
Division 1

Beating Hull KR proved to be a false dawn and another dismal run saw Saints slide down the table. The match programme for the Leigh game pulled no punches, remarking, "Last week's performance against Wakefield was the worst one of the season". However, this home defeat against Leigh by the odd point in 19 was even more diabolical.

Leigh's fortunes had turned round since the appointment of Saints legend Alex Murphy as coach for his second stint at Hilton Park. His old magic did the trick and when the hooter wailed, the sheepskin-jacketed Murphy leapt from the dug out in front of us in the paddock and jigged around with arms aloft, having proved a point on his old stamping ground.

The defeat was all too much for the normally quite reserved people in the paddock, who began to hurl abuse 'upstairs'. And for good measure an apple core and screwed up paper made its way into the directors' box above. "Get your hands in your pockets, you tight fisted swine!" bawled one normally mild-mannered, middle-aged paddock resident. It was heartfelt, because Saints were slipping deeper into the mire and looked set to follow Wigan into relegation.

Although we were ninth, we were far from comfortable because clubs below us like Leigh, Halifax and Oldham were battling hard and had games in hand over us. Out of a division of 16 there was a brutal four-up, four-down system in place so if your side started losing to the teams below you there was only one direction you were heading.

Despondency ruled and some supporters turned on Coslett and his record as a coach. The old men, who held court in Wilf Young's newsagents while waiting for the *Chron* to arrive, would say things like, "Kel's a nice fella, and was an excellent footballer but he's not a coach." Others were more scathing, believing his coaching record to be one of abject failure. "He took Rochdale down, he took Wigan down and he'll take us down," remarked another pessimist.

The prophets of doom were circling and following the previous season's demise of Wigan nobody now argued that Saints were too good to go down. A minority argued that relegation might even do some good, shake the club up and enable a clear out of players from the past. Saints' management needed to be, in the words of singer Nick Lowe, cruel to be kind. I had heard that expression before and seen it applied in practical terms when a relative of mine drowned a litter of stray, feral kittens in a rain bucket in her back garden.

Huddersfield 8 St Helens 10, 15 February 1981
Challenge Cup Round 1

The Challenge Cup offered a welcome distraction from our side's dismal league form. We had been drawn away to Second Division Huddersfield for what should have been a doddle. Going to Fartown was a real experience - although the ground was now in an utterly decrepit state, you could tell it had once been a grand setting, especially against the scenic backdrop of hills and moors. You could almost feel the history and tradition of the place, like walking into a tatty bingo hall that had once been an old Victorian theatre.

Remarkably it was still on the circuit for rugby league's big events such as cup semi-finals and Premiership Finals, which was more to do with its geography than its facilities. White paint peeled off the old-fashioned rusting railings that surrounded the pitch and grass grew between the gaps of the steep stone steps where 33,000 had once watched the free-scoring Lionel Cooper play in claret and gold in 1950.

The Fartown atmosphere was not really in keeping with the quaint, sleepy old *Last of the Summer Wine* type village I had anticipated. There were no avuncular Tykes standing next to me, instead the group of 30-something blokes constantly shouted "Rip his bollocks off, the Lancashire bastard!" every time a Saints player took it in. Something told me they were not going to be taking snuff and joking about Nora Batty before paddling off down the River Calder in a tin bath.

The more mature Huddersfield fans were rather more reflective in declaring that this was the worst St Helens side they had ever seen. Most of the travelling fans – with the allure of the cup trebling our usual away contingent - probably agreed.

Saints' only moves in the game seemed to revolve around dummy-half Graham Liptrot working a run-around with Eric Chisnall at first receiver. Now Chis was an exceptional ball player, capable of prising open the tightest of defences, but we were desperate for a Plan B. Creative loose-forward Harry Pinner tried his hardest to spray it wide, but he needed quicker players running off him really. Inspired by lively loose-forward Tony Johnson, Huddersfield made a real fight of it but we scraped into the next round by a couple of points.

St Helens 5 Hull 3, 28 February 1981
Challenge Cup Round 2

Hull took thousands of fans wherever they played, most of them decked out in black and white, irregular-hooped jerseys long before replica tops became trendy. The Airlie Birds brought a buzz back into a sport that had suffered a fall in crowds due to the recession. Clubs could always be guaranteed a good pay day when Hull FC were in town.

Hull had dragged themselves up by their bootlaces after hitting rock bottom in 1976 when their match at home to Huyton had attracted fewer than 1,000 spectators. Their 'speculate to accumulate' policy was not one all clubs could have carried out as successfully – although some club directors used that as an alibi to stay out of the transfer market completely.

Hull spent their way out of the doldrums, figuring that if they could get a decent side, people would come and watch. Most of their recruits were from the Featherstone-Castleford-Wakefield mining triangle: players such as John Newlove, Charlie Stone, Sammy Lloyd and Steve 'Knocker' Norton and world record buy £40,000 buy Trevor Skerrett. They had a formidable pack and we knew it was going to be a tough game.

As the tie of the round, it had been switched to the Saturday because the second half was being shown on BBC's *Grandstand*. The television cameras did not deter the travelling hordes and as we reached the bottom of St Luke's Road you could already hear their singing from inside the ground. They turned our popular side into a replica of their infamously vocal Threepenny Stand and then spilled into the Eddington End and the clubhouse end where they taunted us with, "You're supposed to be at home!"

They were everywhere. Me and my mate Lic felt like Stanley Baker and Michael Caine in *Zulu* as we retreated to the open bit of terrace next to the main stand for sanctuary, while visiting fans sang over and over their anthem *Old Faithful*, which went:

Old Faithful, we'll roam the range together
Old Faithful, in any kind of weather
When the round up days are over
And the Boulevard's white with clover
For you old faithful pal of mine

Saints took an early lead after eight minutes with a try by Peter Glynn, who had scrambled over following a magnificent break by Chris Arkwright. Griffiths goaled, but Hull responded six minutes later when a magnificent pass by John Newlove created an overlap for Mick Crane to go over in the corner. Lloyd missed the crucial conversion.

21

Then the mud took over and it become a war of attrition and a fight for feet and inches in the middle – there were no further points, but it was utterly compelling stuff.

There were casualties too picked up in the heat of the battle, with scrum-half Neil Holding carried off with a dislocated shoulder and Peter Gorley limping away with a leg injury. Their replacements George Nicholls and Steve Peters performed heroically alongside the other 11, repelling wave after wave of Hull attacks, especially in one 25 minute spell in the middle of the second half, when Saints never got out of their own 25-yard line.

Hull's stand-off Newlove - whose son Paul would later become a legend at Knowsley Road - had a blinder with a perfect pair of hands spraying passes wide to strong-running target men. That none of those runners could get over the line was a credit to Saints' desperate tackling. It was that spirit which saw Saints emerge from the mud victorious to book a quarter-final berth. The black-and-white masses shuffled out in silent disbelief. So did we. We were all mentally and emotionally drained, so heaven knows how the players must have felt. What had passed off in the previous 80 minutes was 'enjoyment' in the way that going on the Big One at Blackpool was, screaming your head off and feeling queasy, only to get back in the queue for another go.

Not all Hull fans took defeat in a sporting manner and one six-foot skinhead wanted to go back to East Riding with a souvenir so challenged me and my mates as we walked across the Black Bull car park.

"Giz your scarf!"

"Why?" asked Lic, playing daft.

"Giz your scarf or I'll knife you," he repeated, this time with more menace.

Maybe winning gives you a false confidence, but Lic replied with a sharp "Piss off". Unbelievably the Hull fan, twice our size and a good eight years our senior, duly pissed off back to Humberside with his tail between his legs.

My scarf was never in danger of getting me thumped – I wore a parka, which could be zipped up to cover my colours when we were at a particularly hostile ground or at home to Warrington. In fact the only time I was remotely under threat was in 1979 when I had opted for a Lumber Jacket – a pretty useless coat for hiding your colours.

Oldham 5 St Helens 6, 15 March 1981
Challenge Cup Round 3

When you saw David Oxley's fixed grin and polo neck on Monday's *Look North* it could only mean one thing – "gentlemen, the draw".

Oxley was a seemingly strange figurehead for rugby league. Although born in the game's heartlands in Hull, he came across as a bit of a toff. However, you can't knock his record because Oxley was at the helm when rugby league dragged itself up from its bootstraps, particularly with a sponsorship drive that boosted the game's coffers. His strategy gave the sport, which had struggled to come to terms with the decline in attendances in the early 1970s, a lifeline. Sponsors were lined up for the championship and most notably the Challenge Cup – which was backed then by tobacco company State Express.

With league leaders Warrington, cup kings Widnes and holders Hull KR in the black velvet bag for the last eight it was music to our ears to hear: "Oldham... will play... (shuffle, rattle) ...number 22... St Helens." Saints looked odds on for another semi appearance – and a step closer towards the holy grail of a trip to Wembley.

We went to Oldham with a real spring in our step, and the town was beginning to whisper Wembley again. In fact it was more than a murmur when we got to the centre of the mill town, all you could hear was Saints fans, including a load of likely lads, singing "Wem-ba-lee, Wem-ba-lee, Wem-ba-lee!" to the tune of "Here we go".

The rickety old Watersheddings ground, surrounded by four old fashioned wooden stands, was jam packed to the rafters with more than 9,000 on. You could barely move to locate your mates so it was just a case of trying to find a cluster of Saints fans and squeezing in. It was a cracking atmosphere nonetheless. Once again it was close, with only a Peter Glynn drop-goal separating the sides at half-time and at the end. We won by the odd point in 11 – but that closeness added to the elation at the final whistle. There was also a little bit of scuffling – with an older lad from our school running down the side street waving a police cone round his head shouting "Come and get it you Oldham bastards!"

The yobs were a mixture of new romantics and casuals with the more fashion conscious having wedge haircuts, wearing Kickers on their feet and being very fussy about not getting their Pringle jerseys pulled out of shape.

As our convoy was leaving the town a mob of Oldham knuckleheads lurked on the traffic island, each of them with a couple of half bricks in their hands, waiting to pelt our coaches. You could see it coming, but the members of the coach in front had other ideas. A gang, led by a lad still gamely wearing an out-of-fashion Mohican haircut and a studded leather jacket with Adam and the Ants emblazoned across it, piled off, scattering the assembled Oldham yobs from their vantage point. It allowed the rest of the coaches a safe passage out without a single brick finding a target. Even those on the Supporters Club coach, who didn't condone that sort of behaviour, looked grateful. In fact our coach, full of family men and women, were cheering. One perfectly respectable bloke declared with a chuckle, "We even won the fight an' all!"

Unluckily for our saviours, their bus driver decided he wanted to be out of town ASAP and pulled away before the conquering heroes returned, leaving them stranded.

Bricking coaches was normally more a threat than a reality, Supporters Club committee members like Enid and Jenny helped matters a lot by making sure it was a calm trip home, insisting on scarves being taken down from windows. It seemed a pointless exercise, because everyone knew who we were. It is not as if Featherstone and Warrington were suddenly holiday destinations attracting buses of tourists.

There had, however, been a case at Oldham a couple of years previously when one fan had decided to drop his trousers and pull a moony at the home yobs. Unfortunately for him a brick took the back window out and the young bloke spent the entire journey home picking lumps of glass out of his backside. Whether the lad dared to go and see Sister Duffy at Providence Hospital to get his injury cleaned up is another matter. How would he explain after dropping his trousers to the no-nonsense nurse? "It is like this Sister…" The Prov, which was the town centre, shut down in 1981 despite a massive campaign and fundraising to keep it open. Irish nurse Duffy had etched more than a few of her own lines in the town's folklore – people still talk about her fondly today.

Hull KR 22 St Helens 5, 4 April 1981
Challenge Cup Semi-Final, Headingley

Although it had only been three years since Saints had last been to Wembley, supporters were keen for a return. Maybe our dismal league form over the previous three seasons had even increased the importance of seeing the Twin Towers. It is amazing how one 80 minute match at the Empire Stadium, with the fanfare that goes with it, would be good enough to wipe away the 30 games of mediocrity we had endure through the season.

There was no longer a place to hide in the draw because there were only big guns remaining. In the first semi-final, revitalised Cup Kings Widnes beat Warrington to secure their fifth Wembley trip in seven years.

A week later Saints took on a Hull KR side we had beaten twice already in the league – home and away – and everyone was hoping they could just pull off something a little bit special.

My superstitions went into overdrive ahead of the game – tracing exactly the same route up to Knowsley Road to get the coach as I had done for the previous rounds and making sure my mam did not get her hands on my scarf to wash it. Given I had worn it constantly since the end of February, it was bogging by now.

We boarded our coaches with a spring in our step, and there were a few more than normal parked up on the training ground. But that was put into context when we got to Headingley; it was immediately noticeable that Rovers outnumbered us by at least three to one in the crowd of nearly 17,000.

Coach Kel Coslett took the players to watch *Raging Bull* at the cinema on the eve of the match. The Martin Scorsese film, starring Robert De Niro as middleweight boxer Jake La Motta, was supposed to motivate them but we needed somebody like him on the field, rather than on the big screen. A few weeks prior to the semi our veteran forward George Nicholls had played a blinder against Rovers, winning the man-of-the-match award for his tough tackling and shrewd distribution. Unfortunately he missed the semi-final after suffering a gashed mouth and damaged ribs in the previous week's battle against George Standidge and Halifax. Georgie Nick wasn't Superman but losing him ahead of the semi had been a big psychological blow.

Although a Harry Pinner try saw it level at half-time, Rovers took us apart in the second half winning 22-5. Man-of-the-match Paul Harkin punished us with his long touch finding kicks and their big pack of international forwards Len Casey, David Watkinson, Roy Holdstock and Phil Lowe gave us a pummelling.

Our pack men were either too old, or the younger ones, like 16-stoner Mick Hope, lacked the aggression needed. Hope had a very upright running style and he blew and puffed going into the tackle, which did not impress some. "Run hard lad, you'll not get hurt if you run hard!" was the encouragement shouted from die-hard supporter Eric Ainsworth from the safety of the paddock.

Our pack lacked fire and somebody who could stand up and be counted when the going got tough. We needed a player of the size and quality of retired forward John Mantle, who could be seen regularly cycling up to Rivington Road School where he taught. The big Welshman still commanded respect and a degree of awe as he pedalled past. Saints had never really replaced him, like for like, when he departed for Salford after the Wembley success of 1976.

As we despondently made our way back to our coach, spirits were dampened further by the awful sight of a handful of St Helens yobs kicking all the windows out of the top deck of a football-special bus. The panes floated through the air and then fragmented into little pieces, scattering on the pavement like crystals of sugar. Everyone assumed that they were Leeds soccer yobs because they had been playing Coventry City at Elland Road that afternoon – and that was the sort of thing we sniffily expected "them" to do. But as the wrecking crew steamed off the bus before the police arrived they revealed some of the so-called 'faces' from the previous scrap at Oldham. The fact that they were from our town and were not Leeds United soccer yobs made the incident seem worse.

For most of the depressing journey back across the M62, most of us gazed out of the coach window in silence – there was not even a post-mortem or an argument, just a hush broken by the odd meaningless cackle from the front. It was no consolation to hear speculative talk that the winners of the previous semi, Widnes, would pick up the cup anyway even if it did turn out to be true.

I felt jealous of one lad in my class, Dave, who despite living in Rainhill, had started supporting Widnes earlier that year and hit the Wembley jackpot at first go. Some rugby supporters living there adopted 'dual nationality'. It happened on the fringes of town and was the same in Haydock and more pronounced in Billinge, where the top enders shouted for Wigan.

Widnes surprised everyone with the way they rallied after selling a lot of their old heads to Fulham. The Chemics' young scrum-half Andy Gregory was hailed as the 'new Alex Murphy' after a cracking try-scoring display at Wembley.

Elsewhere Bradford had come up on the rails to win the Championship, but Billy Benyon's Warrington side should have had it by rights. The Wire's success, in winning the Lancashire Cup and John Player Trophy added to their Challenge Cup run, had created a horrendous fixture backlog in their league programme. It ultimately caught up with them, as they dragged their tired legs around the grounds to complete their hectic run-in of nine games in 23 days.

Saints staved off the threat of relegation, finishing the league season with a flourish beating Warrington, Halifax, Oldham, Hull and Widnes before accounting for champions Bradford in the first round of the Premiership, a game played midweek after a bizarre April snow shower had forced the first game to be postponed.

Saints' season ended in the Premiership semi-final at Hull, who then took on their neighbours in a highly segregated final at Headingley, which thankfully passed off without incident. The previous Good Friday clash between the Humber rivals at the Boulevard had been marred by fighting and brick throwing, and was dubbed 'Black Friday', making both the newspapers and the national television news.

Mudlarks! Saints prop Roger Owen is indistinguishable from Wire counterpart Neil Courtney at the end of this bruising encounter between St Helens and Warrington in March 1982. (Peers)

Dave Chisnall.

5. 1981-82 Maggie, Maggie, Maggie! Out, out, out!

Blackpool Borough 0 St Helens 28, 16 August 1981
Lancashire Cup, Round 1

In some people's eyes it was still summer, the sun was shining, Ian Botham was in the process of winning the Ashes and the school holidays were still on. But for most Saints nuts, summer ended with the first kick of a rugby ball.

Saints had been drawn to play Blackpool in the Lancashire Cup, a team that since some pen-pushing bureaucrat with no sense of tradition had decided to revise the boundaries was the only one officially left in the Red Rose county of Lancashire. It was nonsense – for a good few years 'Out of Merseyside' was daubed on one of the walls at the back of Lowe House Boxing Club near the centre of town. Despite our local radio station being either Radio City or BBC Merseyside, there was still a strong Red Rose feeling across what was, is and always will be south Lancashire.

Some towns escaped the issue – calling Rochdale, Wigan and Leigh folk 'Greater Mancunians' was so stupid a concept that instead they kept their Lancashire label. But in St Helens we were stuck with the aberration that is Merseyside. Some of the town's youngsters welcomed it, believing it trendy to be associated with Liverpool and viewing Lancashire as flat cap and whippet territory.

Merseyside was the butt of black humour at the time – coming as it did in the aftermath of spiralling unemployment in Liverpool and the Toxteth riots, which raged fiercely in July 1981. One joke had a little Liverpudlian lad in class asking the teacher, "What does this word mean, miss? I have heard of sui-cide and homi-cide, but I have never heard of Mersey-side."

At least they had a winning football team to lift the gloom – Liverpool had won the European Cup three times in the past five years. If you feel part of that glory – even if it does primarily belong to some rich bloke who has a big house on the Wirral – it can make you feel a lot better about yourself.

Toxteth was one of a handful of inner-city flashpoints that went up in flames that summer. There was probably a fair bit of copycat violence from what was happening over in Northern Ireland where sporadic rioting was at its peak following the hunger strikes, which had seen 10 republican prisoners starve themselves to death in pursuit of political status. The night after IRA man Bobby Sands died, our television screens were full of images of petrol bombs being tossed at armoured cars.

Although St Helens had a lot of people with Irish ancestry, little of the hostilities from over there fed into our community. One bright spark did, however, see fit to daub graffiti on St Julies RC church in Eccleston, scrawling "Bobby Sands – the 6lb w...ker!" The assumption of the vandal seemed to be that all Irish or Catholics must have been IRA sympathisers.

A lot of Saints fans made a weekend of the Blackpool match – beach, beer, fair and rugby, what more could you want? Long before it was hijacked as a stags and hens resort, Blackpool was a massively popular destination for family holidays before it became cheaper to jet off to Benidorm.

You could see the attraction for all ages; pensioners could just loll about in the daytime, watch the turns, play bingo on the seafront arcades or catch the tram up to

Fleetwood fish market. Youngsters split their time between the beach, rides and the slots. In the summer of 1976 I had saved my 'spend' for ages, then blew the lot on the one-armed bandits and penny falls during a week. As that last penny was slipped into the slot I could hear the big clown in a glass case laughing hysterically at all the fools spending their money with nothing to show for it apart from a gonk on a stick. That is probably how the directors at Blackpool Borough must have felt after the end of the 1981-82 season.

They had injected a bit of cash into the club bringing in, among others, the veterans that had won Fulham promotion - Ian van Bellen, Iain MacCorquodale and John Risman. Superficial changes included the ditching of their traditional tangerine and black jerseys for a hideous green and black kit. They had even changed their nickname from Borough to Milers to tie up with the Golden Mile sponsors.

For all the fanfare and spending, Borough made little impression on the league that year, and got off to a poor start against Saints. The big, bald, bandaged van Bellen found the bone-hard pitch and the baking heat uncomfortable as Saints rattled up 28 points without reply.

St Helens 35 Fulham 4, 30 August 1981
Division 1

Long before Mohamed al Fayed and his millions came on the scene, Fulham were a bit of a joke on the football front. True, they had supplied the great Johnny Haynes, the first £100-a-week footballer, and 20 years later Rodney Marsh and George Best had made appearances down by the river. Fulham had also famously made a trip to the 1975 FA Cup Final with World Cup winning skipper Bobby Moore in defence.

The Cottagers were a friendly football club, tucked in by the side of the Thames in west London. Despite everyone having a soft spot for them - Wolfie from television's *Citizen Smith* supported them, as did Terry McCann from television series *Minder* - they were in the doldrums in the old Division Three of the Football League when soccer had the sense to start at four and go up to the top, Division One. With the football club's crowds around 4,000 they chose an alternative way of opening up a revenue stream – rugby league. And after recruiting a team of northerners, the folk of London flocked to Craven Cottage in their droves with almost 10,000 watching them hammer Wigan in their first game in September 1980.

It looked like the shape of things to come for rugby league. The fans came back for more with 12,000 watching them beat Leeds in the John Player Trophy and more than 15,000 watching them narrowly lose to Wakefield in the Challenge Cup. There was a novelty factor too for away fans – in those days we wanted to go there, rather than moan about how far away it was.

Fulham's first year was like a breath of fresh air in British rugby league, averaging crowds of 6,096. Only the two Hulls and champions Bradford drew higher gates in that first glorious year. Everything looked rosy – but would the big money men from the smoke take over our northern game? Other football clubs now expressed an interest in staging rugby league – among them Bristol City, Charlton, Crystal Palace and Bolton. Portsmouth had balloted their fans with the 9,000 turnout voting 9-1 against, Crystal Palace also applied, but only Carlisle and Cardiff City were admitted into the Second Division for the 1981-82 season.

With people like writer and actor Colin Welland on the board at Fulham, you got the distinct impression that there was an attempt to use our sport's unique northerness as its main selling point rather than the on-field action. Welland was actually the man of the moment – having just penned the Oscar-winning movie *Chariots of Fire*, part of which was filmed at Cowley Girls School in St Helens.

Two of Fulham's props – Tony Gourley and Roy Lester – also made the screen, starring on a grillsteaks advert. But again it was a stereotypical image they portrayed with the patter they trotted out: "What's for tea, Stanley?"

"Grillsteaks, Eric!" The banter continued as they knocked each other about on a muddy field, culminating with the line "Aye, something to get your teeth into."

And they both stared at the camera with their front teeth missing.

Fulham's novelty northern selling point would soon wear off as soon as they started losing regularly in the First Division, which proved a big step-up. Players like John Crossley, John Dalgreen and Steve Diamond replaced some of the veterans who had secured promotion. Some fans felt the departure of van Bellen, who had been a folk hero at the Cottage, meant Fulham had lost some of their appeal.

Saints were first in the queue to give Fulham a bloody nose in top-flight rugby. It turned out to be a painful lesson for their avid balloon-waving supporters to take 200 miles back to London and their players nine miles to Widnes. Saints unusually put flyers out to promote the match and an inquisitive 5,973 shirt-sleeved crowd turned up. Fulham allowed us to throw the ball about with Peter Glynn rattling in four tries from full-back.

The Fulham travellers deserved sympathy not only for what happened on the pitch, but also off it. They had to contend with a dozen menacing looking St Helens skinheads who stood behind them singing "We hate Cockneys" for the entire first half. It is debateable whether any of those balloon-waving families from Fulham had been born anywhere near the sound of the Bow Bells, but they must have left the ground that day with a shocking impression of St Helens if not a little relieved to still have all their own teeth.

Leigh 20 St Helens 6, 2 September 1981
Lancashire Cup Semi-Final

Our season had started full of hope, but just when things seemed to be going well, it all came crashing down.

It was a special night in what was going to be a spectacular season for an unfashionable Leigh club who had been in the doldrums even longer than Saints. Their ordinary squad had been galvanised by the magic of coach Alex Murphy – there could be no other explanation. Their team was made up of solid players with big hearts, like hooker Ray Tabern, props Tony Cooke and big Alf Wilkinson, but in John Woods and Des Drummond the Leythers possessed two players of rare quality. Drummond was the fastest man in the game, as he later demonstrated on BBC Television sport's *Superstars*. Bolton-born Dessie, who did a bit of judo in his spare time, was also deceptively strong both in brushing off tacklers and on defence.

Lightning fast, Drummond had beaten Malcolm McDonald's *Superstars* 100m record that had stood for seven years when he ran a time of 10.85 seconds on the BBC show.

So when Saints took on Leigh in the semi-final we knew we had superstar Dessie to look out for, but the real dangerman was midfield marvel Woods. Critics accused Woods of being too soft, but when he was on his game he could rip a team apart. Poor John Butler, our veteran new signing from Wigan, was left clutching at shadows as Woods swerved and stepped majestically.

With Leigh running so hot, our best hope that night came midway through the second half when the floodlights failed on one side of the ground. Referee Fred Lindop asked both skippers if they wanted to play on. Not surprisingly Woods said yes and although Chisnall apparently shook his head, the game continued and we were despatched from our first competition of the year. Saints lost 20-6, which turned out to be no disgrace as Leigh went on to beat Widnes in the soggy Central Park final.

Wakefield whistler Lindop was, like fellow Yorkshireman Billy Thompson, a real character. Although 'Nelly' Lindop was a walking advert for Brylcreem, he was nevertheless widely respected despite being classed as a real bogeyman.

Rugby league's referees were the envy of most other sports, with their no-nonsense 10-yard stomps down the field if there was any back chat. The respect for league referees is a contrast to that suffered by football officials, who have to put up with a hounding whenever they give or decline a penalty. It was impossible to imagine players running after Billy Thompson and manhandling him. Dissenters would have simply been met with a straightforward point towards the tunnel and a blunt "Go an' get washed."

Barrow 17 St Helens 0, 22 October 1981
John Player, Round 1 Replay

A late Barrow try was enough to force a draw in the tie at Knowsley Road meaning Saints had to make the long Thursday night trip up to what Crumpsall comedian and folk singer Mike Harding called the world's biggest cul-de-sac. The Shipbuilders, who had become one of the league's classic yo-yo sides, regularly being promoted and relegated, were experiencing a revival. They had made a big impact on the John Player Trophy, getting to the final in the previous season and surprisingly stuffing Saints in this first round replay.

Everything about Barrow smacked of decency, from their royal blue shirts with a white vee, their little ground and their loyal vocal supporters to the way they played the game. The crowd for the replay was only 5,289 but it felt like three times that and generated more noise than Liverpool's Kop on a 1970s European night.

They had a strange half-time charity cash collection ritual at Barrow's ground which I also saw at Featherstone. Four people would walk around the pitch perimeter with a blanket and invite the crowd to toss their loose shrapnel into it. There would always be the odd clown who would treat it as a coconut shy and try and hit the collectors with their 2p donation. It was not really malicious throwing – purely a spot of 'divilment'.

Barrow had a number of St Helens lads in their squad over the years including their attacking full-back Steve Tickle and goalkicking centre Ian Ball. Both players were Ray French's former Cowley School protégés signed from rugby union. Ball was the son of former Saints and Barrow full-back Joe, who had died at the age of 37. Like his dad, Ball was small in stature, but made up for that with skill and could certainly kick a ball. Unfortunately he had to deal with the rough stuff during his career and on leaving the game he was scathing about the treatment he had received on the pitch.

Barrow's local hero was an unlikely lad called Eddie Szymala, who worked in the local shipyards. Long before rugby league players spent hours honing their physiques in the gym, Szymala was a body builder. His party piece was rolling his sleeves and flexing the tattooed naked ladies on his bulging biceps to show he meant business. For all Barrow's talented players, they should not have been trouncing us 17-0, with their more mobile pack making ours look cumbersome and clueless.

We were left to contemplate our dismissal from another competition on the way back down the M6. Saints' league form also began to falter after that match, made worse by our five subsequent games being away from home.

For the first time since I had been given licence to roam the run of away matches meant I could not make my 'spend' stretch to attending all the games I wanted to. I had to pick and choose but it seemed irrational to choose to go to Barrow again and watch them lose, but not travel to Bradford where we won. Other longish trips included a narrow win at Whitehaven, a draw at Fev and defeat at Wakefield.

It was not just school kids who struggled with these back-to-back away matches, one bloke who never missed a game turned up at Leeds just after New Year with a bundle of old programmes. He was trying to flog them to any prospective collector on the bus to make enough money to pay the admission price. The recession was biting hard – and folk were having to make tougher choices at home than attending a rugby game. Our home crowds suffered badly during the first three months of the year, with only 2,773 turning up for a game against York.

Some fans simply could no longer afford to go to the match. Heavy industry was being wiped out and some, in particular northern towns, seemed to be vanishing from the economic map. The advice of Tory Employment minister Norman Tebbit was "to get on your bike and look for work." As we moved into the New Year, the must-see television programme was Alan Bleasedale's *Boys from the Blackstuff,* a drama that reflected the impact of mass unemployment on the lives of people on Merseyside.

It seemed that all the town's school kids were watching it – but most just adopted Yosser Hughes' phrase "Gis a job!" and went around head-butting classmates rather than getting depressed about the impact of mass unemployment. At least it made a change from "Can your mam sew?" "Yes" "Well tell her to stitch that!" which was the usual playground prelude to nutting someone.

The long dole queue made the Government massively unpopular, and the current joke of the time was the one about Maggie Thatcher dying and going to heaven. When she arrived at the Pearly Gates, St Peter met her and wouldn't let her in due to her sins on Earth. So the trapdoor opened and Maggie descended to hell. A fortnight later the devil rang St Peter up and pleaded: "Can you take this bloody Thatcher woman off my hands? She's only been here a couple of weeks and she's already closed eight furnaces!"

St Helens 10 Castleford 40, 20 January 1982
Division 1

Saints strengthened their squad with the signing of Gary Moorby, a young second-row bought from Keighley for a Saints record of £37,500. "Gary who?" was my reaction, echoed by most other fans. Even those of us who read the *Rugby Leaguer*, the game's weekly newspaper, had not heard of him. Injuries had decimated our pack, with playmaker Harry Pinner out for a long spell with the loose-forward berth being alternated between Peter Gorley, Roy Mathias and youngster Gary Bottell.

But it was in the front row where we struggled most with veteran Mel James forced out for the rest of the season after picking up a knock in January.

Our other Welsh prop Roger Owen had been 'staying away' from the club, with rumours circulating that he may have been hoping for a move to league newcomers Cardiff City. Owen had produced a barnstorming performance for Wales against England at Ninian Park in November, after replacing Welsh hero Tommy David in the second half. Saints Supporters Club took a coach down to that game at Cardiff, and most of us were shouting for underdogs Wales. However, one lad on our coach changed his mind just before kick off in response to the locals booing *God save the Queen*. Even so, the passionate 10,000 crowd generated a fantastic atmosphere, particularly when Wales rallied to come within a converted try of snatching a draw.

There was a strong suspicion that someone had been whispering in Owen's ear about a move after that international game – or maybe it just gave him a taste of what he was missing at home. The barrel-chested prop was listed at £40,000, but nobody was going to shell that out for a player who seemed injury prone and unproven. His 'stay away' spell did him no good – he was never the same player again and lacked the same fire and passion on his return. Like a lot of union blokes, Owen made the mistake of thinking a forward's game was to plough into the tackler, rather than run at the gap. It ultimately took its toll on his knees – as did carting 16½ stones around the pitch.

Saints' front-row deficiencies meant weeks of chopping, changing and shuffling in the pack with captain Eric Chisnall forced to move up to prop. He played four matches there but seemed unsettled by it.

The patching-up exercise would ultimately cost us dearly once the weather improved. Ice and snow had put paid to all but one match in December, and January's programme had also suffered. We beat Widnes on New Year's Day in a game where only half the pitch was visible due to thick fog.

It was an absolute joke of a match, but referee Stan Wall simply applied the ruling, which was if he was able to see both corner flags from the centre of the 25-yard line then the show must go on.

If you stood behind the posts you could not see to the halfway line, it was the same from the paddock front wall and we had to rely on the 'oohs' and 'aahs' from the crowd on the opposite side to guess what was happening.

Three days later we took a real 30-4 hiding at Leeds on their under-soil heated pitch. Strangely, most of the people on the coach that day were talking about the previous day's rugby union international between England and Australia. They were not talking about the game itself, of course, rather the streaker Erica Roe who ran onto the pitch topless at half-time and grabbed all the headlines.

It attracted so much attention that struggling Doncaster even considered advertising a streaker would appear at one of their games, believing that it would boost the crowd at Tattersfield. Fortunately, that never happened as they realised that it would probably put more fans off, particularly if wives stopped their husbands from going to the match.

Because of the awful weather we then went another two-and-a-half weeks without a match, but regretted that when it came. Mal Reilly's Castleford were noted for their open rugby, but they were also a real Jekyll-and-Hyde team. Unfortunately for Saints, it was 'Classy Cas' who turned up with skilful prop Barry Johnson dictating the game.

Peter Glynn had a nightmare at full-back, constantly missing the high balls that the Cas attack peppered him with. Despite a paltry crowd of 3,338, the crescendo of boos brought the roof down when Saints went in trailing 31-0 at half-time. To add insult to injury Cas came out in the second half and immediately dropped a goal. However, the scoring was stemmed and the match finished at 40-10.

That loss was followed by crushing defeats at Leigh and Hull, followed by a home loss against Leeds. Although there was a win against lowly York in between, it looked grim and Saints appealed for support. An article in the programme urged fans to be patient and stated: "The players don't play badly on purpose." It also made claims that the club had no money to strengthen the squad. The missing line should have read – "so will you please stop asking us?"

Saints had brought in former Workington and Leigh prop Alan Rowley on loan, but in one of the few games he actually played, one wag in the paddock berated him loudly as being "as much use as a chocolate fireguard".

You pick those sayings up as you go along – many must have been passed on from father to son, or older work colleague to young apprentice. There were many expressions that you would not hear anywhere other than the rugby ground. Players having a bad game would always get "Come and stand here with me, yer puddin' bag". Ones lacking a yard of pace were "as slow as a God's horse". Lazy, lethargic players would be condemned with, "I've seen more work in a Beechams".

If you stood in front of someone and blocked their view of the action you would get a dig in the back with the words "Were you made at Pilkington's?"

The refs would have to put up with non-PC insults – "I hope your dog dies" or "I hope your kids have red hair".

Somebody with big teeth would be described as "breaking them in for t' Stores horse," the stores being the popular name for the Co-op whose biggest shop in town was the magnificent Helena House building. There were more vulgar sayings, directed at someone who was really reviled.

St Helens 12 Wigan 20, 13 February 1982
Challenge Cup, Round 1

After gaining promotion Wigan meant business and had sold their player-coach and Great Britain full-back George Fairbairn to Hull KR for a record £72,000. They brought in Maurice Bamford as coach, who had done fairly well at Bramley, Huddersfield and Halifax. The only thing I thought him famous for was his striking resemblance to Polish Solidarity trade union leader Lech Walesa.

Many believed that Bamford's recruitment policy was suspect and he had mixed results from the Yorkshire contingent he fetched over – Jimmy Birts, Mick Scott, Steve Nicholson and Gary Stephens. As their season progressed, higher profile signings had chairman Maurice Lindsay's fingerprints on them, including David Stephenson and goalkicker Colin Whitfield, both from Salford. But the one that really caught the imagination was Rochdale's fast and elusive winger Henderson Gill.

Saints had also expressed an interest in Gill, but they had this habit of losing interest as soon as prices were mentioned. "We have irons in the fire" was the most overused catch phrase by the club.

Gill would go on to become a fine acquisition for Wigan and a crowd-pleaser to boot – he was just the sort of player that would have sent a crackle down the Knowsley Road terraces. Everyone loves a flier – it is that whoosh, and the ability to scorch in for a try from nothing that a genuine speedster has.

The cup match had been brought forward to Saturday because it was being televised on *Grandstand*. BBC no longer showed the second half live, instead games kicked off earlier and were transmitted in a disjointed, edited form that passed as television coverage in the early 1980s. It was a mess and invariably meant rugby league would get between 25 and 40 minutes depending on what other 'more important' sporting events were taking place that day. Tennis, horse racing, golf, football scores and show jumping all took priority. If there was a breaking story after the half-time scores, they simply lopped another five minutes off the rugby league highlights.

The football score flashes dominated games – even if it was only Forfar 4 East Fife 5, Cowdenbeath 2 Corned beef 3– with the screen shrinking to postage-stamp size to bring the earth-shattering updates.

A 2.15pm kick off meant it was nip and tuck for me getting to the game because I had been playing rugby at Hipperholme in Yorkshire that morning. The coach driver got his foot down and we were duly inside the ground with five minutes to spare. I felt really inhibited going to Saints with my school blazer on – it just did not feel right. I was half expecting the headmaster's hand on my shoulder when I bawled abuse at the referee!

My mam would have gone up the wall had she caught me swearing in public. When I was about six or seven my brother had got me in lumber by saying "One cough, two cough, three cough, five cough... which cough's missing? Go and shout it to mum!" I did just that and got a clout for my troubles. You have an insatiable thirst for swear words when you are a kid – and my mam insisted that artichoke and asparagus tips were the worst in the book. How would we know any different – those vegetables were never on sale in Benyon's, the Mayfair or Krazy Kuts in the early 1970s.

Me and my mates stood in the paddock, next to the dug-outs, and that was not a place you could eff and blind with impunity. The previous week Nellie Kennedy, a real Saints stalwart of the paddock, had given my mate an old school ticking off after he had bellowed "you dirty little, fat f...er" to Kevin Dick, Leeds' chunky little scrum-half.

Anyhow – we all felt like swearing after Wigan beat us in every department to win 20-12 and knock us out. New £60,000 centre David Stephenson grabbed the headlines by scoring two tries and a drop-goal. Their fans went home happy – although the ones going back by train had an unusual send off as some St Helens yobs set fire to the Burgy banks near to the train track.

There were suddenly signs that the sleeping giant of rugby league was about to open one eye and have a peep around when a mammoth 17,500 turned up at Central Park to see the Cherry and Whites narrowly lose to cup-holders Widnes in the second round.

For all their signings the Riversiders only just managed to consolidate their position back in the First Division, a feat Fulham were unable to match.

By the time Saints visited Craven Cottage in March, Fulham were already battling with Featherstone to avoid the drop. Saints again won 17-2 in an instantly forgettable, damp squib of a game. There was none of the fervour and passion on the terraces that had been there in the Londoners' first season.

More worryingly for the rugby outfit, the football club under former England and Newcastle striker Malcolm MacDonald had started to gather momentum especially reviving their West London rivalry with QPR and Chelsea. As the Cottagers' Saturday afternoon soccer crowds grew, the reverse was happening with Sunday's rugby men.

It was a massive lost opportunity for rugby league to establish a firm foothold in the south – but despite the optimism of that first term, the odds were really stacked against them. Ironically, had the import ban been axed then instead of a couple of years later, Fulham would have possibly been the best-placed club to attract top-drawer Australians. They would have spent that crucial first term in the top flight more productively, but instead it was the beginning of the end for Fulham's life at the Cottage. Although they bounced back up the following year, they were caught up in the yo-yo syndrome that afflicted those teams outside the top 12.

Inquisitive Saints fans made a day of our first trip to Fulham and the Supporters Club took four coaches, rather than the usual one or two. One of those buses bizarrely took an impromptu detour past Buckingham Palace, Hyde Park and the Houses of Parliament to please a family grouping at the front of the bus who wanted the full London day out treatment. Those on the back seats drew more amusement from passing a Chinese restaurant called Ho Lee Fook.

A few of the usual suspects went to watch training the following Tuesday where we smugly taunted regular die-hard Mr Morgan, who had missed his first game in donkeys' years having only just had an operation. We shouldn't have really and he responded to us young lads with a huff "Buckingham Palace! Wait till you get to my age and are having trouble with *your* testicles, you'll not want to sit on a coach for five hours each way then."

Huyton 5 Carlisle 19, 11 April 1982
Division 2

Huyton – for a St Helens lad in the 1980s – was beyond the pale. Prejudiced view or not, you thought of rough estates where scallies sold knocked-off sides of bacon and socks and a place where hot wired cars ended up being burnt out. The place was only famous for being former Prime Minister Harold Wilson's Parliamentary constituency.

With it being Easter Sunday I was free of Saints duties and cajoled my mate's brother into taking us to Huyton.

He did not seem too keen and when we got there and parked the car I understood why. An unwashed face appeared with those immortal words "mind your car for a quid, la?" It is more than a threat than a service. I got the impression that even though John had handed over a crisp pound note, he was still anticipating seeing his beloved motor propped up on at stack of house bricks on his return at half-past four.

Visiting Alt Park for the first time felt like walking onto the set of television's gritty drama *Play for Today*. Although the small town, which is part of the largely impoverished Knowsley borough, is situated roughly midway between St Helens and Liverpool, its accent and sporting culture was scouse and it is soccer territory.

People who push the theory of selling rugby league to Liverpudlians should have visited Alt Park – the locals hated our game and viewed it as a 'woolly back' sport. The neighbourhood scallies let the club know their feelings by routinely vandalising the ground - concrete terrace slabs were broken, fences torn down, plate-glass windows shattered and the toilets trashed.

Coach Geoff Fletcher once joked about the lions escaping from the nearby Knowsley Safari Park and finding their way to a local estate, where some Huyton kids cornered them. He quipped: "The lions were bloody petrified!"

The club had enjoyed a nomadic existence since first appearing as Wigan Highfield in 1922 before moving to White City for a season as London Highfield in 1933. They returned north as Liverpool Stanley, playing at the Stanley track between 1934 and 1951. They then became Liverpool City and moved to Knotty Ash, minus Ken Dodd's Diddy Men, in 1951.

Huyton came into being in 1968, and although they never won anything they had some half-decent lads from St Helens, Leigh and Widnes playing for them in the mid-

1970s which saw them finish seventh in the second division - above the likes of Barrow, Hull and Leigh - in 1975.

But by the late 1970s they had become the league's whipping boys. Although coach Geoff Fletcher's dedication never waned, it was a thankless task. The former Wigan, Oldham and Leigh prop kept on plugging away, putting his faith and hours of hard graft into keeping rugby league alive in the Liverpool suburb.

Fletcher is a real character – deriving his nickname 'Piggy' from the pigs he kept on a smallholding at the rear of Saints' Eddington End - and he was not one frightened to express an opinion. He actually grabbed the headlines in the *Daily Mail* in the 1980s after getting his wig swiped by Huddersfield's second rower Graham Swale. Long before it became fashionable for bald blokes to shave their heads, Fletcher wore a toupee off the field, so while he was out playing Swales whipped it out of the changing room as a joke. There was probably a frank exchange of views afterwards between Fletcher and the prankster.

New boys Carlisle were going very well in their first season in the Second Division and had already gained promotion by the time of their maiden visit to Huyton.

A large contingent travelled down from the Border outpost and they were left shell-shocked by the near derelict state of the ground, but also by the abuse they received from the handful of scallies who had bunked in through the gaping holes in the fencing. Bizarrely some locals even popped their heads in between the slats of the terrace, which had also been smashed to smithereens by vandals.

The visitors had to contend with 'woolly back' jibes and to the tune of *Tavern in the Town* were treated to a chorus of:

There's a woolly over there,
baggy pants and greasy hair,
With a Tesco T-shirt halfway up his back,
You're a f...ing woolly back!

There was always banter between Scousers and St Helens folk back in the 80s. Folk in town would often answer derogatory woolly back jibes by calling Scousers mushrooms – namely "big heads and brought up in shite!"

Carlisle won the game comfortably. Huyton finally got sick of throwing their seed onto barren land, rubble and broken glass and upped sticks to Runcorn at the end of the 1983-84 season.

St Helens 13 Hull 14, 21 April 1982
Division 1

Saints' cup exit effectively killed off a season that had started so promisingly, but at least our league form began to pick up and we won eight out of the next nine games.

There had been upheaval with unsettled veteran skipper Eric Chisnall being transferred to Leigh. It was sad to see Chis go as he had given the club good service, but sometimes you have to let go. And anyhow new heroes were emerging and different names were being carved into school desks with a compass, not least Roy Haggerty who was an unorthodox, rough-and-ready handful from Thatto Heath. Although he had forced his way into the side in the centre he was switched to loose-forward for the Hull game and later proved a more effective operator in the pack.

36

Away teams' matchday programmes always stated that Haggerty "needs to develop physically" in their pen pictures of him, which my Widnes supporting mate thought was a euphemism for him being a weed. But Haggerty didn't rely on bulk to break tackles, rather his power, sidesteps off both feet, change of pace and sheer tenacity. His scything midfield runs against Hull were a revelation as he helped himself to a try and the man-of-the-match award. Haggerty, however, was an enigma – and would do daft impulsive things if he had a rush of blood to his head. Against Hull he had a top game but then tapped a kickable penalty, which ultimately meant we lost a great match 14-13.

As the years rolled by Haggerty became the subject of so many stories – a sure sign of a genuine local hero. Some were true – when he was substituted against Dewsbury in 1986 he was first in the bath while the game was still in progress. Unfortunately for him Saints sustained a late injury and Haggerty was called back into the fray. Out he strode down the tunnel, with his head covered in white, frothy shampoo suds.

An armful of tall tales appeared after he toured Australia with Great Britain in 1988. One of them now does the rounds of the after-dinner speaking circuit and goes that all the Great Britain players were enjoying breakfast the morning after their first night in Australia when Roy appeared late from his room and ordered bacon, egg and beans. The waiter returned to the table and said, "Sorry sir, we have no bacon". To which Roy replied, "You what! A country full of sheep and you're telling me you have no bacon."

The Championship race between Widnes, Hull and Leigh went to the very last game of the season with Alex Murphy's unfashionable side beating relegated Whitehaven in midweek to clinch the title. Almost immediately Murphy dropped the bombshell that he was leaving Leigh again in their hour of glory, just as he had done after guiding them to the Cup success of 1971. He had been earmarked as the man who could get the Wigan ball rolling again and the rugby league world relished the prospect.

Hull went on to win the Challenge Cup Final replay, beating Widnes at Elland Road with captain David Topliss deserving his man-of-the-match award for a fine two-try performance in a great night for a sport still battling to get the recognition it deserved. The positive images of our final made a refreshing change because the night before Leeds United had been relegated with their yobs trashing West Bromwich Albion's ground to leave football's First Division with a keepsake.

Fighting was daft really – but perhaps it is due to the testosterone that kicks into lads after the age of 12. Most pre-arranged fights at school were poor – they would always start with words such as: "me and you behind the bike shed after school". Those sort of fights would not necessarily be over some big argument, most times they would be to determine the pecking order of who was 'cock of the year'. News of the impending bout would spread like wildfire, so everybody would go out to watch at the last bell. They were usually wrestles and were broken up by the teachers before they really got going. The best ones were those heat-of-the-moment flare-ups – and immediately you would get a crowd in a circle yelling "scrap, scrap!"

My only serious fight came in the fourth year against a stocky lad whom I must have annoyed for some reason. Out of the blue, he belted me with two beauties right on the button, busting my nose and sending my glasses flying. I had to fight dirty to level it up, kicking him in the face and then wrestling him to the ground in a headlock. It all went so quickly, but you could hear the gasps from the big circle. He gave up as soon as it went to ground as he knew what was coming and we shook hands. I had 'won' on a submission but it was a pyrrhic victory as I spent the rest of the afternoon sticking bog roll up my bleeding nose.

Fighting away from school was always worse – and if you were one of those lads that hung around outside shops you would get into scrapes. Most of them were inter-district, and lads off Hard Lane Estate would always go down to Bleak Hill for a fight. Hard Laners even had their own logo at that time, which was an H and L joined together in the same way that the NF merged theirs. You got the same skirmishing in the south end of town. The only ones that ever hit the local newspapers were the tussles with Scousers that occasionally took place in Taylor Park.

St Helens 18 Wales XIII 18, 5 June 1982
Testimonial Match

Roy Mathias had been a great servant for the club and was awarded a testimonial, which unusually involved playing two matches. The first was in his hometown of Llanelli, where he performed with distinction before coming north. It was a painfully long journey down to Wales on a hot summer day – and with no real air-conditioning on the coach, we were all bortered in sweat.

It was an unusual experience going down to a town where English was the second language and hearing the locals talk. You would pick up the odd word in eavesdropping, like St Helens, followed by laughter. One paranoid woman off our coach was convinced they were all "calling the English." The same woman ran on at the end of the game and asked for Welsh prop Glyn Shaw's trademark sweaty headband for a souvenir – which was just a piece of tatty electrician's tape!

Fair play to the locals, they flocked to pay tribute to one of their Scarlets old boys although it had to be played at the Llanelli's non-league soccer ground not Stradey Park where he had learned his trade. Rugby union considered that league was still unclean in those days – but most fans simply saw rugby and did not take on the prejudices of their masters. The Welsh team contained all the old favourites past and present, including dual code international David Watkins.

South Wales was crying out for a decent rugby league team. Unfortunately the experiment at Cardiff Blue Dragons was floundering in their first season. They had pulled in 10,000 for their Ninian Park opener against Salford. But crowds quickly dwindled to 3,000 then to just above the 1,000 mark, which looked daft inside a big soccer ground.

In some respects Cardiff were almost there and their signing of ageing Welsh internationals grabbed some headlines. Paul Ringer's biggest claim to fame was getting sent off for a high tackle playing rugby union against England at Twickenham, Steve Fenwick was a goalkicking former British Lion and Tommy David was a rugged, but mobile flanker.

The trio were joined by ex-pat Welshmen who had been on the northern circuit and some veteran league boys like former Saints stalwarts George Nicholls, Ken Gwilliam and Tony Karalius. But somehow they were missing something else to really make the team tick and encourage open minded rugby fans in the Principality to turn out.

Some of it was not Cardiff's fault – the Welsh public, unlike those who watched Fulham, were rugby literate and could not be fooled into turning out to watch their side play Huyton, Bramley and Doncaster. They wanted to see Widnes, Saints and Warrington, the top teams, who also had decent Welsh converts in their ranks.

Slasher's testimonial match, played on a roasting hot day, ended in a draw. As we sweltered our way home winding through some breathtaking countryside we imagined what nightmares summer rugby would present. That said I was glad of the match to break up the summer boredom and two coach loads made the long trip.

It had been a far from eventless summer with May and June being dominated by Britain's war with Argentina, following the military junta's invasion of the Falkland Islands. That South Atlantic skirmish was followed by warfare without the guns - soccer's World Cup in Spain. Unusually England had managed to qualify following the dismal failures of the previous two competitions. They were joined by Scotland and Northern Ireland. It meant we had to put up with three soccer records in the charts. England's song had Kevin Keegan prominent on vocals as 'Ron's 22' vowed: "This time we'll get it right." They didn't. People's favourites Brazil were outstanding, but Italy won the competition.

Slasher's second benefit game at the start of the following season was against leading amateurs Pilkington Recs at Knowsley Road. It turned into quite a stormy affair with Recs' veteran former Swinton prop Kevin Whittle and Mathias renewing old tussles in a touchline dust-up. So much for it being a friendly – had it been a regular game Mathias would have surely been sent off after landing several blows on his opponent and leaving Whittle with a cut above his eye.

Mathias deserved a bumper benefit – and he continued to put something back into local rugby league on an amateur basis after retiring. You can still see him on the touchlines of Burtonwood Bridge's games in the North West Counties League.

However, it was not so rosy a summer for another of our well-liked Welsh converts. Coach Kel Coslett was told at the end of the season his services as coach were no longer required. It was a shame because Coslett - the club's record points scorer with 3,413 - had been given a tough job to do with the side in transition. Coslett seemed to be getting the house in order by bringing the youth on board when he was shown the door. He later said that if he had failed to get anything out of his side the following year he would have admitted defeat and walked away, but he did not get that chance. Billy Benyon, the former Saints 1960s and 70s centre, took over the coach's reins. Supporters looked forward to his return and he promised he would restore some pride to the Saints jersey.

Geordie prop Paul Grimes drives the ball in the 11-10 Challenge Cup quarter final defeat against Featherstone in March 1983 (Peers)

Alex Murphy in a lively discussion with referee Robin Whitfield. (Peers)

6. 1982-83 The Invincibles

St Helens 7 Carlisle 7, 29 September 1982
Lancashire Cup, Semi-Final

September Man is standing near
To saddle up another year
And autumn is his bridle.

Great words, but those lines from train driver Dave Goulder's fabulous song *January Man* had no meaning to rugby league fans then. For us September was more like a spring month - one of hope, fresh start and new beginning for the year ahead.

We had good cause for optimism and with Chris Arkwright, Steve Peters and Roy Haggerty showing the green shoots of our recovery. Saints got off to a good start in the Lancashire Cup, beating Widnes and Barrow away from home to make the semis.

We were drawn at home in the semi-final against Carlisle, who had beaten cup holders and favourites Leigh in the last round. Still, it seemed straightforward enough, but, marshalled by the tough tackling Denis Boyd, Carlisle came to Knowsley Road determined to do a job and we were lucky to escape with a draw.

The Bordermen had bolstered their promotion-winning side with three then unknown Kiwis - Ian Bell, Dean Bell and Clayton Friend. Scrum-half Friend scored a dazzler of a try, taking the ball from a scrum 35 yards out, beating three men on his dash to the line. Or so I was told – my glasses had been broken in a coach crash the previous Saturday and they had to be sent away for repair. In those days they took yonks to mend, and even then the opticians would have to send us a postcard to say when they were ready. It meant I could not see a thing at the game, just white blobs and darker shades moving in the distance, although I could detect the raised tempo by the noise from the crowd. My mate gave me the full commentary of the match – but it was probably a waste of time me being there. I broke my glasses again a year later, this time just before Christmas, which surely would have meant me 'missing' a few games. I took remedial action by buying a cracking pair of binoculars from the Magpie's Nest – the famous second-hand shop on North Road – and although I had the mickey taken out of me, at least I could see what was going on.

We beat Carlisle in the Brunton Park replay. The tight game ended up 9-8 with Harry Pinner's three drop-goals and another one-pointer from Neil Holding proving crucial as we booked our first final since 1978. It was more like watching rugby union, a game which awarded three points for a drop-goal and in those days only one more for a try.

The game was not without fireworks, with Chris Arkwright and Dean Bell sent off for fighting. Brunton Park was neat enough, but it didn't look like the ground of a team that had once played in football's top flight in 1974-75.

Having 'watched' one game I could not see, my loyalty or stupidity was tested further four days after the replay. I had picked up a bug, and was sick as a dog on the morning of the home game with Leigh and could barely lift my head. When my mates came knocking an hour before kick-off I was straight out with them. I took in little of the game, but kept thinking "any minute now I am going to puke over the non-playing Des Drummond", who was watching the match on the bench to the right of the dug-out. I held out despite my mates trying to make me throw up by talking about a particularly gruesome scene from the video nasty *Driller Killer*. My mate's dad had just bought a video – a Betamax for extra quality – and a group of classmates tended to bunk off in their dinner hour to watch X-rated films such as that, *Suspiria* and *I Spit on your Grave*. Apart from the obvious, watching video nasties was one of several ways 16-year-olds misspent their youth - others headed down to the amusement arcade Lucky Strike to play Space Invaders or Donkey Kong.

St Helens 0 Australia 32, 17 October 1982
Tour match

The Yorkshire television area always had better rugby league coverage than Granada which was possibly due to the cluster of big city soccer giants west of the Pennines.

However, our Redifusion set had a couple of spare buttons that you could twiddle to pick up distant channels HTV and YTV with a very fuzzy picture.

The Australians kicked off their first tour for four years with a fiery opener against Hull KR, which was shown on Yorkshire the following Monday. Unusually it was not the punch-ups and the sending-offs that caught my eye. Through a haze of haphazard dots we saw the ball switch inside to a centre built like a taller, leaner version of the Incredible Hulk. This imposing figure stormed 70 yards down the middle for a try - it was a young Mal Meninga introducing himself to British rugby league. He looked like something else.

Most of the guys on tour were unknown over here because there was no satellite coverage or any widespread circulation of videos from down under. *Open Rugby's* evangelical editor Harry Edgar had tried telling us how good they were going to be, but sometimes you have to witness it before it goes into your brain.

It was a memorable tour, which made Saints' policy of fielding a scratch side against the 'Roos when they came to Knowsley Road even more insulting. Saints had a proud record against the Australians, but with the Lancashire Cup Final taking place the following week, someone chose to field a weakened side. Fair play to 'A' team lads like former Bold Miners prop Bryan Gelling and Mick Glover, who had a really good go in that match, but the policy was an insult to the Australians and coach Frank Stanton described it as a mockery. The idea to rest players dented the prestige of the club and left us ill equipped to deal with the challenge of the following week.

To complete the farce, Meninga's name was spelt incorrectly in the programme and before the game both teams lined up to the 'national anthems' played on a record player. Nobody had told Saints that *Waltzing Matilda* was not the Australian anthem, while Saints got the England football team's version of *God Save the Queen* from the aforementioned football World Cup record. As we left the ground, feeling cheated, strains of *White Cliffs of Dover* came out of the crackly tannoy. You couldn't make it up.

We couldn't really gauge how good the Australians were on that showing against Saints, but they were to sweep away the cream of British rugby league with such style, pace and skill on that tour.

Great Britain's preparation for the series included going to Venice to lose to the French. Although the players seemed to enjoy their trip on the gondolas in Venice, you could imagine them singing *Just one Cornetto.* But they were well and truly sunk when the Australians arrived on our shores.

The first test was taken to rugby league's capital and played at Hull City's football ground. A massive 26,771 crowd was shoehorned into Boothferry Park to witness a 40-4

Australian victory. It sent shock waves through a game that had put up blinkers to the gulf that was clearly opening up between the two nations. The sight of Mal Meninga cutting through and knocking experienced Leeds centre Les Dyl off as if he was a little lad more or less summed it up.

The British game had buried its head in the sand, blissfully ignorant of the way the Australians had developed their game. No longer could anyone say that although Australia had the pace and the fitness, Britain had the skill to combat it. That myth was left, much like Dyl, in a sorry heap on the turf.

They had second-rowers like Wayne Pearce supporting breaks as though he was a three-quarter – and you had backs like Meninga and Eric Grothe who were capable of bundling over our packmen like nine-pins

Long-haired, bearded winger Grothe was nicknamed 'rolling thunder' and looked like a well-fed escapee from a hippy commune, but he terrorised the touchlines on tour, bumping off all-comers. Scrum-half Peter Sterling's blond flowing locks and great support play made him stand out, while his Parramatta half-back partner Brett Kenny demonstrated his silky running skills without seemingly exerting himself.

I wanted a second look and made it to Central Park, Wigan for the second test. It was packed, even up the big banks at the side of the Kop end that were never populated.

Although Britain changed their squad radically from the one that they had spent all summer preparing, the Australians still emerged triumphant to wrap up the Ashes. They did it despite playing with only 12 men following the dismissal of fiery prop Les Boyd.

Central Park was the easiest ground to get to from St Helens on the train but one passenger on the return trip made the journey time seem three times as long. Completely plastered, his self-proclaimed talents knew no bounds.

"I could drive a train," he declared, pointing at the driver, who was visible through the window at the front of the carriage. "Look at him the lazy bastard, all you've got to do is sit there and pull a lever."

He took another gulp from his party can, as I tried to read my programme to avoid eye contact. Brummie comedian Jasper Carrot, who was popular at the time, used to do a gag about the 'nutter on the bus' – well here he was sitting beside me. Then another pearl of wisdom "That *Meringo's* a big get, in't he? I could sort him out up a dark alley, though. No sweat. I'd need a f...ing monkey wrench, though."

The tourists left these shores unbeaten, earning the tag 'The Invincibles' and leaving an indelible mark on British rugby league. The lifting of the international transfer ban two years later would see many of that touring squad return to play spells for British clubs, but their role would be as missionaries as well as mercenaries. Rugby league in this country would never be the same again.

Britain had to at least address its appalling preparation for the series for a start. How could you have three different skippers for a three match series? Veteran scrum-half Steve Nash skippered in the first test and then prop Jeff Grayshon in the second. Then David Topliss was dragged back from a holiday in Spain to skipper the last one at Headingley, after Ken Kelly had been told he had the skipper's armband. It smacked of an amateur night out and we half expected to see Toppo run out wearing a pair of Union Jack shorts, whilst bursting into a chorus *Viva Espana* during the national anthems.

We need not have worried, Topliss had a good game and at least Great Britain showed a lot more fighting spirit in that last test and scored a try. Lee Crooks got an adrenalin rush and a brawl ensued. Livened up by their first competitive match, the home crowd sang to their visitors "Go home you bums!" to the tune of *Auld Lang Syne*. I don't think they meant it – the 1982 tourists were just the shot in the arm our game needed.

Warrington 16 St Helens 0, 23 October 1982
Lancashire Cup Final, Central Park

I was playing rugby for the school that morning against Eddy Camp, who included future Saints star Bernard Dwyer in their ranks. My team lost and Dwyer ran through my powder puff tackles for three tries. Dwyer was a natural athlete as a schoolboy, a top rugby player at both codes, a sprinter and he even beat me in the discus during the St Helens Schools Athletics Championships at Ruskin Drive that year.

The afternoon match was a much greater disappointment than the morning's encounter. At the ground I joined my mates, who were optimistically positioned in the Central Park paddock, tucked in beneath the makeshift podium where the winners would pick up the trophy.

The game was still in the balance at half-time; then Warrington introduced experienced former Saints prop Dave Chisnall. He succeeded in niggling playmakers Neil Holding, Graham Liptrot and Harry Pinner, upsetting Saints' rhythm and knocking them off their game. Big Dave was good at that sort of thing – he was a very shrewd footballer too and knew how to play the game.

Creatively we had better players, but alas my hopes of breaking my trophy duck were dashed by some ferocious Warrington tackling. And after 80 minutes the ribbons tied to the fancy old silver cup were primrose and blue, rather than red and white.

You had to feel sorry for our coach Billy Benyon, although he was not the sort of bloke to wallow in self-pity. Benyon had been sacked by Warrington, despite taking them to within a whisker of the title in 1981, and certainly wanted his side to prove a point. Sadly, the team lacked their coach's fire and commitment that day.

To cap it all for Saints, a frustrated Graham Liptrot was sent off for dropping his knees onto the back of his opposite number Carl Webb. Lippy's action was probably a result of a combination of factors, one possibly being the fact that he had suffered a broken jaw against the Wires the previous March.

For the second week running Saints were nilled, losing by 16 points. When the hooter sounded the Saints fans under the podium turned on our chairman Tom Ashcroft. "Get your bloody cheque book out!" we hollered, before being moved on by the police to stop our barbed comments upsetting the assorted worthies, sponsors and hangers-on seated above us in the directors' box.

Once again a Saints season that had started so well was beginning to unravel. We desperately needed to strengthen the side if we were to compete in the big games.

The Wigan board, namely Messrs Lindsay, Hilton, Robinson and Rathbone, had no trouble putting their money where their mouths were. They had stumped up the cash to turn their club around and had cottoned on to the fact that if they could get it together on the pitch, then 10,000 Wiganers would flock through the turnstiles. Things were beginning to bubble on the banks of the River Douglas with Alex Murphy at the helm.

The crowds had started rolling back and the team had been boosted by the addition of big Kiwi forward Graham West, who was pictured in the *Post and Chronicle* hooking up sheep carcasses from the abattoir. The Riversiders went on to win the John Player Trophy against Leeds in front of nearly 20,000 spectators at Elland Road, which was a bit of an iffy choice for a neutral venue. It made no odds, Wigan won and were back in the big time and the rugby league world seemed to welcome it.

Leeds 13 St Helens 23, 27 February 1983
Challenge Cup, Round 2

In the opening round of the cup Saints beat a barely resurrected Carlisle team 52-0 in a game that very nearly did not take place. The north Cumbrian club had collapsed and the game at Saints looked likely to be their last.

After a relatively poor start to their season Carlisle's crowds had dropped and players concerned about their futures abandoned ship, leaving stand-in coach John Atkinson to scrape a team together. Their former coach Alan Agar had joined Featherstone and turned up at Knowsley Road as a mere spectator, but was called into action as a substitute because Carlisle had kept hold of his playing registration. He would return to haunt us.

There were shocks in the opening round – Widnes were out, lowly Hunslet had unbelievably beaten giants Hull KR and Wigan lost at home to cup fighters Castleford. It meant the competition was wide open.

Following the debacle of the Lancashire Cup Final defeat, Saints' form had picked up. The signing of no-frills prop Paul Grimes from Whitehaven had added fire to our front row. It was a mutually beneficial move because coming to Saints added a new lease of life to the career of the experienced Geordie, who had first turned professional with Leigh in the late 1960s after answering a newspaper advertisement.

His rampaging runs with a dipped shoulder were his trademark and brought cries of "Go on Grittar!" from a bloke in the paddock who insisted on calling him after the previous year's Grand National winner.

The anticipation in town was illustrated by 11 coaches being filled for the trip to Headingley, with hundreds of others making their way in cars. Leeds were also cock-a-hoop following their first round victory over Widnes, so it made for a sparkling cup tie.

At the Thursday training session before the game the players all seemed confident and even had a planned move called 'Lancashire comeback' which seemed fitting for the occasion - Yorkshire (and Widnes) seemed to have dominated our game for too long. The move involved Harry Pinner missing out the first man and sending blockbusting Roy Haggerty scuttling into the hole created by the defence falling for the dummy runner.

The match lived up to all expectations, but it remained tight especially when Chris Arkwright was sin-binned for a late tackle on Leeds's veteran playmaker John Holmes. No-nonsense Arkie couldn't seem to help himself against Holmes and always seemed to leave him a stinging reminder across his face.

The Leeds fans hated Arkie, some thought he was just a head-hunter, but there was a lot more to his game than the odd clout he dished out. 'Tosh' could break the line with his long-striding, forceful running and then display his handling skills.

While Arkie was in the sin bin – using the time to jog a lap of the cricket oval - Leeds closed Saints' lead to five points. It was really edge-of-the-seat stuff until Roy Haggerty's second try - followed by a mass brawl - brought down the curtain on this classic cup tie.

It was one of those wonderful days for the players and travelling fans – we sensed the side was on the verge of something special and the supporters were unusually vocal. Strains of *When the Saints go marching in* increased in volume towards the end – it was music to our ears even if it sounded like a cinder trapped under a closing door.

The music in the top 40 at that time wasn't that easy on the ear either, with the likes of Dollar, Bucks Fizz and Tight Fit cluttering up the charts. There were also the new romantic bands like Spandau Ballet, ABC and Duran Duran battling for ascendancy with keyboard groups like Ultravox, Visage and Human League. The idea of a load of blokes wearing make-up, making a din with synthesisers, was a shock to the system. Wiganer Limahl fronted chart-toppers Kagagoogoo with a haircut like a badger. What had we done to deserve the 1980s?

There was still some good music beginning to emerge from Liverpool, with the development of Echo and the Bunnymen, the Icicle Works, China Crisis and a Flock of Seagulls. Most of the decent young bands would get their first blast on BBC Radio 1's *John Peel Show*, which all the alternative kids listened to. Those kids would then sketch the band's names on their rucksacks to claim them before they became popular. Once the bands hit the charts the fans usually accused them of selling out and scrubbed out their names!

St Helens 10 Featherstone Rovers 11, 12 March 1983
Challenge Cup, Quarter-Final

When your side is playing well, the cup draw brings the familiar cry of "anybody at home!" and mid-table Fev, was perfect.

The formbook was with us, but the omens were not. For successive years in 1958 and 1959, the Colliers had knocked a great Saints side out of the cup at the same third round stage. That was a team of Saints legends Moses, van Vollenhoven, Greenall, Murphy, Prescott, Huddart and Karalius.

Featherstone is only small town - a village really - built on coal and expanded around the crossroads on the road from Pontefract to Wakefield. But it was a village with a tremendous rugby-playing tradition and punched well above its weight – sometimes literally. In the mid-1970s they won both the Challenge Cup and the League title with its notoriously strong pack prominent before it was dismantled and sold off to Bradford and Hull. They had replaced them with another big unit, but had experienced harsher times including a spell in the Second Division. Folklore suggested they called down the nearest mine shaft to recruit a new forward and 11 of that squad worked down the pit for a living. They were a team of few stars but included Peter Smith, the hard-working international forward, and dynamic running second-rower David Hobbs.

Fev were a very solid outfit marshalled by ginger-haired loose forward Terry Hudson, who was at the hub of all operations. Their thick-necked forwards Gibbins, Hankins and Siddall simply flattened us in the middle of the park and we seemed unable to work any space out wide.

It had been a tight game, but we had recovered from an early deficit to take a narrow two-point lead when Roy Haggerty scuttled through for a try. It was still nip-and-tuck but in the closing 10 minutes Keith Bell broke from deep, supported by winger Marsden and put in John Gilbert who cut inside to seal the match in Featherstone's favour. It seemed to happen in slow motion – it was an awful, gut-wrenching feeling. This was supposed to be our year – and that was underlined by the fact that cup favourites Hull were in the stand watching Saints, believing we were the only team left in the cup to beat. Saints' souvenir shop had apparently already ordered loads of scarves and hats anticipating a Wembley rush.

I was absolutely pig sick walking home and it was even worse for happening on a Saturday with a boring Sunday to follow, moping around the house, listening to the gloating commentators on Radio Leeds talking about "Plucky Fev".

Perhaps it was just destined to be Featherstone's year, as they went on to beat Bradford in the semi despite Ellery Hanley showing unbelievable strength to hand off half the Rovers team on his length-of-the-field run to the try line. Fev then rocked the rugby league world by beating hot favourites Hull in the showpiece final at Wembley. Hull were the team of all talents then and were backed by massive five-figure crowds every week, but defeat by the Colliers broke their hearts and also their period of ascendancy in the domestic game. Although they would be dogged by other factors, it would take Hull 22 years to win the Challenge Cup back. For Fev, however, it was their last big day in the sun – and with hindsight nobody would begrudge them that.

Despite those blips it had been Saints' best season for years finishing fourth, behind Hull, Hull KR and Wigan. Saints seemed to be so close to glory, but that made that cup knockout even harder to take. Although Saints could play some classy rugby, the side still lacked a vital ingredient that would turn that promise and adventure into success and silverware.

Our town needed something to put a smile on its face. The job market was non-existent with unemployment nationally well over the three million mark and most school leavers were going straight onto the government's Youth Training Scheme.

Whole swathes of the centre of town were lying empty including the large patch of waste ground from the back of Boundary Road to the bit where you reach the town centre at the end of Westfield Street.

On one crumbling wall – probably where the Mecca Bingo building stands now – a piece of poetic graffiti philosophically urged "Jesus Christ, if you really exist, why do let the suffering persist?"

Some of my classmates mumbled about attending Young Socialist meetings, and you would see handwritten, dog eared notices fly-posted around town, near the Tech college. It was simpler to think about where Saints' next big signing would come from, rather than contemplate whose fault it was that there was land empty and building workers on the dole.

The Tories, boosted by the Falklands Factor and the divided Labour and SDP opposition, were returned to power that summer with a thumping 144-seat majority.

Roy Haggerty scores in the 24-14 win over Hull in the 1984 Challenge Cup second round. (Peers)

Saints' stand-off Steve Peters in action in the Challenge Cup second round against Hull in 1984. Andy Platt offers support, as Hull's Fred Ah Kuoi moves in to complete the tackle. (Peers)

7. 1983-84 One stupid mistake

St Helens 26 Warrington 30, 14 September 1983
Lancashire Cup, Round 2

In rugby union scrummages and line-outs are effectively the key to all that happens in a match, so much so that former BBC union commentator Bill McLaren would go into fits of ecstasy if a team had won one against the head. You also heard rugby union crowds shouting "heave!" at the set piece scrums, to encourage those cauliflower eared lumps in the front row as they locked horns.

Admittedly League scrums were a mess, but there was still a competitive edge to them. The tussle would usually start with both scrum-halves needling each other as to who was putting the ball in, irrespective of the ref's instruction. Some of the best scraps on a rugby field were between the small guys at the mouth of the scrum – like when Steve Nash and Tommy Raudonikis in the first Ashes test in 1978 scrapped like a pair of birds in a cockpit before they got their marching orders.

But it was in the front-row where the art of scrummaging was seen in its messiest form, with both open-side props clashing heads, pushing and pulling each other around to give their hooker the best chance of striking the ball. In the late 1970s you would regularly see the likes of Tony Karalius or Keith Elwell virtually sitting on the floor holding onto their props' shirts for dear life.

Hookers usually bore the brunt of officialdom when refs were instructed to clamp down on technical offences like "loose arm" or "foot up". Contrary to the rulebook, the ball never went straight in the middle of the tunnel and then out at the loose-forward's feet. Instead it was dropped towards the open-side's feet and sometimes it was even tossed behind the prop's legs, usually going unpunished if refs wanted to get on with the game which was usually the case unless they were on one of their seasonal purges of scrum offences. The crowd would always bawl out "feeding", which was as common as "Gerrem onside!" in the 1980s.

It is difficult to pin down exactly when scrums ceased to be competitive – it is like asking when twinnie loaves disappeared, when people stopped getting ½p back for returning milk bottles, when Clock Face crisps stopped being sold or when white dog muck vanished.

But the rule changes in the summer of 1983 saw the beginning of the end of the scrum as we knew it. The downgrading of scrums and the introduction of a turnover on the sixth tackle was one of a number of rule changes introduced. The other big one was upgrading a try to four points.

There were, of course moans, especially from Yorkshire where they built their ordinary teams around the strength of their scrum. Saints fans universally believed that the changes would benefit our side. We got off to a good start in the league beating Hull KR and Warrington. We then met the Wire at home in the Lancashire Cup second round. There was a lot of rivalry between the two clubs, and they were not popular visitors - some Saints fans referred to them as 'scummers'.

"Saints are no great shakes", Wire coach Kevin Ashcroft declared in a radio interview before kick-off, just to add more fat to the fire. There were too many ingredients in the melting pot and the stormy match inevitably erupted into a mass brawl, with punches even being thrown from the other side of the terrace wall. Once the dust settled Saints'

Steve Peters and Roy Haggerty had been given an early bath. Warrington had wingers Phil Ford and Mark Forster sent off along with prop Mal Yates. They also had Bob Eccles and Mike Gregory sin-binned and were close to fielding a sevens team at one stage. Yet despite our numerical advantage Warrington still went on to win 30-26, as we dumbly played it down the middle instead of working the ball wide.

Saints had hit one of those awful, demoralising patches and a crushing 32-6 hammering by Oldham was our fourth defeat in five games - not even the famously delicious Watersheddings' meat and potato pies took away the sour taste.

The club needed new players, but our gates only averaged around 4,500 so money was not there to compete with Wigan and the Hull clubs in the transfer market. There were no sugar daddies in town willing to bankroll our club. Instead it was the small man and woman who did their bit, with every penny counting. I did a Big Ten lottery round covering 100 houses scattered from Dentons Green to Windlehurst taking commission of £2.25. It was less if somebody palmed me off with a couple of Irish 10ps or pesetas when they had been coppering up on the dark Thursday night doorstep. Some weeks that was compensated by people giving me a tip and Windlehurst folk particularly were always quite generous and cheerful.

The round was a labour of love – it was a way of helping the club and a cut-price season ticket was thrown in. It was also a way of getting into conversations with fellow Saints fans in the days when website conversations belonged to *Tomorrow's World*. That doorstep chatter broke up the monotony, but on the flip side it made my round take twice as long. One 40-year-old bloke would collar me for nearly an hour every week. He was one of those fellas that had always worked, provided for his family and had spare money to watch Saints home and away. But then he lost his job and now followed Saints only on the radio. His 15p was now his link to the club he loved.

It was a crying shame, but unemployment had made him really angry, a bitterness that was directed evenly between a poorly performing Saints, particularly Clive Griffiths, and Maggie Thatcher, who he insisted on calling "that blue bitch". After the Oldham defeat he was predictably livid and following a long build up concluded, "I could play for t' Saints, I am doing nothing else, I've no job. What a shower - I feel like going down to training to chuck f… ing bricks at them."

Barrow 12 Widnes 8, 1 October 1983
Lancashire Cup Final, Central Park

Barrow, who had been relegated the previous season, had done well to reach the final, beating our conquerors Warrington in the semis. They were not given a snowball in hell's chance against cup kings Widnes, but I went along to shout for the underdogs. There was plenty of Barrow support, but a gang of bone-headed Wigan Athletic football followers on Wallgate set upon one group of exuberant fans. One shaven-headed Barrovian vainly protested his innocence as the coppers bundled him into the back of their Black Maria with blood streaming from his face after coming off second best against a Latics hooligan mob. It was an awfully long way to travel to miss the game, especially one of such magnitude. It was the only sour note of the afternoon.

Widnes appeared too powerful in every department but Barrow ripped up the formbook and won the cup 12-8. It was so pleasing to see a club as proud and as down to earth as Barrow win what was then a major competition. In my short time of supporting St Helens, unfashionable clubs like Featherstone, Leigh and Barrow had all won cups. Surely it would be our turn soon?

St Helens 29 Bradford Northern 14, 23 October 1983
Division 1

Some players dream of going out in a blaze of glory beneath the Twin Towers – but a good portion just get one last smack in the nose and go home and throw their boots in the bin. It was the latter that sadly brought the curtain down on Saints' Welsh international prop Mel James's 11-year career.

The former Swansea heavyweight came off the bench midway through the second half at home to Northern, barely a couple of minutes later he was being led off with the physio rubbing the magic sponge over his bloodied face. That was his inglorious farewell to professional rugby league.

Remarkably Big Mel had first hinted at retirement after the Wembley defeat of 1978, but soldiered on to start another six seasons. He had been a solid servant since signing from rugby union, but now we needed to move on. His replacement had arrived earlier that month when we swapped Gary Moorby for Leeds prop Tony Burke. At the time coach Benyon believed Burke "would add a touch of devil to the pack". It also allowed Andy Platt, who looked every inch an international of the future, to take up his place in the second row. Saints' pack now had plenty of mobility especially with the emergence of young Paul Round.

The close season had seen another member of our 1976 cup winning team leave the club, with Peter Glynn joining Salford and their goalkicking full-back Steve Rule coming in the opposite direction. We hoped Rule's kicking was a lot straighter than his nose – his flattened hooter veering sharply to the right.

Our team was still very much made up of St Helens lads, because money was still tight, Saints were lucky that the town was so awash with talent and those players were usually expected to sign on purely for local pride. Unfortunately that didn't pay mortgages, rent or food bills and over the years Saints had missed out on some fine local players who had gone elsewhere – Test players Ian Potter and Brian Case, who gave their best years to Warrington and Wigan, spring to mind.

St Helens had a very good amateur network with clubs like Pilkington Recs and Blackbrook leading the way, while new club Thatto Heath were emerging at Sherdley Park after being set up by former Saints full-back Frankie Barrow.

Pilks played at City Road and wore the red, amber and black colours of their forerunners St Helens Recs, who had a great tradition in the game in the first half of the century until their demise in 1939. The Glassmen had supplied many players to the professional clubs, but in the mid- to late 1970s their core of star men stayed as amateurs rather than take up the offers to turn professional. BARLA internationals Peter Glover, Joey Hull, Sid Wright, Billy Simmonds, John McCabe and Jeff Gormley were integral cogs in the Recs machine that dominated the amateur game – regularly winning the National Cup, Lancashire Cup and the North West Counties League.

City Road was a regular Saturday afternoon haunt for me between 1979 and 1983 – and you really do see the game in the raw at that level, with just a rope separating you from the action. You feel the heavy, bone-crunching tackles put in by the like of Ken Cross and Arthur Manning. You also hear every instruction and insult. Recs stand-off McCabe was pound-for-pound one of the hardest men I have seen on a rugby field, but also a very gifted footballer. He signed for Huyton at the back end of career before returning to the amateur game with Thatto Heath.

Recs came within minutes of toppling Castleford in the 1978 Challenge Cup, with Mal Reilly's side needing a very late try that day to save their blushes in front of a big Knowsley Road crowd. Recs also only narrowly lost a couple of cup ties against Wigan in 1977 and 1979.

A lot of outsiders really don't know how widespread the amateur game is in the sport's heartlands. There was always this common misconception usually from sports fans in the south that all rugby league was professional and nobody in their right mind would want to play this game purely for pleasure. Nor do outsiders know how much genuine dedication players, coaches and the 'Touchline Tommies', who run on with the bucket, show from week-to-week. Unlike union international players, league's amateurs had to raise their own funds if they wanted to take their place on a tour, buy a blazer or a pullover.

Disgracefully the old colonels influencing the RFU still prevented a free gangway for those playing amateur league to union and vice-versa. This was as clear an indication as any that those barriers were simply an instrument to continue their vendetta against league and nothing to do ensuring their game maintained Corinthian values, for it was amateur league players they were restricting. It was sheer hypocrisy particularly when you threw in the 'boot money' scandals that had come to light and the lavish expenses that were doled out to certain players.

Kent Invicta 7 St Helens 40, 6 November 1983
John Player Trophy, Round 1.

The Garden of England was an unusual setting for the start of Saints' John Player Trophy campaign. Kent Invicta had been set up in the southern outpost of Maidstone to follow in the footsteps of expansionist pioneers Fulham, Cardiff and Carlisle.

All three of those clubs had been beset with problems, on and off the pitch. Despite the warning signs Invicta, based at Maidstone United FC's London Road stadium, were determined to press ahead. The RFL understandably was also keen to see the game expand at all costs, but it was incredible to just put a club into an area, without any local culture of our game at school, youth or amateur level and expect it to develop.

Kent had knocked together an average looking squad, including veteran of the Fulham pioneers Ian van Bellen, and they did a least make efforts to base the team in the south.

There was one slight twist, with Kent signing Mark Elia, a young New Zealander who apparently had come to England to play cricket. Immediately it created enormous publicity as the media initially thought they had signed Mark Ella, one of the famous Wallaby rugby union international brothers. For good or ill, Elia was destined to make headlines in his own right in years to come.

Kent's supporters seemed quite keen, but there were too few of them, and enthusiasm doesn't pay the bills. A small cluster of Maidstone United supporters turned up out of interest, and they sang "Football League, here we come!" to a really bad tune. They had been non-league giants, who eventually got their wish to be admitted to the Football League. But they were only there three years and folded in 1992.

Kent's flirtation with rugby league was even shorter lived, and the following year they were implanted into Southend, Essex. There, their feeble crowds, including one of 88, were lost in the massive Roots Hall football ground and they were removed from the league after just one season.

The novelty factor meant Saints Supporters Club took about three coaches to the posh, quaint little town on the banks of the River Medway. A few checked out the souvenir shop where they sold badges with a black horse on their Invicta badges – strange given it was the white horse county.

We won quite comfortably with former Cowley lad Colin McIntyre grabbing a brace of tries. Watching the players train the following Tuesday it was disappointing to see him brought down to earth with a rollicking from one of our senior players during the tick and pass session. "Just because you've scored two tries doesn't make you a f…ing superstar!" I suppose that sort of thing goes on in any workplace with the new kids on the block. One of my mates had left school that summer to do was doing YTS – and said his colleagues tried the full range of pranks on him. In his first week they instructed him to fetch a glass hammer, left-handed screwdriver, told him to go and ask the supervisor for a long stand and sent him to the pie shop at break for some navy cake. It could have been worse - a lad I knew started at Proctor and Gamble Pharmaceuticals in Skelmersdale and he was sent up to the labs where he was told to ask a young assistant if he could borrow her fallopian tubes!

Warrington 10 St Helens 18, 19 November 1983
John Player Trophy, Round 2

The fall-out from our previous stormy encounter with Warrington was still being felt two months down the line. A ring-rusty Roy Haggerty was playing his first game back after a harsh six-match suspension handed out following that battle of Knowsley Road.

The game was a cracker and nowhere near as bad-tempered as the previous clash, with Neil Holding's peach of a try being the highlight. Saints crucified them with drop goals, with Harry Pinner kicking two and Barrie Ledger and Holding notching one apiece.

The result was not the only talking point - Saints came out onto the pitch wearing something looking like a tracksuit. It turned out to be our new away kit, light blue with a darker blue chevron and sleeves. Chevrons really were so 1980s. The kit had to be changed to enable our sponsor's logo, St Helens Glass, to be emblazoned across the players' chests in white lettering.

A couple of weeks later we would see the disappearance of our old white shirts with a simple red vee which we had worn for well over 20 years, to be replaced by red sleeves and red chevron.

It was a rarity then to change strips – years later it happened every season to tie in with the market for replicas. Although our subsequent kits, bar one, remained relatively decent, plenty of clubs ditched their traditional kits in order to fit in too readily with sponsors' demands. Sponsorship was now an essential part of a game that could not rely purely on gate money to survive.

Wakefield 31 St Helens 22, 8 January 1984
Division 1

Relegation battlers Wakefield were one of the first sides to bring over an Australian star after the import ban was ditched. Wally Lewis's signing, and the Australian entourage he brought over with him, gave Trinity a real shot in the arm. With his one handed, 30 yard spin passes, Lewis was a revelation and his hat-trick was the key factor in their 31-22 victory over us. Lewis scored those tries despite the best efforts of his opposite number Steve Peters, who seemed to belt him as hard as he could at every available opportunity. Peters – a player who could play scrum-half, stand-off or centre – was tough nut in Saints' ranks. It was like playing with a seventh forward – and in those days we needed it. The big-hearted former Blackbrook lad would tackle all day and was a sound passer of the ball. He just lacked half a yard of pace and a kicking game that would have made him an international.

One player not lacking in pace was winger Barrie Ledger, who had developed into our best winger since Roy Mathias. Ledger scored an absolutely belting try at Belle Vue that afternoon, taking the ball on the right-hand side, deep in his own 25 before going on a diagonal run across the pitch, tempting and beating the tacklers before straightening up for the last 30 metres to touch down on the left. We led at half time, but failed to score in the second half and contributed to our run of six defeats out of seven. Only three successive games against strugglers Whitehaven, Fulham and Salford eased Billy Benyon's men out of the mire.

Wakefield - for all their investment in 'King Wally' - still finished second from bottom in the league and were relegated. It was hard to believe that these former giants of the game, playing at the ground that was the setting for the classic Richard Harris film *This Sporting Life*, were now little more than a yo-yo side. It was another reminder of how fragile success was in rugby league and how the old certainties were changing.

St Helens 16 Leigh 10, 12 February 1984
Challenge Cup, Round 1

Saints' John Player hopes were killed off by Widnes in a nondescript semi-final at Wilderspool and our league form was patchy, which meant that all our eggs were once again placed in the Challenge Cup basket.

And in the opening round a very well drilled Leigh side, coached by former Saints scrum half Tommy Bishop, looked on course to smash every single one of those when they took a 10-0 lead.

It got worse when hooker Graham Liptrot took a smack in the face and was led off the pitch holding a towel to his face and all feared that his jaw had been smashed again. Incensed, I paced up and down the paddock manically, calling for summary justice to be dispensed to the culprit. I had not even seen who had allegedly done it but in that blinkered, partisan way immediately blamed their battle hardened veteran second rower Tony Cottrell. The robust former BARLA international had joined the Hilton Park outfit late in his career after an illustrious stint with amateur giants Leigh Miners Welfare. He was a bit of hard knock, a street-wise rough diamond. Thankfully word filtered out that Lippy had *only* suffered a fractured nose.

Fortunately the players did not respond to my fist shaking tantrum from the paddock and stuck to their game, settling down with a couple of penalties and then a try by Andy Platt to level the scores.

The game was still delicately poised on a knife-edge until Holding nipped in for a well taken try, picking himself up from a heap of bodies to do a daft high stepping dance behind the line, which looked even more ridiculous when shown on *Granada Reports* the following day. It had been a magnificent cup tie, and Saints had shown real character in coming back.

St Helens 24 Hull 14, 25 February 1984
Challenge Cup, Round 2

Hull were still a fine team, backed by a huge support, but the previous year's shock Wembley defeat had wounded them. But in leading try scorer Garry Schofield they had recruited a truly gifted try poacher. The 18-year-old had a knack for sniffing them out, but it was not going to be his day today. Skipper Harry Pinner had a blinder, sending speedy second rows Andy Platt and Paul Round tearing through countless gaps. 'Haz' also helped himself to a try and four drop goals.

I watched the video of the match round at my mate's house and thought that Alex Murphy's summarising skills were hilarious. After Pinner hoofed over his last one pointer the Wigan boss declared, "They'll probably give him the Town Hall clock!"

Did *Grandstand* viewers down south really envisage the workmen from the corporation scaling the old building to dismantle the historic timepiece and transport it in crates to adorn the Saints skipper's back yard? Murph was full of sayings like that. "If he's got a bad leg, I wouldn't mind two of them!" would apply to a player who is supposed to be injured. "It's like walking day in Belfast" would greet a try when a winger simply had to collect the ball and touch down. And when a player butted an opponent Murphy combined Kojak and comedian Bobbie Ball's catchphrase to remark "Who loves you Tommy!"

Saints' mobile pack was playing well with tall, rangy and awkward looking handful Paul Round coming on leaps and bounds. In later years he was dubbed 'Rambo' after the Sly Stallone Vietnam avenger on account of his willingness to get stuck in and have a go. One match saw him take a stray knee to the head making a tackle – which clearly concussed him - but tried to go back onto the pitch despite wobbling around like a New Year's Eve drunk.

With the back-row bolstered Peter Gorley had moved successfully up to prop, which gave him new life. The quiet man was under rated, but he would make surging, tackle breaking runs, and always have the ball available. Week in, week out Eric Ainsworth, a long standing Saints fan who stood in the paddock, would beseech the side's half-backs to 'Follow Gorley, and you'll get a bagful!'

Peter must have looked enviously at his brother Les who had signed for 'Cup Kings' Widnes and helped himself to a drawer full of medals, including two Challenge Cup winners. Some Saints fans argued that 'We had signed the wrong Gorley', preferring the battering ram charges and abrasive approach of Big Les, then the mobility of Peter.

St Helens 7 Wigan 16, 11 March 1984
Challenge Cup, Quarter Final

The rain fell hard on the morning and afternoon of our crunch quarter-final tie, which was the last thing we wanted because Saints' light, mobile pack suited the firmer grounds. We were a top of the ground team, but to make matters worse they allowed an under-17s curtain raiser to cut the pitch up even further making parts of it look like a paddy field. Maybe I am just looking for excuses for yet another heartbreaking loss and the end of another Wembley dream.

The game revived the halcyon days of the 1960s and despite the rain it pulled in Saints' first 20,000 crowd for well over a decade. Full houses like this had been regular features in the 1950s and 1960s, but nobody envisaged those days returning in the era of colour television and videos. The big crowd was due to the Wigan sleeping giant rumbling – their hordes had tipped up over Billinge and made up almost half of the crowd. We took a spec up on the 25-metre mark on the Popular Side – the bad news started for me just before kick off when a lad I knew from school decided to tap me on the shoulder to tell me that the rain had revealed I had an egg in the nest. I could cope with being 17-years-old and bald, but not losing to Wigan. It just wasn't my day.

In many ways the showdown saw the 'Good, the bad and the ugly' sides of rugby league. The good was the way in which Saints matched the Wigan pack in the middle, and then took their chance superbly when speedy wing Barrie Ledger waltzed in for brilliant try in the corner, magnificently goaled by Griffiths. At 7-4 it was close, but we thought our side had just done enough in the boggy conditions to clinch it. It was like trench warfare without the bullets and bayonets – with both sides just doing the basics and forcing the opposition to fight for every yard. It was that muddy Wigan had to borrow our change strip in the second half as their first half kits had become obliterated. "Murphy, Murphy what's the score?" taunted the Saints' popular side, where the over-sized dugouts were now located.

We sensed that Benyon's men had the tactics and personnel to keep that lead as the conditions deteriorated, but then came the bad. Griffiths, who had been found a place on the wing for his kicking expertise, moved inside to launch a sixth tackle punt. But, in an unfathomable display of tactical ineptitude, the Welshman wellied the ball to the side of the pitch that he had left unmarked. Speedy teenage makeshift winger Shaun Edwards collected the ball and darted into the hole created, racing the length of the field. Although he was just about held, but our defence was ragged, allowing John Pendlebury to plunge over from the next play. It was a killer blow and our players' heads hit the floor, allowing Australian Mark Cannon to seal it with another. Saints fans streamed out stunned and dejected, whilst the Eddington End packed mostly Wiganers, erupted with jubilation. All you could hear was 'Wig-un! Wig-un!' with the first syllable excruciatingly elongated. The Pie-eaters were on a roll, but a big dollop of good fortune was fuelling their momentum.

One old bloke, who had left early to beat the crush, was happily making his way home assuming we had won asked me the final score as I overtook him on Rivington Road. '16-7 *to them!'* He looked so wounded. Here was an old man in his 70s who must have lived through the depression and the Second World War, yet still could be almost reduced to tears by defeat in a rugby match.

It said a lot about the history between the two clubs, especially in the Challenge Cup, but more about how much we invest in the team we claim as our own. What it means to ordinary people, who crave just a glimmer of glory to brighten up dull, monotonous days. It is only a game – but success on a weekend can send you to back work or school on a Monday with a spring in your step. It can make the wait for your Giro on a Wednesday almost bearable – especially if you have spent your last couple of quid going through the turnstile. A small share in your team's weekend triumph can make you almost feel important in a world that often makes us feel useless and isolated. In Saints' case it is glory that many in the town may have taken for granted in the past – but were now just craving a little flashback.

Billy Benyon's post match interview with Gerry Burrows on Radio Merseyside was excruciatingly painful to listen to. All he could utter was, "One silly mistake has cost us today. One stupid error…" He didn't name Griffiths, but that is clearly whom he blamed and the Welshman was sold to Salford before the start of the following year.

So that was the good and the bad. The ugly came in the hooliganism that marred the occasion, with two sets of lads blatantly using the cup-tie as an excuse to fight each other. The ground was packed so the only place to fight inside the ground was up at the open restaurant end where the heavy rain thinned the crowd and allowed both groups to periodically swing punches and aim some kicks at each other. A mob of Wigan thugs had caused pandemonium en route to the ground, smashing one of the big windows in the Top Nags as customers cowered under the tables inside. In the town centre, the Rope and Anchor had a television set thrown through the window and according to press reports 'police were called because rival fans poured their own beer and threw dominoes and bottles at each other.' Dominoes were never usually the choice of weapon in a saloon bar brawl you see in the westerns. Billy the Kid drew a mean six shooter but he was terrible at throwing a double six.

Clearly the protagonists weren't true rugby fans but seeing fighting on that scale made our sport's statements on the malaise of soccer seem very hollow and sanctimonious.

The *St Helens Leader* – the town's newest free paper which didn't even cover Saints week-to-week – suddenly discovered the way to Knowsley Road and splashed the shock, horror hooliganism story on the front page. It seemed that only bad news was new for them.

Widnes 19 Wigan 6, 5 May 1984
Challenge Cup Final, Wembley

"Lydon strikes faster than the Miners!" read one big banner nailed to a couple of washing line props in the Widnes end. Centre Joe Lydon vindicated the banner writer's faith in him by scorching in for two long range tries. Wembley was always good for home made banners – great as long as some oaf did not put one up in front of you. The previous year Fev had 'Hull have the Kiwis, but Rovers have the polish' and you would always see one about Joan Collins with only the name of the full back changing!

Wigan had overcome a strong challenge from a plucky York team to get to Wembley for the first time in 14 years – and on the motorway going down their success-starved supporters outnumbered their Widnes counterparts by at least three to one.

Familiarity had bred a degree of contempt on behalf of some of Widnes' fickle armchair supporters but having made it to the Twin Towers with monotonous regularity – seven times since 1975 - Wembley could quite rightly claim to be their twin town.

After everything I had heard about Wembley, my lasting impression of the inside of the ground was a feeling of disappointment. 'Welcome to the world's largest urinal' should have been posted outside. The stairwells were deep with 'second hand ale' by the interval and at full time a waterfall was cascading down the steps. It was ok if you had a sturdy pair of shoes, but one woman in front of me came a cropper after unsuccessfully tried to negotiate a dry passage in her open toed sandals.

The match was a battle of wits between two Saints legends - Alex Murphy and his old protector Vince Karalius. Vinty performed with distinction in the great sides of the 1950s and 1960s before tasting further Wembley glory with his home town Widnes team in 1964. Many of our older fans still recounted the exploits of 'the Wild Bull of the Pampas'. He had made his money from scrap metal and had coached the Chemics in the 1970s before moving to the Wigan hot seat. After that he spent a period out of the game after going into the tax exile on the Isle of Man. The word exile made him sound like

Napoleon, although Karalius too, was a natural leader of men, but this one never met his Waterloo!

Pedestrian Wigan just did not perform, particularly overseas players like flamboyant Australian Kerry Hemsley, who had been flown back for the final. Hemsley looked an unusual character – a cross between a member of *ZZ Top* and an American wrestler.

Murphy lambasted his overseas players particularly after the game and vowed Wigan would be back next year. They would be, Murphy wouldn't!

Our solitary Saints Supporters Club bus was completely lost among the sea of coaches on the vast Wembley car park. All coaches look alike and two or three members of our posse failed to find the coach and made their own way home. But as we were waiting a drunken Wigan buffoon on the next coach decided to strip off and start manipulating his buttock cheeks to make his backside talk. It was on of those 'car crash' sights that you look at even though it knocked you sick. The old women on our bus could not believe anyone was capable of such vulgarity and shielded their eyes.

Hull KR 21 St Helens 16, 7 May 1984
Premiership Semi-Final

Rovers' fearsome pack led by giant flat nosed Kiwi Mark Broadhurst laid the foundations to their Championship success. Going to Craven Park was a tough task, but Saints were playing well and had confidently won at Warrington in the first round.

Bank Holiday Grandstand televised it with an idiotic 11.30am kick off, meaning another early start on the M62 for our growing band of fans. In Harry Pinner's absence, Chris Arkwright had been moved to loose forward where he gave a tremendously gutsy display. Arkie had plenty to motivate him after just being notified that he was being withdrawn from the Great Britain Tour squad to Australia after he had been measured up for his blazer. It must have been like checking off 23½ points on a pools coupon, only to find out your collector had not put it on and pocketed the money.

Medical advice claimed Arkwright's troublesome knee wouldn't stand up to the hard grounds on the gruelling Australian tour and yet other players with similar injuries made the trip.

Arkwright's actions spoke louder than words, grabbing an early try in this game, and Saints led at half time. Sadly a late try by Rovers' centre Mike Smith was enough to end our dreams.

Players, coach and fans alike - we were all gutted, the team had given their all, but that just wasn't good enough. The curtain came down on a season that despite promising much, left us with a trophy cabinet gathering more dust. Rovers fans told us so too, singing in their own inimitable way, "You've won f... all again, St Helens, St Helens!" The song rang through our heads as we sped back down the M62 to signal the closing of another chapter.

Summers were generally boring pre-Super League, but some of them stay with you forever. For me the really hot one of 1976 still conjures up imagery of scalding swarms of ants with kettle water, lolling outside Benyon's corner shop with frozen jubblies, Lasse Viren winning double gold at the Montreal Olympics, and the West Indies cricketers making a mockery of England skipper Tony Greig's promise to make them grovel. Six weeks school holiday felt like it was forever then.

Similarly 1984 was such another memorable hot Olympic summer – Orgreave, Frankie says T-shirts, Zola Budd and Mal Meninga's signing etched it permanently onto my memory.

British athletes Daley Thompson and Seb Coe were among the big Olympic winners, with the British vest-wearing Springbok Zola Budd being the highest profile loser. The bare footed distance runner legged up America's blue-eyed girl Mary Decker in the 3,000m final. There were tears all round apart from those who enjoyed a bit of schadenfreude, particularly after all the shenanigans in getting her over here.

St Helens light-flyweight John Lyon, the Commonwealth champion from the Lowe House Boxing Club, made the quarter-finals before being beaten by eventual gold medal winner Paul Gonzales from the host country.

For the third Olympics in a row politics had intervened with all the Soviet Bloc countries, bar Romania, boycotting the Los Angeles games in retaliation for the America's non-attendance at the previous Moscow event.

Politics dominated the summer. The miners strike over pit closures, which had started in March, developed into a long war – and polarised opinion nationally. It started following NCB's chairman Ian McGregor's declaration that 20 pits were 'uneconomic' and would have to shut, leading to a possible loss of 20,000 jobs. The NUM saw it is as the thin end of the wedge and then that was it, the miners were called out on strike without a ballot.

Stories in the local press told of the hardship of striking miners at Bold and Sutton Manor collieries, who were being forced to sell cars, televisions and video recorders. Support groups had been set up taking daily collections of food, clothes and money from other parts of town and beyond.

To those who believed what they read the *Daily Mail*, the miners were bully boys being led by a megalomaniac Marxist with a political agenda, but to others they were just honest working men, fighting for their jobs, homes, families and communities.

The battle outside Orgreave coking depot south of Sheffield between 5,000 striking miners and police from 10 counties, including cavalry, was the incident that really grabbed the country's attention. Even people who had never even met any miners had an opinion one way or the other after that.

Frankie Goes to Hollywood provided the musical backdrop to the summer with singles *Two Tribes* and *Relax*. The latter had been banned by the BBC's Mike Read earlier in the year for its explicit lyrics, and promptly went to the top of the charts.

The video to Two Tribes, which depicted US president Ronald Reagan brawling, biting and gouging in a cockpit with ageing relic of a Soviet counterpart Konstantin Chernenko, was also banned. It was quite a haunting song, particularly the use of the siren, and especially for those who believed the world stood on the brink of nuclear war. CND had grown into a massive protest movement. On the other side of this highly-charged debate were those in favour a strong western response to a Soviet threat and they were pro-Reagan, Maggie, Rambo and the independent nuclear deterrent. To them CND stood for communist, neutralist, defeatist!

Aspects of the Two Tribes video were shocking but most people just bought the record because it was a lively pop tune and Frankie were 'in'.

Aside from the summer's musical and political distractions – there was only one story. Mal Meninga, the giant Australian centre, who we had seen wreak havoc two years previously, had signed for the Saints. Former Saints player Ray French, who was Down Under to cover the Great Britain versus Australia test series for the BBC, actually delivered and collected the contract to and from the big man. Saints had been interested in star players before, but they had always just slipped through the net. 'Let's just wait and see', said some. That cynicism was excused because we were well accustomed to half hearted bids used to temporarily appease fans' thirst for a big name. But despite Leeds and Wigan's interest this time we had got our man and there was a tangible air of anticipation in the town.

The previous seven barren, trophy-less seasons had been a long hard slog for the team, town and its supporters. We may not have won anything, but the bulk of our fans had remained loyally hopeful that our developing young talent would one day produce a change a fortune. But we needed a catalyst – Meninga would surely be that man.

On the eve of the season Wigan coach Alex Murphy was given the bullet after a heated exchange with chairman Maurice Lindsay on the day of the Wigan Sevens – which apparently involved a telephone being thrown. A fair few of us gloated!

8. 1984-85 Miners, Meninga gnomes and scally hats

Bradford Northern 30 St Helens 10, 30 September 1984
Division 1

The previous year Saints had ditched their training ground in favour of the new fangled synthetic pitch down at Queens Park, known as Reccy Park. The large open space to the north of the town centre had been filled with flag wavers when the Queen came up to open the scented garden for the blind during her Silver Jubilee Tour in 1977. While she was here she didn't take a swig of 'corporation pop' from the drinking water fountain that used to be positioned between the bandstand and children's swings. Those dispensers, in the days when people would have thought you barmy to pay for bottled water, were a godsend on a hot summer day, but have all gone now. The shock of AIDS probably saw them off really – by 1984 everyone was probably a little confused and ill informed about this new illness. The previous June saw film star Rock Hudson diagnosed with the ailment and the tabloids were packed with 'gay plague' horror stories, and the sixth form common rooms full of juvenile jokes. Older people, women in particular, could not believe that 1950s Hollywood heartthrob Hudson could be 'one of them.'

Anyway, such grim stories were of no concern once the season got under way. There were happier stories to lift us and a real sense of anticipation among Saints fans was building up. That expectation was reflected in the increased turnout of fans at training sessions. Usually there were only a handful – the real experts were John Morgan and Gordon Lawrenson who were always there rain, hail or shine and both could always tell which players were not pulling their weight. "He'll never be a footballer as long as he's got a hole in his backside," was one of Mr Morgan's favourites. Another – directed at a slow three-quarter we had – was "He's too much lead in his arse for a centre!" Former Saints and Salford scrum-half Bob Prosser and die-hards Neil Connolly and Ged were also regulars at training, as was milkman's mate Dickie, even if he did tend to be the butt of the jokes.

Some women supporters had turned up at Reccy Park to view the talent when the first of our trio of Australians arrived, Paul Hamson. Maybe they expected a caricature of a bronzed Bondi Beach muscle man - but one middle-aged woman turned to the other and within earshot of Hamson balled, 'My God, I thought these Australians were supposed to be 'andsome. He's as ugly as sin!'

Of more concern was Hamson's playing, which didn't really come up to the standards we had anticipated. It was a pity really because he was pleasant enough, but he was like one of those kids that had all the right kit, knew what to do, how to train and what to eat – but ultimately had expectations beyond their capability. Surprisingly Hamson never re-appeared in Britain as a coach, armed with a clipboard, collection of certificates and overhead projector charts. He made his debut in the 84-12 win over new club Mansfield Marksman in a pre-season friendly. He then came on as sub against Bradford, in a match that saw Saints throw away a 10-point lead to concede 30 unanswered points.

One of the highlights was a long-range score from another newcomer – this time from a lot closer to home. Sean Day joined from Culcheth and was a rarity having turned up at training with an anti-hunting tee-shirt reading 'For fox sake stop the hunting!'

The Bradford game, and the one at Hull KR the preceding week, was typical of a lot of displays we endured in Yorkshire. It was the last match Saints played before Meninga arrived, and was like the lyrics of Blancmange's *The day before you came.* After Mal galloped in on his white charger, nothing would ever be the same again for our fans who had 'never had it so bad.'

St Helens 30 Castleford 16, 7 October 1984
Division 1

I should have been the first proper Saints fan to welcome Big Mal to Knowsley Road. My mates had been talking about his arrival all morning because we knew he was due to arrive in Britain that day. At dinner break we took a speculative shufty up at the ground after calling into Burke's bookies for a fixed odds coupon and the 'Crispy Cod'. As we stood there eating our splits on the stone wall facing the training pitch a biggish blue car suddenly swung in from Dunriding Lane to our left. It was Big Mal, being chaperoned by Margaret Burrows from the Lottery Office!

My three mates Kingy, Si and Wello, without any hint of hesitation, were over the wall to greet him and get his autograph on tatty bits of greasy chip paper. How's that for a proper welcome to St Helens? Like a big chicken I stayed on the other side finishing my chips - the wall remaining a symbolic dividing line between star player and fan. It sounds daft but it was almost like I wanted to put him on a pedestal although I did spend all afternoon, and subsequent months and years, wishing I'd spoken to the giant.

Meninga's first match saw a crowd of 7,500 turn up – not spectacular, but twice the size of Saints' previous home game's gate. We did not to go home disappointed as Big Mal thundered through for two tries in a convincing 30-16 victory.

When the ball was worked his way he was simply devastating as he brushed off the attempted tacklers. It was just like giving the ball to that oversized kid at under-14 level – with similar results.

From scribbling his name on a few chip wrappers Mal now penned the opening lines on the first page of another chapter in the history of St Helens RLFC. But never satisfied, unbelievably there were still grumbles from some supporters. "He'll have to improve his bloody goalkicking!" mumbled one elderly fan coming off. Meninga's style of pointing the ball towards the posts and then toe-bunging it was a bit suspect, but that was the least of our worries.

St Helens 31 Leigh 10, 10 October 1984
Lancashire Cup Semi-Final

My mate Dave Davies was stood on what has become 'the Scaff' on the half way line of the Popular Side when he started the very first chants of "Veivers! Veivers!" It caught on instantaneously and was a spontaneous response to the little known Australian plucking the high balls out of the air and then returning them majestically to set up the counter attack. Everybody thought Veivers had only come over to polish Mal's boots, carry his bags and go boozing with him for seven months. After shaky debut, the blond full-back from Brisbane played a blinder against Leigh – and was to become part of the furniture at the club over the next 10 years. The chant stuck with him for the duration.

His eye for the ball was brilliant and his bottle didn't go under the pressure. Those "Veivers!" cries greeted his every move and singing generally swept down the popular side, radiating from the half way line. There had never been so much singing at Knowsley Road in decades. John Woods, who at 27 had become Leigh's 13th coach in 14 years, took plenty of stick from the half way line. To the tune of Boney M's *Hooray, It's a Holiday*, he was taunted with:

John Woods, John Woods,
Johnny, Johnny Woods
When he gets the ball,
he does f...k all,
Johnny, Johnny Woods!

Saints won to go through to the Lancashire Cup Final and we filed out of the ground elated, making a beeline for the Black Bull. The Bull was handy for a midweek match, but with licensing hours being what they were it was always shut between 2pm and 7pm on a Sunday when most games took place. The pub was my first regular haunt and I spent most of my school lunch times in there. The lounge had a snug area where the older customers drank in the evening. The bar had a separate pool room where young lads, usually from West Park Sixth form, would stick beer mats in the pockets and play as many games as you wanted for the same three 10p pieces, as long as no-nonsense but amicable landlady Rita didn't catch you.

Alcopops had not been invented and so if you wanted your beer to taste like pop you got a lemonade top on it. The strongest booze you could get in a bottle was Greenalls Old Chester or Old Glory, which were fine, but definitely an acquired taste. The Bull also had a function room where The Housemartins played not that long before they became they hit the charts with *Happy Hour* when Fat Boy Slim was plain old Norman Cook.

Like most of the town's public bars the Bull's daytime customers were largely old men dotted around the best seats near to the radiators, but with a view of the television. There they would sit passing time, watching the racing or the western on BBC2 and muttering the occasional two-word sentence at each other. Even though a gas fire had replaced the old coal fire, one old cock still insisted spitting into the grate. You would hear the tsst as the green globule of spit fried on the bars of the fire.

Another regular always sat next to the bagatelle table, but as soon as someone approached he would pick up the cue to instruct the young lads how to play the game. Most us were not that interested; we only went on for a knockabout because that, unlike the pool table, was free. Bagatelle is an odd game with holes in the table that you had to knock the balls into from a curved cushion. It is virtually extinct in pubs nowadays.

The bar side was an overwhelmingly male environment – apart from the barmaid, the only time I saw a woman in the public bar was when one fetched her husband's dried up tea between two plates, wrapped up in a towel. It was a form of protest really on her part, and she thought it would shame him. But "Mardi" as we called him because of he was always singing some dreadful old song about "Mardi Gras", was already sozzled and lapped it up and even asked for the bread and butter!

Wigan 18 St Helens 26, 28 October 1984
Lancashire Cup Final, Central Park

The Saints bandwagon continued to roll, as we rattled the points past Hunslet, Halifax and Oldham. Some weeks it was just too easy, but there was always another talking point and other players in the spotlight. The crowds were up and the town walked with a collective spring in its step. It wasn't a one-man effort, but because Big Mal attracted the opposition's attention it was creating extra room for the other players to really turn it on. The final had been due to take place at Warrington's 14,000 capacity Wilderspool which normally would have been ample size to host the traditional county finale. But rugby league was experiencing a real boom in South West Lancashire and Knowsley Road and Central Park were the only rugby league grounds big enough capable of holding a 20,000 crowd. We tossed for the venue and Saints lost, requiring us to venture into the lion's den and wear our change blue strip. Despite the heavy drizzle over 26,000 rolled up for the cup's first Sunday final.

Saints' first half display went like a dream with Mal Meninga scoring two and creating one for Sean Day, which combined with a blockbusting effort from Roy Haggerty, gave us a 24-2 half time lead.

If you look very closely at Shaun Edwards' forehead nowadays, when he is television summarising for rugby union games, you can still see Meninga's hand print from that day. Big Mal was unstoppable – so the 18-year-old makeshift full-back Edwards had a decent excuse and it did not leave any permanent damage on the lad's confidence.

Wigan mounted a ferocious second half onslaught with Graeme West, Henderson Gill and Nicky Kiss scrambling over for scrappy tries.

The tension mounted and Gill went so close to scoring, but he was held up and then crunched in a tackle and stretchered off. Our only second half score was a Day penalty, which settled our nerves a bit. The boy from Culcheth looked more like a soccer player than a rugby league player, but he gave a nerveless display and his kicking was a feature in the win.

Saints held on for their first trophy win since May 1977. It was only the Lancashire Cup, but it meant so much and blokes in their 40s were welling up when proud skipper Harry Pinner raised the ornate piece of silverware. We ran onto the pitch afterwards to congratulate the team during their lap of honour and not even the handful of Wigan knuckle draggers, who followed us singing "We hate *Scousers!*" could knock the smiles off our faces. There had been a small pocket of trouble during the game, with cans of beer being thrown in the skirmish, but it was no big deal.

There was only one other grumble - the television coverage. We wanted to share our 'Big Mal' experience with the rest of the world and show them what delights had been delivered upon us after seven years of misery. For the first time the BBC had decided that they weren't going to show the final on *Grandstand* on the same day. Instead, they cobbled together highlights, which showed little more than the tries the following week. The Beeb had chosen the year when both County competitions had more interest than ever to curb their coverage. The all Hull Yorkshire Cup Final had also drawn a 25,000 plus crowd at Hull City's Boothferry Park. League was yet again getting the smelly end of the stick as far as television coverage was concerned. On a tatty piece of A4 foolscap, ripped out of my History 'A' level folder, a petition duly went round and was fired off to BBC. Whoever was charged to read it and respond to the document probably didn't even get past the "We the undersigned" bit at the top. It lost what tiny credibility it had when people added Alf Hart, Don Kiddick and M. Mouse to the list of objectors.

Meanwhile Saints marched on through October and November undefeated, and playing superb rugby.

Bradford Northern 12 St Helens 12, 2 December 1984
John Player Trophy, Round 2

Odsal was a tip – the huge bowl had been carved out during the ice age, its huge banks had been added to in 1923 by the dumping there of household rubbish. It all created a unique setting for a rugby match. It was vast, and had staged the famous cup final replay of 1954 in front of a 102,000 plus crowd. Because they had had that remarkable physical capacity in the past, endless time was spent in the early 1980s discussing the prospect of building up Odsal as the 'Wembley of the north.'

One end of the ground was the huge open terrace, and behind the other posts was steep clay banking which was impossible to stand upon. It looked terribly grim.

The bowl was so vast and open to the elements that it made for a terrible winter venue. The changing rooms were so far away from the pitch, that the players remained on the field in a huddle at half time. Odsal also hosted speedway, meaning the pitch had fold up corners – bizarrely although the speedway has gone those raised corners remain a feature of the pitch today. It is possibly the most awkward feature for visiting wingmen, who had to get used to a kicked ball stopping or rolling back in the corner behind the try line.

For the John Player tie hordes of fans journeyed over the Pennines, and mostly stood up at the big open end behind the posts. Our hosts were treated to several renditions Dvorak's *Largo from the New World Symphony* or more familiarly known as the Hovis advert theme. Saints were now taking a large following away from home, and it was a real transformation from the one coach load of hardy souls from only four years before.

It was a terrific, nail-biting cup-tie with Saints getting a draw against an Ellery Hanley inspired team despite the dismissal of Roy Haggerty for a high tackle. Saints won the replay quite comfortably in front of another boisterous 10,000 crowd.

All seemed rosy when Saints then demolished an Australian packed Leeds team in the league with Harry Pinner and Chris Arkwright to the fore. The match had been quite close until the last 20 minutes; then the men in the red chevron simply tore them to shreds, winning 48-16 at Knowsley Road with a wonderful brand of flowing rugby. Saints felt invincible and we savoured every second of it. If, like in Jim Croce's song *Time in a bottle*, you could capture and keep for posterity a period in time, that special autumn of 13 unbeaten games and great nights in the Black Bull would certainly be in there. They were great days to be a teenage Saint.

The club missed a trick when it came to marketing at the time as a lot of the young lads were wearing scally hats. It was a trendier version of the bob cap, but the idea was to split them in half, so one half would be blue for the rejuvenated Everton and the other green and white for Celtic. There were a few permutations between the two Merseyside clubs and their Glaswegian counterparts. Had Saints thrown theirs into the marketplace they would have sold a few hundred, even if they would have been instantly cannibalised and sewn up with a soccer team. The scally look of slightly flared cords or jeans, and a mullet haircut was in vogue in town.

Some of the town's youngsters may have looked to Liverpool for fashion, football, music and Zone Tickets, but older folk in town longed to go 'Back to Lancashire!' Some felt the town's identity was being eroded by the proximity to our larger neighbour and believed soon our distinctive dialect would be overtaken by Scouse. Others were a bit more dismissive of the militancy associated with the city, believing that would deter businesses from coming to the 'Merseyside region'. A *Militant* Tendency influenced

Labour council ran Liverpool at the time with the sharp suited motor mouth Derek Hatton to the fore.

St Helens 8 Halifax 14, 22 December 1984
John Player Trophy, Quarter Final

We looked forward to Christmas – a festive period that had Band Aid's *Feed the World* as its back drop – but then our bubble was pricked by a collection of largely unknown Australians. We all thought their player-coach Chris Anderson was some Aussie has-been, over in England for a career swansong at a slower pace. Nobody could have even imagined then what this Kangaroo coach in waiting was about to achieve at unfashionable Halifax. That afternoon they closed us down, and surprisingly went on to record a famous 14-8 knock out.

Apart from Anderson's coaching prowess, there were other explanations doing the rounds as to why the wheels had come off Saints' season in such an unlikely fashion and in front of the BBC cameras.

Drink was top of the list. It is hard to know the truth because St Helens is a terrible place for gossip and Chinese whispers. Some players felt that the wild allegations that did the rounds across town blew matters out of all proportion. There were sufficient grounds, however, for the club to slap an alcohol ban on all players, saying those caught drinking within 48 hours of a match would be dropped.

Like any industrial town, St Helens folk liked to have a few drinks and let their hair down. The town's most famous boozer was Joe Johnson, who could sink a ridiculous amount – and did a lot of supping for charity. He was regularly featured in the *St Helens Star* in the 1980s and among his exploits was out drinking an entire rugby union team at a spring fete. Another famous challenge involved supping a bucket of beer quicker that two Thwaites' Brewery dray horses. Apparently Joe finished first and then snatched the trough off the pair of nags and gulped that down, froth, snot and saliva from horses' mouths and all. Once he had his 'railings' out it is claimed that he could sup 60 pints in a session, although he did have a puking bucket to bring it all back up in. However, some health campaigners got wind of these exploits so he then drank water for charity.

Drinking was part of most sports' cultures, but you would not list any of our players as Champagne Charlies. There was obviously some discontent in the camp with press reports suggesting that Phil Veivers was threatening to fly home, while our leading scorer Barrie Ledger was put on the list at £70,000. Saints' feeling of invincibility had slipped, and Wigan took full advantage four days later at Knowsley Road on Boxing Day.

Although Saints got back on the horse at Widnes with a New Year's Day win, a bad winter set in with proper thick snow bringing sport to a grinding halt. A break in the season was the last thing we needed really, with January's league programme decimated Saints were unable to erase the memory of those Christmas defeats and recover from that mini implosion.

St Helens 3 Hull KR 8, 21 February 1985
Challenge Cup Round 1

All we had talked about since Mal's arrival was getting to Wembley but champions Hull KR at home was a tough opening hurdle. The ice and snow had shunted this game back and it was eventually played on a Thursday night. It was as tense a tussle as you could imagine. Some things in life deliberately put you on the end of a cliff, leave you clinging on desperately and agonisingly by your fingernails. Just when you think there may be a hope of pulling yourself up, some clodhopper comes trampling along with size 12 toe cappers to send you plummeting. Sometimes, like in this game, the eventual fall is so inevitable that the drop and collision at the bottom of the rocky crevasse is preferable to the agony of clinging on.

Saints held a 3-2 lead and were tantalisingly close to going through when the combined efforts of Gavin Miller and Gary Clarke sent us tumbling out. That result was not in the script back in those heady autumn days when we all envisaged our date at the Twin Towers. If we couldn't get to Wembley this year with big Mal in the side, when could we?

The following Wednesday Saints suffered a 46-point drubbing at Hull and it seemed like we were back to the early 1980s mode of thinking again – a side going through the motions to pick up their losing pay. At least Ste Lea, a young stand-off from Bold Miners who had a limited run up at the club, gave classy Australian scrum-half Peter Sterling something to think about after cracking him a few times.

But Meninga was copping most of the verbal flak from opposing fans, especially after his star billing of the autumn. The knives were out from Saints supporters too and at the Boulevard one irate and hoarse speccy kept yelling "Do something Meninga, you fat pig! You're not here for a bloody holiday." Saints' difficulties were not Big Mal's fault, so it was unfair for him to take all the stick, even if he was on a reported £1,200 a game. It was simply that he was supposed to be our saviour! After walking on air in autumn, the harsh winter had brought us crashing back down to earth.

Featherstone Rovers 13 St Helens 14, 3 March 1985
Division 1

Featherstone, with its hostile crowd and tight little ground, was a difficult place to visit at the best of times. And this was anything but the best of times – in fact it was the worst time to visit a mining village that had endured a year of hardship. The strike was coming to its bitter end that very day with a specially convened meeting of the NUM national executive narrowly voting for an orderly return to work. Despite that whole year of sacrifice, the miners went back to work defeated and without an agreement on pit closures. It effectively sounded the death-knell for the British coal industry and dealt a severe body blow to the idea of collective working class action.

The strike affected Featherstone more than any other club – they had even given fans season tickets 'on the slate' conditional on them being paid back once the strike was over.

It was neither the time nor place for a handful of outsiders, who knew little about sacrifice or struggle, to start taunting the locals. Sadly a coach of young lads from St Helens, fuelled by Dutch courage from a can, did just that. They got a hiding behind the back of the stand for their troubles from local blokes aged 16 to 60, including many wearing orange labelled NCB donkey jackets. After being given a bit of time to lick their wounds, they were rounded up and escorted out for their own good by private security guards with what appeared to be wolves on leads. They did not have policemen patrolling at Fev's Post Office Road ground – then again they would not have been that welcome in a mining town in those days.

The police did, however, have to attend that afternoon because one St Helens lad was slashed across the back with a kitchen knife. It was obvious something bad had happened because a crowd gathered at one of the corners backing onto the row of terraced houses following one skirmish

The game was a real bruiser also, littered with off-the-ball incidents one of which resulted in Graham Liptrot getting his jaw broken for the fourth time in his career. He was clobbered by Fev's lumbering second-row Neil Clawson, who just caught him late and high, and once again Lippy's career looked under threat.

The Colliers thought they had clinched the win with a Keith Bell drop-goal, but Holding's late penalty snatched it by the odd point. In the grand scheme of things the result of a rugby match was not that important on that raw, murky afternoon at the crossroads on the road to Pontefract.

St Helens 47 Hull 18, 22 March 1985
Division 1

With spring on the way, Saints put their miserable mid season blip behind them. Leigh's chunky hooker Gary Ainsworth, who had come in on loan to replace Lippy, pepped up play in the loose. Our clash with Hull marked the turning point of our fortunes.

The game was switched to Friday night to accommodate *RL Action*, who showed highlights of that night's match later that evening in the Granada, Border and Yorkshire areas. This series was far better than the one that had first appeared in 1981, which televised one of Sunday's clashes, showing it very late on a Monday night, usually after awful networked American programmes like *Quincy*, *WKRP in Cincinnati* and *S.W.A.T.* had been shown.

For good or ill *RL Action* gave the first big break on television to one half of the Richard and Judy phenomena. Richard Madeley co-presented the show with long standing rugby league broadcaster and writer Keith Macklin.

The Hull match turned out to be a cracking game that did much to take the edge off the sour taste of winter. Skipper Harry Pinner played a blinder, and the team's overall passing and support play was tremendous.

Leading 17-12 at the break Saints took complete control in the second half. The try of the match saw Neil Holding race from the base of the scrum, feed centre Phil Veivers, whose lobbed pass found Barrie Ledger. The nippy Saints wingman cut inside four Hull defenders, on a diagonal inside run towards the posts, before releasing to the supporting Steve Peters. He combined with Big Mal to leave Sean Day with a walk in at the corner.

Our 47-18 triumph cancelled out the 46-24 defeat they had embarrassingly given us at the Boulevard some weeks previously.

It was a perfect evening with the only minor blemish being one police officer's bid to kill the noise on the half way line, where Saints' choir was located. The veteran cop was possibly in league with clean-up campaigner Mary Whitehouse or God's cop James Anderton and concerned that bad language would be picked up by the TV microphones, which were dangling from the temporary scaffolding above our heads.

He deliberately plonked himself in the middle of us and was on a one-man mission to clean it up the scaff. It was daft really because it simply agitated blokes who stood there for donkey's years without causing a hint of trouble. It also encouraged the younger lads at the very back to taunt him with the tune from *Laurel and Hardy*. Despite the occasional stare from the grey haired bobby - which did not stop the singing – it was a loud, lively night.

Perhaps they should have sent him down to Luton, where the previous week had seen some of the worst hooliganism to ever take place in a football ground. There the police had to retreat as Millwall fans brandishing anything they could rip out of the stand, attacked the police. It was the game that prompted Thatcher to instigate the idea of making all football fans carry identity cards. Luton took no more chances and simply banned away followers from attending their games.

Leigh 30 St Helens 26, 21 April 1985
Division 1

Despite the winter's troubles, Saints had picked up enough points in the spring to be in with a fighting chance of winning the championship. Alex Murphy was back at Hilton Park for his third stint there but it was a far cry from three years previously when Leigh had been champions. Murphy had returned too late in the day to preserve their First Division status. Saints fans in the crowd showed no mercy, with cries of "going down, going down!" ringing around Hilton Park.

To win the league Saints had to beat Leigh and leaders Hull KR had to lose at Barrow on the last day of the season. The Robins kicked off an hour earlier and by half-time news filtered out that they had already won their match, and therefore the title. Some Leythers must have unsubtly let that result seep into the dressing room at the break – because our players' heads dropped and we just let it drift away. We were left to think of the stupid games Saints had lost that had cost us the title, like the daft defeat at Oldham by a couple of points and the sloppy midweek game at Castleford.

Although it had been the best league campaign for 10 years, we really were left thinking of what might have been. The displays of the autumn had really spoiled us rotten, but at least Saints were coming good for a run in the Premiership. Our rivals Wigan had bigger fish to fry having made it to the Challenge Cup Final for the second year running.

Hull 24 Wigan 28, 4 May 1985
Challenge Cup Final, Wembley

'Classic' is perhaps the most over used word to describe sporting events – but the 1985 Final was worthy of that description. It had the lot - thrilling rugby, long-range tries, a brilliant comeback and a gripping finale. That Wigan won, clinching their first Challenge Cup for 20 years, was a minor drawback for most of us neutrals who had gone down for the day out. Some of us were prepared to let them have it on the basis of the sparkling rugby they played that afternoon.

Games such as this really helped to boost our sport's appeal to a wider audience and *Grandstand's* millions lapped it up. It was a PR dream, particularly on the wings where John Ferguson, the Aboriginal wingman who had flown back for the final, crossed for two superb tries after that little shimmy then dart left the defence clutching at thin air.

On the other flank crowd pleaser Henderson Gill polished off a magnificent long-range try before turning to the camera with a big cheesy grin.

The Lance Todd trophy went to Brett Kenny, another pupil of the Australian class of 1982. He nonchalantly strolled onto the pitch with his hands in his shiny red tracksuit pockets. Despite his casual manner, Kenny played with such a devastating effect and was the difference between the sides.

Wigan clung on despite a Peter Sterling inspired comeback and the hooter was greeted with understandable jubilation. Wigan fans flooded onto the supposedly sacred Wembley turf, much to the dismay of the players, who wanted to take their lap of honour unhindered and unmolested by the giddy hordes.

As we left the ground we all mocked one kalide Wigan fan, who had fallen asleep face down on the grass embankment outside the ground. He had missed the match and his side's finest hour and to make him feel worse supporters leaving the ground took advantage of his drunken stupor to empty rubbish on top of him as they passed him - he was buried beneath a pile of discarded ale cans and chip wrappers.

One of his Wigan colleagues inside the ground was worthy of more pity. Just as the big cup was being raised a boozed-up Hull fan stood a few yards to the left of me and my mates – decided to urinate up this pie-eater's back. A bizarre scrap ensued, particularly as the stupefied Hull fan still had one hand full as the disgusted Wiganer gave him a good slapping!

St Helens 37 Wigan 14, 7 May 1985
Premiership Semi-Final

Some days the rugby league planners made some barmy decisions, but the one to make Wigan play their Premiership semi-final three days after their Wembley win was perfect for us! Initially they wanted the game to take place on the Monday, which was just crazy – we wanted to claim some credit for winning! Wigan were nursing knocks, suffering from tired limbs and hangovers from the effects of Wembley that we thought they would not bother. Wing Chica Ferguson didn't – he flew straight home without even picking up his Wembley pay packet while compatriot Brett Kenny played as if he was already on the plane. Surprisingly Wigan's adrenalin helped them in the opening stages roared on by a good section of a mammoth 20,000 crowd. They had brought thousands to welcome their homecoming heroes, so much so that Saints' Cumbrian prop Peter Gorley could not get through the heavy traffic coming over from Wigan and pulled over just off the East Lancs Road near Carr Mill Dam and jogged the last three miles of his journey.

The game was close for a spell but once the tired legs of the Wembley victors buckled, Saints stepped up a gear and coasted home 37-14. Saints were in the Premiership final for the first time since 1977.

St Helens 36 Hull KR 16, 11 May 1985
Premiership Final, Elland Road, Leeds

Back-to-back champions Hull KR were the most consistent team of the season and had also won John Player Trophy. Fortunately, when they came up against us in the Premiership Final they were missing their inspirational Australian loose-forward Gavin Miller, who had done more than most to knock us out of the cup earlier in the year. Saints' key Australian Big Mal was there and had a crucial impact on the game.

The Final was taken to Elland Road to give it a bit more prestige and to generate more receipts from the extra seats, but Headingley would have probably have provided a better setting than a quarter full football ground. It was a big ground to fill and the barriers that separated sections and steel fences around the pitch were alien to our followers. It was set up like a war zone – built to police Leeds United's infamous followers from the Service Crew and anybody who wanted to have a pop at them.

Most fans were lumped together into the Kop, which was huge – probably treble the size of our Eddington End. Our group had mixed well with a gang of Rovers fans in the bar before the game but when Saints scored their first try a mob of boneheads waded into us, fists flailing. We escaped from the front line just as the 'Towners' arrived mob handed, waving a big Union Jack with 'Town Baddies' painted across it. Police kept a peace line to enable us to concentrate on the game. The most serious incident after that was an orange being tossed back-and-to until it was too soggy to be thrown any longer.

The match was too good a game to get distracted by that sort of juvenile rubbish, with Gary Ainsworth scuttling in to give us a great start. Our second try by Phil Veivers looked to be from a forward pass, but we got the benefit of the doubt from referee – and future Saints kit man - Stan Wall officiating his last game. There was no doubting the brilliance of our third with a surging break by Mal Meninga only halted by a crunching, high, tackle by Rovers' full back George Fairbairn. However, quick hands, particularly from centre Steve Peters, saw the ball whiz across our back line for Barrie Ledger to waltz in at the other corner.

Determined Rovers hit back, but Meninga's first interception of the afternoon from a David Hall pass ensured that Saints went in at half-time in front.

The opening stages of the second half saw Rovers test our defence, but crucially it didn't flinch an inch. Then came that pivotal moment – and one that is etched upon the memories of those Saints fans stood up there on the Kop that day. Meninga latched onto another loose David Hall pass before steaming fully three-quarters of the length of the pitch running towards us, holding off Fairbairn for a crucial try. It broke the Robins' resolve and Harry Pinner sold an audacious dummy to score by the posts and then the flying Ledger grabbed his second, sparked by Neil Holding, to seal the 36-16 win.

The victory was a perfect end to a season that had seen us finally escape from the doldrums. Much of our success was the due to our young local players maturing and the coaching of Billy Benyon, but nobody can ever underestimate the role Meninga played in the 'Return of the Saints'. Big Mal had completed his afternoon's work and his stint for the Saints with two crunching tackles. Unfortunately he hurt his own shoulder with the last tackle that lifted Kiwi test centre Gary Prohm off his feet. Mal was left wincing, holding his shoulder. Surely he did not feel pain like a mere mortal? It was his last act for Saints, as he left the field a few minutes from the end to tumultuous applause.

His all-too-brief stint at Knowsley Road will always be remembered - Mal earned his Sainthood, and the honour of being cast into clay in the form of Meninga gnomes!

The big man was apparently offered everything from becoming the licensee of the Seven Stars, massive cash incentives and accommodation to return to St Helens. Perhaps it was better for our memories that he didn't return and went out in a blaze of glory. That is the way we will always remember him - picking up trophies in that light and dark blue chevron jersey.

Taking a shine off the day was the desperately sad news from Bradford City's Valley Parade where 56 football fans had perished in a fire in the stand. Viewing the horrific television footage on the evening news bulletin on the Black Bull's telly it was hard for supporters to take in that these ordinary sports fans had set out just like us that day. The incident occurred but a few miles from where we were rejoicing and celebrating. We just shook our heads – we had all stood and sat in grounds like that, and much worse, in our time and we counted our blessings.

Mal Meninga in the thick of the action on his St Helens
debut against Castleford in October 1984. (Peers)

Harry Pinner and Barrie Ledger raise the Lancashire Cup at Central Park, after
beating hosts Wigan in October 1984. (Peers)

A moment to savour! Mal Meninga scorches over the Elland Road turf, leaving Garry Clarke and George Fairbairn in pursuit, to grab a crucial try in the Premiership Final against Hull KR in May 1985. Note elated commentator Elton Welsby cheering from the touchline. (Peers)

A Mal Meninga break ends in a crunching tackle by George Fairbairn in the Premiership Final. But with the cover pulled out of shape, St Helens scored from the next movement. (Peers)

Skipper Harry Pinner is chaired by Andy Platt as he raises the Premiership Trophy.
Also in the picture are Barrie Ledger, Paul Forber, Gary Ainsworth and Phil Veivers.
Steve Peters and Neil Holding are at the front. (Peers)

9. 1985-86 The morning after the season before

Wigan 30 St Helens 2, 2 October 1985
Lancashire Cup Semi-Final

Proper town centre pubs seemed to be diminishing by the day in St Helens in the mid-1980s – and some of those that remained had makeovers, which invariably involved a plastic plant arrangement. The age of the off-licence, videos and the decline in manufacturing jobs probably contributed to the change in drinking culture. The Scarisbrick had been turned into a second hand record shop, The Cotham Arms had shut, the Washington and Volunteer knocked down to be replaced by a car park and chemist respectively.

To celebrate leaving school a crowd of us did a Thursday night crawl round the town centre to see what was out there. We started off at half past five from the Sportsman's, a Boddingtons pub with a Saints tradition, in Duke Street. It used to be the Talbot Arms, and in the 1920s Saints used to change there before going to the match in a horse drawn wagon. A pub sign painting of Vince Karalius is a reminder of its Saintly heritage. From the Sporties we moved over to the Turks Head and the Anfield Arms in Cooper Street then eked out a route to Chessies (Exchange Vaults), run by cockney John Sines. The Clarendon, which was thriving then with its own newspaper, and the Traveller's Rest were next stops before our posse headed past the dole office and police station to rejoin Duke Street for the Lamb, Rope and Anchor, Duke of Cambridge and the Rifle Corps.

From there it was a walk across the waste ground and rubble to the Sefton, Wheatsheaf and the Royal. We looped out to the Cricketers, the Golden Lion, the Float and the Liverpool Arms.

The latter two were in Green Bank and opposite a block of maisonettes that made up the since demolished St Thomas' Square. Thicker than a Green Bank butty was still a common expression in town at the time. Town was full of daft expressions like that – "She looks like Tilly going for liver" was applied to a young woman who looked a bit of a mess and "I've seen more meat on Good Friday" would describe a skinny person.

The Phoenix, then run by former Saints and Cronulla scrum-half Tommy Bishop, was our next stop followed by The Bridge, which has since been flattened to make way for the new road that passes the new cinema. You had to go under a subway to get back to the bottom of Bridge Street where we hit the real towny pubs, of which the Market was packed with it being a Thursday 'pay day'. To get into The Nelson in the mid-1980s you had to wear 'kecks' – so we had no chance, not even wearing a pair of 501s, which thanks to Nick Kamen were massively popular at the time.

It was straight up to The Angel, which was a nice but pokey little split bar/lounge pub with a sloping floor. The name Angel suited it, when it re-opened as the Brasserie Chalon some years later most of the town's drinkers referred to it more bluntly as 'the swinging tit'.

We headed up the stairs at the Fleece, which was the town's poshest hotel before it was demolished to make way for W.H. Smiths, and just made it across town to the George and then the Alfred before the last bell. We all looked as though we had been dragged through a hedge backwards. On our way home I was thrown head first into Harry Pilkington's fountain that used to disfigure Church Square. What was the point of that fountain? It always seemed to be dry and full of old cans and chippy wrappers.

When the water was working it only took an odd bottle of washing up liquid from Money Save to make it foam over.

While Meninga was here it had been like we had been supping the finest Greenalls Original every week. What followed after his departure was like taking a sip of that open can the morning after a party – the beer was flat and somebody had put their dog end out in it.

While Saints fans had generally wallowed in celebrating 'how good the Meninga party had been' during the summer, Wigan used their summer more productively strengthening their hand with the signings of top drawer Australians like Greg 'the Wall' Dowling and Steve Ella, the game's top try scorer Ellery Hanley from Bradford and Great Britain forward Andy Goodway.

Saints signed three hit and miss Australians - Gary Greinke, Ross Conlon and Brett French. Enough said! French did show some flashes in his stint for us, but the others weren't in the same class as the Wigan signings.

Saints' Lancashire Cup semi-final illustrated the painful point perfectly. Twelve months previously at the same ground Saints had looked magnificent, as we had stormed to our first trophy in seven years. Now we just looked pitiful as we lamely surrendered the cup, slumping to a 30-2 defeat. Prior to the game one of our forwards allegedly said, in anticipation of his confrontation with Greg Dowling, "I have been knocking down walls for years!" Talk is cheap - Dowling was one tough cookie and was still upright after 80 minutes. After this mauling the writing was on the wall, not just for Saints, but also the rest of the league.

St Helens 8 New Zealand 46, 27 October 1985
Tour Match

The 1985 test series with the Kiwis really caught the imagination, with some sparkling tries in the opening two games and the series level going into the final match. Saints' Harry Pinner skippered the Great Britain side magnificently throughout, and he was one of the many home players who suffered facial cuts in the brutal third test at Elland Road. Andy Goodway had been stretchered off after being clobbered by Kurt Sorensen and later David Watkinson left the field in a bloody mess after a mass brawl from a scrum, which ultimately saw a member of West Yorkshire Constabulary enter the field. Lee Crooks saved the series with a magnificent touchline penalty after a pulsating encounter.

In contrast, the Kiwis game at Knowsley Road, was a complete non-event and we suffered a 46-8 drubbing, our biggest defeat by the Kiwi tourists in 34 years. Many of the 8,000 crowd drifted off before the final hooter, all thinking something drastic needed doing. Even though performances did pick up slightly in November, the die had already been cast.

In early November all Saints fans were summoned to the town hall for an extraordinary meeting. We all thought it was going to be the announcement of a new signing or a club takeover bid. Would we get there and see the chairman magically tap a table with a wand and make Mal Meninga appear from behind a velvet curtain? Not on your Nellie!

We smelled a rat as soon as we saw the lottery office women armed with clipboards taking names and addresses. Those fears were confirmed as soon as chairman Lawrie Prescott opened his mouth, with his nasal tones revealing that Saints were starting a fund raising scheme, the Saints Alive Society. Fans would be asked to pay £2 for a weekly draw with top cash prizes, with funds raised being used to buy players. There was a crescendo of boos, with cries of "Skinflints" and "Dip in your own pockets for a change!" hurled from the town hall balcony. We thought that our board was that tight you imagined some of them still had half-eaten packets of Spangles in their pockets.

Only the appearance of highly respected former England centre forward Nat Lofthouse, who had overseen a similar scheme at Bolton Wanderers, stopped it being turned into a complete shambles. Blokes like Lofthouse were held in high regard on account of the things he had done on a football field. Had 'the Lion of Vienna' not spoken so well then the galleries would have emptied pronto, but even the most sceptical stayed to listen before voicing our objections loudly outside.

Saints' board had to produce something else out of the hat rather than a promise of jam tomorrow, produced from our own collective pockets. Meninga's exit had created a void, not only on the field, but also in the hearts of the supporters who needed a hero to worship. It was that role Saints' directors now sought to fill as ridiculously, the board thought they'd already filled the playing void with the signing of French and Conlon, who quite simply weren't in the same class as mighty Mal.

Then the shock news came like a bolt from the blue, coach Billy Benyon was sacked and Alex Murphy was back at the club he had been drummed out of in 1967! The previous season Saints played brilliant open, football on the way to two trophies and runners-up spot in the league. Understandably, there was a real crackle of emotion in Benyon's voice in his interview with *Granada Reports'* Elton Welsby shortly after he had been given the news. He said, "There is only one word for it – I have been sacked by St Helens Rugby League Club - for being successful!"

Benyon had constantly pointed out weaknesses that needed to be corrected, but players he requested were not available, according to the board who failed to back his judgement. The coach was the scapegoat for a club seeing a widening gulf opening up between it and rivals Wigan.

Most felt really sorry for Benyon and some supporters like Ged, a real home-and-away die-hard, stopped going in protest. Despite any reservations we had about Benyon's treatment, Murphy's return got people talking rugby league in the barbers, bus queues, bookies and public bars once more. His record and sheer presence justified all those alliterative adjectives that his name was always being paired with. Magical, magnetic, mercurial Murphy was back at the scene of so many triumphs as a player in the 1950s and 1960s.

As he walked along the touchline in his opening game against Dewsbury, the half-way line of the Popular Side chanted: "There's only one Alex Murphy!" As he grinned, waved and clapped his hands above his head in response, the prodigal son provoked real infectious enthusiasm.

Folk in town hoped he would be "Murphy the Messiah", as the back page of the *Daily Mirror* declared. We needed something to lift the gloom as a lot of us were still unemployed, with figures standing around the 20 per cent mark. St Helens was a couple of per cent worse off than other towns like Warrington who had been able to diversify and were temporarily boosted by the grants that came with their New Town status. The town's unemployed signed on at the Crab Street office every fortnight. The worst time was 9am, not because you had to get out of bed early, but because you had to wait for the counter clerks to open up the depressing, blue painted, soulless building. It led to a dole queue winding down the road towards the Travellers Rest. If you were under 21 you drew about £23 a week in supplementary benefit. If you lived at home, virtually half of that would go in keep, leaving the rest for Saints money, a few pints on a Friday and Saturday and a few quid to one side to save up for a shirt.

One Tory MP suggested the unemployed should go for long walks and eat porridge if they were bored and hungry. I was not averse to a good walk, especially up Billinge Lump or around Crank. Tales abounded about the caverns up there, with the mysterious goings on people talked about. I never saw any big white rabbit up there anyway.

The only plus side I saw about being on the dole was being able to use the library – which was a superb resource in the centre of town. I was in there every day reading the papers and the books. They had a strange choice of publications in the periodicals rack, stocking the *Vietnam Courier* and *Pravda*, which smacked a little of political posturing. I doubt anybody read them.

The Gamble Institute building also had a great music library, which for £4 a year enabled you to take out six records out at a time. Each time you borrowed one you had to check them with the assistant, who would mark any scratches onto a paper disc that would be kept with your ticket. Free time was the only positive side of being on the dole then - the worst bit was not the lack of money more the uncertainty of where it would eventually end and the inevitability that a move away from the town might be the only answer. The previous summer Paul Weller's The Style Council had released *Our Favourite Shop* featuring a song called *Homebreakers*, which summed up our feelings.

For young people, it seemed that every position advertised in the job centre required 'experience', but it was impossible to get that if nobody would give you a chance.

That said if you were lucky to be in work, and grafting hard, it seemed the last thing you wanted to hear was other people's hard luck stories. There was even a hint of resentment and that raised its head at a supporters' forum when one of the speakers from the floor suggested a cut-price ticket for the unemployed if they showed their dole card, similar to the reduction pensioners received.

"You are kidding, most of them are thriving!" argued one woman.

Wigan 38 St Helens 14, 26 December 1985
Division 1

Murphy didn't have a magic wand and consequently Saints' displays remained erratic and mediocre. Midway through the second-half of the John Player tie at home to Doncaster, Saints trailed and the crowd booed and slow hand clapped.

Thankfully the players pulled their fingers out and Saints made it through and went on to crush Hull in the third round by 57-14. That emphatic victory lulled Saints into a false sense of security. We did not know it then, but Hull were already a busted flush and their long serving coach Arthur Bunting departed.

Saints' bad form and injuries led to a string of crushing defeats that made Murphy's promises on taking the Saints job seem very hollow. Murphy's men were humiliated - live on *Grandstand* - in the pre-Christmas John Player semi-final against Hull KR at Headingley.

The funniest part of the day was a handful of my mates having a row with Ross Conlon's wife who sat behind Saints' tiny contingent with some other wives and girlfriends. 'Big Al' Rigby who was a well known character in town and a Saints regular then insisted on calling Mrs Conlon's husband Ross *Condom*. He was only doing it to lift the gloom of a depressing afternoon, but she was getting very irate as she kept shouting down "Con-Lon" to correct him and eventually said "If you're going to slate him at least get his bloody name right!"

Defeat against Rovers was just a prelude to an utterly miserable festive period with Wigan slaughtering us on Boxing Day. In 12 months the Pie-eaters had overtaken Saints and then put their foot on the gas. Wigan had entertainment and flair stamped across their back line with the likes of Steve Ella, Henderson Gill and Ellery Hanley.

And while Saints' board talked about signing giant South African centre Danny Gerber, and having irons in the fire elsewhere, Wigan were buying players. They added Springboks Rob Louw and Ray Mordt to their playing staff, which already included fellow South African Nicky du Toit.

The trend troubled some, including the outspoken left wing Labour Euro MP for Wigan and St Helens, Les Huckfield, who felt it may have been a way of bypassing the sporting boycott imposed on South Africa's apartheid regime. Although the boycott did much to advance the toppling of that vile regime, it was hard to see how the Wigan trio were 'ambassadors for apartheid,' particularly as the three Springboks were playing alongside the likes of Henderson Gill and Ellery Hanley which would have been an anathema to any Afrikaans white supremacists.

St Helens 8 Bradford Northern 18, 19 January 1986
Division 1

As we went into 1986 those irons in the fire began to go cold again. On the field we slumped to further defeats, leading to a real talk of crisis in the air as we slipped closer to the relegation zone. The pat answers trotted out from the club were that fans needed to be patient, injuries were the main cause of our playing difficulties and we would only buy when the time was right. Murphy could motivate players but he could not fill the gaps left by injured players nor could he put pace on slow legs. At the end of the day he had to leave the players behind in the tunnel, he couldn't do it for them.

Saints fell to a sixth successive defeat at home to Bradford in a really piss-poor and effortless display. When the hooter sounded I was incandescent with rage and ran over towards the tunnel where the directors had to go down. When they appeared I screamed at them, waving my arms like Magnus Pyke, incoherently urging them to do something. I even pretended to rip up my season ticket, though was not mad enough to rip up the tickets – just the blank vouchers at the back that wouldn't be used anyway.

Saints stared Second Division rugby in the face as rumours abounded that the players didn't want to play for Murphy. Letters in the *St Helens Reporter* illustrated the depth of concern in the town. One called for the displacement of "the present archaic over-manned board". Another read: "Saints' team is the worst in anyone's memory... complete lack of effort, guts, interest and professionalism is there for all to see." "Is there any one out there with the money and ability to do at Saints what was done at Wigan?" appealed one despairing Saints fan. Someone even placed an advert in the *St Helens Star* bargain classified section "13 action men £2 each," followed by Saints' telephone number. Apparently they received quite a few calls at Knowsley Road before they finally twigged it. On the Bradford display £2 would have been too high a price.

The transfer deadline came and went with Wigan splashing out £100,000 on ace Widnes centre Joe Lydon, while we took Tony Ogden on loan from Oldham, a player who would never play for Saints. Saints may as well have signed Corrie's Stan Ogden - the difference in aspirations was there for all to see.

However, the fall out from the Lydon deal did have an unexpected silver lining for Saints. Widnes coach Eric Hughes, unhappy at the selling one of his club's best talents, resigned and joined Saints as a player in February. It proved to be a good move for both parties, giving Hughes' playing career a new lease of life as Saints' league form improved dramatically.

Dewsbury 19 St Helens 22, 24 February 1986
Challenge Cup Round 1

Our postponed cup game with Dewsbury was shifted to Headingley on a Monday night after the infamously cold Crown Flatt ground showed no sign of thawing out.

A paltry 1,948 crowd saw one of those games that Saints did not fancy and we trailed 12-6 after a first half display of missed tackles and clueless attack. A middle aged bloke beside kept shouting abuse at the players "What's up Saints, is the money not on?"

That was nothing to what Alex Murphy was about to say and a cluster of us went and stood outside the dressing room to listen to him give the players a rollicking. The air was blue - it was the way he did things and as coach of Wigan in 1983 Murphy had got himself into lumber when Granada had filmed him effing and blinding at his players after their defeat by Hull KR.

At the time there were gasps from television viewers who saw him in glorious form berating his Wigan side that had not only lost, but allowed his star youngster Shaun Edwards to take a good hiding. Looking around the dressing room he barked "There are too many f....ing fairies in this team."

They managed to bleep him out on *Granada Reports*, but later, on *RL Action* we had the uncensored version, which seemed to offend some viewers more than the players the language was directed at. In those days – even after the watershed - there were very rarely f words, only a few bs and never any cs on the telly. That is one of the reasons why Murphy's unparliamentary language was so shocking. It also shattered a few illusions because Murphy is a legend and as such was on a pedestal. That said swearing goes with the territory, and it was the way 'Murphy the Mouth' tried to make his players respond. It clearly worked with some, but others felt it degrading.

Although Saints hit back in the second half with tries by Neil Holding and Roy Haggerty, Dewsbury shocked us once more with a try, goal and a drop-goal and we looked dead and buried. Thankfully Haggerty grabbed a late try converted by Barrie Ledger – which meant we sneaked through by a three point margin.

Wigan 24 St Helens 14, 8 March 1986
Challenge Cup Round 2

Saints seemed to have overcome their stickiest spell and we went to Central Park in an optimistic mood. And that didn't seem to be misplaced when Kiwi centre Mark Elia, who had joined Saints in January, latched onto a precision Graham Liptrot pass to stroll 70 yards down the left flank to score an outstanding try.

Our skinny Australian centre Brett French scorched in for another corker giving Saints a 10-4 lead at half-time. It was too good to last - Neil Holding, who had been having an outstanding game, tried to open it up only to gift Wigan centre David Stephenson an interception try which caused Saints to buckle, eventually losing 24-14. Again it was their charismatic strike players Hanley and Gill who provided the finishing touches.

After that Wigan, who had already won the John Player and Lancashire Cup, looked set for a clean sweep given the talent they had available. But then quite inexplicably the wheels fell off, coinciding with a couple of games missed by Steve Ella.

They were knocked out of the cup at home by eventual winners Castleford and had to settle for those two early season trophies. It was two more than Saints, but it was not good enough to prevent the departure of their joint coaches Colin Clarke and Alan McInnes. Wigan's directors demanded a better return for their lavish investment.

Saints played their part in stopping Wigan's glory trail that season with a marvellous Good Friday victory over them. Saints had played out of their skins, but the visitors looked to have pinched it until Mark Elia plunged over for a last ditch try. When totted up at the end of the year that win cost Wigan the title, the championship going to unfashionable Halifax, who had emerged from the doldrums in spectacular fashion.

Saints finished the season on a brilliant run of 13 unbeaten league games, including victory at Hull KR where Mark Elia helped himself to a hat-trick in his farewell game. The long striding Kiwi was a firm favourite and he would return to wear the red vee again.

One of those less memorable games included a jammy win at York's muddy Wiggington Road ground in March. There were only 1,900 spectators there and many of those were fuming that we had 'stolen' this game. Rightly or wrongly, because of York's scenic setting and sense of history, you expect a more cultured fan in the Minster city. Unfortunately one teenage thug decided to avenge this defeat by pushing a young Saints fan to the ground before robbing his scarf. The poor kid was distraught as he made his way back to one of the three Supporters Club coaches. Stewarding that day was former Desert Rat Gordon McCully – who we all called Percy because of his likeness to the *Coronation Street* character Percy Sugden. He loathed bullies and insisted our driver stalked the streets until the culprit was found – it did not take long and the York lad was caught and dragged upon the coach by four Saints followers. There he was made to hand over the stolen colours and apologise to his victim before being kicked off the coach on the outskirts of York with the words, "Yorkshiremen - you're full of piss and wind!" ringing in his ears. I bet he never stole again though!

Remarkably Saints were just one win off winning the league ourselves, which was a remarkable turnaround from the low base in the bleak mid winter. Sadly, we slipped to a surprising 38-22 defeat at home to Leeds in the first round of the Premiership, which meant we had to hand over our trophy.

Perhaps we should have had greater things to concern us that spring. In April the roof had blown off the Chernobyl nuclear plant in the Soviet Union. Just to show how devastating this nuclear power could be, it even affected the hill farmers of Wales. A lot of people started giving lamb a wide berth; others started asking questions about the nuclear plants closer to home like the ones up in Cumbria. Some even cracked jokes – the one that did the rounds was "Why don't you wear Russian Y-fronts? Because Cher knob'll fall out!"

There were other issues of concern – with the Americans using British bases to launch bombing raids on Colonel Gaddafi's Libya that same month. All the current affairs issues and a few more light-hearted ones were discussed on Alan Beswick's late night phone-in show on Red Rose Radio and on the night of the Libya bombing he played Mike Harding's emotive *Bomber's Moon* song. Beswick's show made for compulsive listening. Although the Lancashire station was not naturally our local one, loads of St Heleners listened to Beswick play devil's advocate with a string of often tongue-tied callers.

The outspoken Warringtonian had a seven-second delay button to cut out swearing – and he needed it too. On one occasion he took the controversial step of banning everyone with a Scouse accent from ringing him because of the bad language frequently used by people from that city. It was all good stuff – and on his day Beswick was the best in the business at this game. The show was addictive, but it went on until 2am, which meant many people went to work bleary eyed in the morning.

10. 1986-87 Only a point

St Helens 50 Leigh 18, 31 August 1986
Division 1

The only consolation that a rugby-less summer offered was that you could spend more money on beer and having no Saints meant Friday and Saturday nights out became an even bigger focus for the week.

Most under-25s headed into town on a weekend and the Market and Nelson in Bridge Street were always packed out. Drinkers would alternate between the two pubs all night, with lads piling out of one to try the other at the sound of those immortal words 'It's snooin' wi talent over t' road.' Town had a handful of nightclubs, with Cindy's being the biggest and most popular, but others went to Park Lane, Pepe's, upstairs at Jesters and the newly opened Crystals.

Jesters modelled itself on a fun pub and they insisted on getting the staff to dance on the bar to sing or mime, usually to that dreadful 1980s anthem *Shattered Glass* and sometimes more bizarrely the 18 verses of Rolf Harris' *Court of King Caractacus*.

Most single people – lads and girls - invariably went clubbing to have a laugh and if you were lucky 'cop off' or at least have that objective in the back of your mind as a vague possibility! Clubbing was also a way of extending the evening's drinking as pubs in those days called last orders at 11pm. The alternative was to get a 'stay behind' at one of the less central town pubs, but that was mostly for older regulars or piss artists. It was also classed as cheeky work to roll up five minutes before the last bell, having spent all night boozing elsewhere, and then expecting a late drink.

Nobody went to Cindy's simply for the beer. The ale there was served up from those awful hard plastic glasses and any cracks in them were luminous in the disco light – as were your white socks, which were 'in' at the time. The carpet was invariably so sticky that it was like walking on floor tile glue and the music was so loud that conversation was impossible. The DJ would give a code if there was trouble on the dance floor and then the bouncers would run in and sort it out. If you were in the way as the miscreants were bundled out, your ale went flying all over the place.

For all its faults the big white building in Duke Street was an institution in town and hundreds of St Helens relationships owe their formative moments to a chance rendezvous at the side of the dance floor. None of them started with any of the dubious chat up lines that some of my mates claimed they tried, like 'Do you want to go halves on a bastard?'

A bricky I worked with called Little Dave swore by the place saying "It doesn't matter how ugly you are, you can have a face like a bag of spanners but you will always get your leather at Cindy's. It might cost you a few quid in drinks mind!"

Cindy's was the place where folk went to let off steam after a crap week at work or isolated at home on the dole. In a town, which probably still had quite demarcated male and female jobs, it was one of the few places you met members of the opposite sex. If you had not copped off by the time the sloweys came on you either went home to watch *Hit Man and Her*, or over the road for chips or a fight. Plenty of blokes leaving Cindy's in the early hours could identify with the line from The Specials song *Friday Night, Saturday Morning* which goes "Wish I had lipstick on my shirt, instead of piss stains on my shoe."

Cindy's provided some light moments, on one occasion I saw two lads arguing with each other in the men's toilets after one of them had tapped up a girl. It transpired that one lad's luck was in and he was going back to her place, but was wearing Y-fronts. He desperately tried to persuade his mate to give up his boxer shorts, which looked more fashionable, or cleaner, than the underwear he had thrown on that night. Bizarre!

We usually had a laugh afterwards, eating our chips while mocking the paintings in Graham Smith's shop window over the road from Cindy's – there the self-proclaimed egg and sausage artist sold his paintings of the aforementioned foodstuffs "to ladies for kisses and tickles". What a character he was!

It was not always fun and games outside the chippy – I saw quite a few scraps there. On one occasion this stocky lad offered this other one out, but before they started the main protagonist took his Lacoste shirt off to reveal a body that looked like the after picture on a Bullworker advert. It was a combination of him not wanting to damage his designer gear, which people were precious about in the 1980s, and him wanting to intimidate his opponent or pose with his physique. The other lad decided discretion was the better part of valour and legged it.

Some went out of town for their entertainment to places like Mr Smith's in Warrington or on so called 'coach dos' from Birchley Street at the side of the Town Hall up to Peppermint Place or Cinderella's near Blackburn. A lad who I had gone to school with was arrested for fighting following one such coach do. In court he was asked "Why he went to Blackburn to cause trouble?" to which he dumbly replied, "Same reason you go t' Spain for your holidays!" and the stipendiary magistrate was not impressed.

A rare chance to see Knowsley Road in July came as St Helens staged an event called *Soap Aid* in an attempt to raise money for famine relief in Ethiopia, just as *Live Aid* had done in the previous summer. The cast from leading soap operas, *Emmerdale Farm*, *Brookside*, *Coronation Street*, *East Enders* and *Albion Market* entertained the crowds. Marillion and Icicle Works gave some musical clout to the proceedings.

The event was well meaning but riddled with cock-ups. Ian McNabb, lead singer of Liverpool band the Icicle Works, came away with a shiner after being refused entry at the post-gig function at the Fleece. Marillion's 20-minute set was marred by running battles between a gang of 'town scallies' and the security guards, prompting lead singer Fish to break off singing to cry "this is supposed to be a concert not a f...ing battle ground!" in his best Scottish accent.

My mate Tommo found it all quite depressing. He had also gone to the *Radio One Roadshow* in Church Square some years previously, which had also been marred by violence between gimps and skinheads. "They'll never bring anything to St Helens ever again. They'll just think the only thing we want to do here is kick shit out of each other!" As you travel around the country you realise every town is just the same on that score.

Violence is part of everyday life – but is also a way of dispensing summary justice. Saints' new try scoring centre Steve Halliwell found that to his cost on the opening day of the league season. He had joined Saints from Leigh, where he had topped the try scoring charts with 48 touchdowns the previous year.

Rumours abounded that a lot of his former Leigh colleagues were spitting blood about the way he had departed after winning his big prize and was clearly a marked man when fate had it that the two teams should meet at the beginning of the season. The kick off went straight to Halliwell, who was immediately clobbered by a very heavy challenge. Groggily he wobbled off the pitch with less than a minute on the clock.

It settled a score, but coach Alex Murphy was furious claiming someone should have been sent off. "Everyone in Leigh had been talking about what was going to happen all week!" he claimed.

St Helens 112 Carlisle 0, 14 September 1986
Lancashire Cup Round 1

Record scores are supposed to be something of a landmark, but you could not help feeling sorry for the Border city men as Saints ran in 112 points without reply. This result was a landmark score for us but it must have been terribly demoralising for the Carlisle players and their hardy band of loyal supporters who had stuck with them through a pretty turbulent short existence.

For all our fans' mock pity, we all urged our side to pile on the agony with Steve Halliwell crossing for a hat-trick, with Barrie Ledger and Neil Holding scoring four apiece. Paul Loughlin hoofed over 16 goals and scored 40 of those points – both club records in what was little more than a training run. Lockers was a good strong running centre and local lad to boot, although coach Murphy had an unusual way of geeing him up. In one radio interview Murphy praised Lockers by saying: "He's been getting some stick, with people calling him Dobbin... but today he showed what a good player he is!" Dobbin? If the fans weren't calling him that before the interview, they certainly were afterwards.

Although Carlisle were no real test, Saints were looking good. Three emphatic away wins at Salford, Leeds and Hull KR, followed by a 38-16 home victory over champions Halifax perched us on the top of the league with a massive 'points for' tally.

The team had been bolstered with the signing of two Australians, stand-off Brett Clarke and prop Pat Jarvis from St George, Sydney. Clarke was a small, nippy bag of tricks for the opposing defences to deal with, even if he did have a tendency to run up his own arse. Jarvis was a big man, who would hit the defensive line hard, making the ball available. Anglo-Australian Halliwell was also making an impact with his scoring, despite having the worst mullet haircut in rugby league and "running as if he has got a bit left in", as my mate crudely put it.

Wigan 22 St Helens 16, 1 October 1986
Lancashire Cup Semi-Final

Saints were still unbeaten when they drew Wigan in the Lancashire Cup semi-final. It was one of those nights – and Central Park really needed rubber walls as the mammoth 28,186 crowd was shoe-horned in. At least they had the sense to put the kick off back a little bit, but if you were shorter than 6 feet 2 inches your view became obliterated as the crowd piled in.

There was controversy galore because Saints were playing out of their skins in the first half, and had the upper hand when the floodlights failed to the inevitable cries of "Get a bloody shilling in t' meter!" or "Lecky must be a new thing in Wigan!" Conspiracy theorists alleged that this was a dirty Wigan plot to knock us out off our stride. The players went off for an early half-time and played a longer second half when the lights were restored.

Whatever the facts are the floodlight failure did have an effect, with Wigan pulling back level after the enforced break. And then it happened! With time running out Neil Holding's clearance kick was charged down, and within the blink of an eye Ellery Hanley was heading for the whitewash. It was game, set and match to the Pie-eaters yet again! Saints fans were in uproar believing there had been a hint of offside, knock on, hand ball or lbw, but it didn't matter - Wigan were on their way to the final and more cup success.

Wigan's biggest strength seemed to be their ability to keep playing for the full 80 minutes, without resorting to panic football.

In the summer Wigan had brought in ace New Zealand test coach Graham Lowe, who had some strange sartorial touches – one of which involved wearing a beret! The only time anybody from our game had worn such a garment before was when Neil Holding did his Frank Spencer impressions at the *Rugby League Roadshow* that was rolled out for players' testimonials.

Wigan were the consummate professionals on the pitch, but they spoiled that image by inputting the ridiculous slogan of 'Ere Wig-O' into their new computerised scoreboard. Wigan were now universally known as 'Pie-eaters' and were taunted by everyone in the game. The term 'Pie-eaters', however, had nothing to do with their capacity for crust crunching on Poole's finest. If that was the case St Helens folk would equally be in the firing line with our love of Pimblett's, Burchall's and Lievesley's.

No, pie-eaters, apparently dates back to a miners' strike in the 1920s when Wigan colliers were starved back to work first and were therefore forced to eat 'humble pie.'

St Helens 8 Australia 32, 2 November 1986
Tour Match

It was hard to believe that there were actually 26 players were walking onto the pitch ahead of this tour match. All eyes were fixed on just one of them with chants of "There's only one Mal Meninga," reverberating around the ground.

Although Mal had lost a little favour in Australia, along with his centre test berth, he was still revered in our town and 15,370 had turned up to pay homage. Our players even showed their appreciation by gifting him an interception try to mark his return. Despite losing 32-8, the display was a spirited one and a huge improvement on the previous two tour displays.

It was quite a bruiser with big prop Steve Roach going off after a couple of minutes with a dislocated elbow. Saints were terrier like in their approach with Chris Arkwright in particular letting Wally Lewis know he was in a game. His partner in crime was his best mucker Paul Round, who really got stuck in when he came off the bench. To cries of *'Rambo, Rambo'*, Roundy was sin binned along with Kangaroos' full-back Gary Jack after a brawl.

Britain had drawn the previous season's bruising test series against New Zealand but it had been a cracking series. Hopes were high that this season they could close the gap still further and there was a real thirst for international rugby league, so much so that the first test was taken to Old Trafford. The handful of rugby league fans who 'boycotted' the game arguing that they didn't want to give money to football were left with egg on their faces as over 50,000 turned up, despite torrential rain, to watch Britain go down.

The game's highlight was a wonderful try by Joe Lydon, coming just as the crowd had begun to turn up the noise. With "Here we go" rising in volume, Lydon linked up brilliantly from full-back, beating Australian counterpart Gary Jack for pace on the outside to score in front of a Stretford End that was bouncing all over the place.

The great feeling was extremely short-lived as from virtually straight after the restart the 'Roos took control of the match again. Britain kept fighting though – and at one stage there was a tussle between two of the game's real men of steel Kevin Ward and Greg Dowling. It would have been quite a scrap had those two gone toe-to-toe, instead Dowling simply pointed to the giant electronic scoreboard which was on its way to recording a final score of 38-16.

The pre-match entertainment featured a race between some of the game's speed merchants with Saints' Barrie Ledger taking on, among others, Barrow's Les Quirk and Warrington's Mark Forster. Ledger was called up to the main event for the following test at Elland Road to win the last of his two caps. Unfortunately there was not a lot he could do as Great Britain were hammered in what turned out to be a complete washout, with Britain losing 34-4. To make matters worse the Kop was already quite full when I got on the ground, which meant I watched the game from the exit stairs. The gate was over 30,000, but I had stood on that ground with much bigger crowds for Leeds United games and still had a better view. The problem was that rugby league fans tended to get their spec, and refuse to move into the gaps in front of them. Football fans tended to fill every available nook and cranny by a gradual process of nudging and shoving. Rugby league fans were far too polite to push and too stubborn to move – so where we were all packed in like sardines at the back, there must have been loads of room down the front for the rest of them.

Some argued that this is why Wembley's capacity was always smaller for rugby league games; the other theories being that it was to allow more families or rather insultingly rugby league fans were generally fatter and therefore took up more room!

The third test at Wigan was a lot more competitive – with Great Britain unlucky to lose after the Kangaroos' fortuitous penalty try nudged them back in front at a crucial stage. It was still in the balance until Wally Lewis sealed the game with a super solo effort. The Australians had matched the Invincibles of 1982 in going through the tour undefeated, but the biggest story of the day unfolded after the match. A grinning Wigan chairman Maurice Lindsay, looking like the cat that had got the cream, revealed to the BBC cameras that they had signed Australian skipper Wally Lewis. They didn't need Lewis, and were acting like a millionaire sticking another Porsche on the drive for pure bravado. Thankfully, 'King Wally' never materialised in the cherry and white hoops of Wigan and for that we were all very grateful.

There had been major transfer developments at St Helens, which centred around unsettled long-serving club captain Harry Pinner, who had been listed at £95,000. Pinner, who had enjoyed a testimonial the previous year, had skippered Saints through some of the club's toughest times. His ball-playing skills and tactical nous had been a much sought after commodity throughout the early 1980s with Wigan, Widnes or the host of other 'money' clubs keen on enticing him away from his home town team.

Saints could have cashed him in, but instead they simply imposed a huge asking price to ensure that he stayed put. It is hard to imagine what Saints would have done without him in the early 1980s – Pinner had his knockers on the terraces but he had always been our shining star man who led the way when the night was darkest.

Coach Murphy now had other plans having played Chris Arkwright in the loose-forward spot during the course of our unbeaten league run. Pinner was now dispensable and it was for the best all round that he moved to Widnes in exchange for their test forward John Fieldhouse.

The problems at Knowsley Road were minor compared to the ones afflicting the local Labour Party, which was split down the middle. The press constantly outlined local difficulties, divisions and splits with the friction stemming from the intention of some party members to deselect the town's MPs, John Evans and Gerry Bermingham. One leading member, who was subsequently suspended from the Labour Party, even began a campaign of letter writing and was dubbed 'the St Helens Phantom poet,' for sending dubious mail to his comrades in St Helens South.

The National Executive in London simply looked at the irregularities, and suspended the local district and constituency parties, which in turn meant Evans and Bermingham remained safe as MPs. It became quite absurd once branch meetings were suspended. With it being against party regulations to hold factional caucuses, a left grouping held a meeting in the TUCURC under the banner of the North West Ferret Breeders Association. The guest speaker advertised on the little red tickets was Gerry Coughdrop, which was clearly the nom de plume of Gerry Caughey. The leading Scouse firebrand had earned his reputation during the 1970 Pilkington strike and had his followers, but political opponents and Labour moderates viewed him as a left-wing bogeyman.

Most of the town's solidly anti-Tory public looked on bemused by the shenanigans and bad headlines that afflicted the party they supported. That said, Labour votes in the town were still weighed by the sackful. The common belief was that "If they stood a pig on the Town Hall steps with a red rosette on, he'd still get in."

Castleford 22 St Helens 26, 6 December 1986
John Player Trophy Round 2

Having beaten Whitehaven in the opening round, we looked set to go out at Castleford, where we trailed 16-0. Rather than get disheartened we decided that should Saints grab a consolation score in the second half our contingent would do the most demented of dances, purely to get on telly. The BBC was obsessed with panning the cameras into the crowd to focus on some little lad eating a Curly Wurly or an old, toothless granny shaking a rattle and smoking a pipe.

We only realised how stupid it looked once we got home and watched ourselves swirling around like dervishes on the video. Folk watching us at home must have thought we were doolally. At least we had something to celebrate because Saints came out a completely new side in the second half swept Castleford off the park with some magnificent free flowing rugby. Keeping the ball alive at every opportunity has always been the Saints way – it is not a recent phenomenon.

Scrum-half Neil Holding started the proceedings with a chip over the full-back collecting the ball on the other side to race in for a trade mark score.

Great work from young hooker Dave Harrison, who was having the game of his life, sent Andy Platt in for our second. Winger Kevin McCormack then intercepted and went the full length of the pitch, waving to the crowd as he crossed for a try.

The game tipped our way from there and although Castleford did rally to make it a nail biting finish, we had them especially when a three man tackle dumped their enforcer Kevin Ward into touch, his leg buckling beneath him as he went.

The big news in St Helens at the time was the prospect of the town's biggest company Pilkington's being taken over by the large conglomerate BTR. Adverts around the town declared 'Pilkington's. The world's leading glass company, let's keep it that way!' However one board on the edge of the town centre had been defaced with a thick white painted slogan of 'What about all the redundancies?' referring to the reduction of the workforce over the previous decade.

However, a lot of people in the town were genuinely worried that a successful BTR takeover would see them asset stripping, leading to more redundancies in a town already devastated by high unemployment. So even those who did not particularly like Pilks preferred the devil they knew.

St Helens was built on coal and had sand a plenty to the north, so the town had the raw materials for glass production. Making the stuff was something our townsfolk had been good at, but opinion on Pilks seemed divided in the town.

Some argued that they were a good firm that really looked after its employees and were described as 'paternal capitalists.' Some looked at the figureheads like Sir Harry and Lady Mavis as the town's equivalent of the Royal Family. However, St Helens group Old Ma Cuxsom and the Soapchoppers actually wrote a less than deferent song about Lady Pilk after she had insisted that the bridge near her home over the East Lancs Road was painted blue after the council had changed it to grey. That song appeared on a Radio One John Peel session, with musical aficionados hearing the chorus of "La-ady Pilkington, take a running jump, off your bridge!"

Others also viewed the company less than favourably, claiming for years they had enjoyed a monopoly of the labour in the town and their presence had possibly prevented other companies from settling here. St Helens was not quite a one-horse town, but the lack of a diverse number of big companies contributed to the town's local unemployment difficulties in the 1980s.

No matter what you thought, opinion seemed unanimous that a BTR takeover would have been bad for the town. A popular front campaign, that included the unions, local newspapers, councillors, MPs and small businesses, was launched, pledged to keep the conglomerate out.

St Helens 20 Warrington 22, 14 December 1986
John Player Trophy Round 3

Just when things were going so well, a Les Boyd inspired Warrington team 'beasted' Saints out of the competition after a real cracker of a match. Wires led 14-8 at half time, but Saints nudged back in front. With the nerves of nearly 12,000 spectators reaching breaking point, Warrington edged us by a couple of points. Our pack was subdued by the power and tenacity of the Warrington forwards, particularly their fearsome Australian duo of Bob Jackson and Boyd. The latter created three tries, and also acted as a joint refereeing adviser to Mr D. W. Fox – and was in the lanky legged referee's ear throughout the match.

A Kangaroo tourist in 1978 and 1982, Boyd was a formidable opponent, packing 16 stone of muscle and bone into his chunky 5 feet 9 inches frame. The rugged prop had sought refuge in Britain after suffering two mammoth suspensions that had effectively wiped out his seasons in 1983 and 1984 down under. Ill-discipline threatened his career – but he played some of his best rugby in an Indian summer in the UK at Wilderspool.

It was definitely a case of the little and large show, for having a blinder on his dad's old stamping ground was tiny scrum half Paul Bishop, one of those cheeky scrum halves whose face would stand clogging. It was a bit of an eye-opener really because Bish came into the Nelson Hotel later that evening and as he stood there supping his pint he just looked like some scrawny young lad with a 1980s perm and the scally tash to go with it. And yet he had taken the knocks from blokes who were a good six stone heavier than him all afternoon and showed no ill effects. He was one tough rooster – a chip off the old block and a shrewd footballer to boot.

After beating Saints, Warrington went all the way to the John Player final, before losing to Wigan at Bolton's under soil heated Burnden Park football ground on a freezing cold day.

It seemed strange going to Bolton for the final as geographically it was only a few miles from the rugby league heartlands of Leigh and Wigan, yet its sporting culture was completely different. There the round ball game was king with Bolton being home to one of, what was then a string of unfashionable Lancashire clubs, including Blackpool, Preston North End and Blackburn Rovers.

Despite their proud football tradition and history, memories of Tom Finney, Stanley Matthews and Nat Lofthouse seemed to be all that remained at these clubs, who seemed to have been left behind by the advance of anonymous little southern clubs like Watford, Oxford, Luton and Wimbledon who cluttered up the top flight in the mid 80s. It summed up everything that was wrong with Britain in that decade. England's bread used to hang by Lancashire's thread, but now it was all about service industries and the stock exchange. Luton, with a plastic pitch and cardboard cut out fans were in the top flight, but they were a club whose only claim to fame before they banned away fans, was that one half of Morecambe and Wise supported them.

St Helens 4 Wigan 12, Boxing Day 1986
Division 1

The boring *Spy Catcher* book about M15 was the cue for the latest anti-Wigan joke.
'I see they've banned that book in Wigan.'
'What, *Spy Catcher*.'
'No, Pie snatcher!'
It was along the same lines as that other mid 80s joke: 'I see Bruno's opponent has killed himself!'
'Who, Witherspoon?'
'No, with a knife!'

Our unbeaten league run had continued for 25 matches despite our slip up in the John Player, but now we faced the acid test - Wigan. Murphy, in his own inimitable way had used his newspaper column to urge the town to turn up and get behind the team on Boxing Day 'instead of staying at home stuffed with turkey'. Unfortunately, the fans responded, with 21,214 turning up, only for the players to freeze on the big occasion allowing Wigan to ruin yet another Christmas.

The atmosphere prior to the match was boisterous, with the only sour note being the racist taunts directed at Wigan's wing Henderson Gill from a small pocket of the Popular Side. All credit to the charismatic test winger, who simply turned and faced the small section of offenders, grinning at them until the cheers from Saints supporters far outweighed boos. That sort of 'monkey chanting' by a tiny minority happened at a few games in the 1980s, and only really fizzled out when Saints themselves signed a black player. It seemed to be a complete contradiction as some of the Saints fans who spewed out this rubbish, also hero worshipped Mal Meninga, who had also been subject to racist abuse in Australia.

At Saints it ranged from petty things like Roy Powell, the Leeds second-rower, having "Bruno, Bruno!" or Harry Belafonte's *Banana Boat Song* chanted at him. He was such a gentle giant, he just smiled and carried on with his game. Most people viewed that as harmless fun, but the monkey noises some wingers had to contend with were a bit more disturbing. If it was any consolation, the level of racism was quite soft in town, based on ignorance due to a lack of contact with people of a different coloured skin rather than any deep-seated hatred. Generally, the only black people you would see in town back then were in a restaurant or occasionally in the doctor's surgery. Some saw no difference between abusing somebody who was black and calling one for being fat or having red hair. I suppose Widnes physio Vivian Gleave, who was one of the first women to regularly have to go onto a rugby field, was not too chuffed at having to run the gauntlet of "Get your tits out for the lads" every time she went onto the field to treat a player. Women physios are so commonplace now and crowds even more mixed, that such chanting would be greeted with incredulity.

Defeat by Wigan saw Saints slide to further consecutive defeats against Widnes and Halifax.

St Helens 18 Swinton 16, 21 January 1987
Challenge Cup Preliminary Round

Rugby league's Challenge Cup mathematics used to be simple prior to 1980 when there were only 30 professional teams. All they had to do was throw in the winners of the previous autumn's BARLA County Cups and you had the perfect formula. The expansion of the game, embracing Cardiff, Fulham, Carlisle, Mansfield and Sheffield, meant the game now needed six preliminary ties to make the maths work.

It was a free-for-all and the luck of the draw whether your name would come out of the hat for one of those. Some argued that clubs of St Helens and Wigan's stature should not be forced to take part at that stage, comparing it to the FA Cup, where the big clubs only joined the competition at the round three stage.

However, it offered loyal fans of lower clubs a rare chance to see the top teams. There was not much prospect of the sort of giant-killing which was much more frequent in football, where the underdog could get a fluke goal and then pack the defence for the rest of the match.

Rugby league underdogs have no such luxury, and there is no place to hide on a rugby league field and shock results are infrequent. Swinton, however, came within the shavings of an upright to adding their name to the giant-killing roll of honour narrowly being edged out 18-16 by Saints in the Preliminary round.

Another bad winter set in but we beat Dewsbury on a cold February night at Crown Flatt in the First Round proper after several postponements. However, the biggest cause of celebration that week emerged from the gloom, partial frost and mist of Oldham with Wigan's team of all talents being turned out of the cup by the Roughyeds thanks to a late try by Paddy Kirwan.

Oldham 14 St Helens 24, 14 February 1987
Challenge Cup Round 2

It was another bitterly cold day at Watersheddings and straw had been scattered across the pitch to keep out the frost. Every day seemed to be cold and wet in Oldham, an old-fashioned mill town carved into the side of the Pennines. The Roughyeds were riding the crest of a wave following their marvellous victory over Wigan and they led 8-6 at half-time. The Saints fans, packed up behind the back of the posts, shuffled nervously because after all the ribbing we had given Wigan, it would be just our luck to suffer the same fate.

Crucially Oldham were down to 12 men, after hooker Ian Sanderson was sent off for a high tackle on Neil Holding. Saints moved the ball about a lot more in the second half, and used the one man advantage to send Kevin McCormack and Paul Forber over for good tries. Holding then scored a peach of a try - after taking the ball from the scrum, he dummied to the invisible man on the wing, beating the now overweight former Great Britain full-back Mick Burke for pace to score. The intensity of the first half and prospect of losing had made the victory even more pleasing. Raucous cries of "We're on the march with Murphy's Army!" repeatedly rang around the ground, each time rising in volume. It was a great feeling.

We were really buzzing and a few days later we beat Warrington 42-22 to go top of the league. On *Granada Reports*, Murphy had been asked a question about Wigan to which he replied, "You're on about the Pie-eaters again, well they'll spend the money but we'll take the title." Wire coach Tony Barrow was less than happy on the same programme, complaining about the dismissal of his substitute forward Tony Humphries for a late, high tackle on Holding. He accused Holding of doing his "usual dive" to fool the ref, then "was up running around like a spring chicken!" It was just an unfortunate statistic, but Holding had unwittingly got two players sent off in the space of five days. Undoubtedly Holding, like all scrum halves, played the old soldier from time to time – but if a robust forward like Humphries cracked you, you knew about it.

Leigh 8 St Helens 14, 14 March 1987
Challenge Cup Semi-Final, Central Park

Chris Arkwright's hat-trick helped crush a spirited Whitehaven side to move us just one step away from Wembley. The Cumbrians brought a big following, intent on milking the magic of the Cup, but Saints had too much class despite the threat posed by the menacing, powerfully built, bald headed figure of Norman Lofthouse on the wing. In the last four we drew Leigh, with the other semi pairing off the boil 'cup kings' Widnes with reigning champions Halifax. Our game was obviously a bit of a needle match, with Alex Murphy having enjoyed such a Jekyll and Hyde relationship with the Leythers, and our former boss Billy Benyon being charge of Leigh.

But after 33 minutes it looked really straightforward with cries of "easy, easy!" greeting Saints' third try as Andy Platt powered over to make it 14-2. Kevin McCormack and Chris Arkwright had grabbed the early scores to put Saints in the driving seat. We should have known that semi-finals are very rarely 'easy'. Instead of crumbling Leigh grabbed a try just before the interval to set up a nail-biting second half.

To settle my nerves I nipped for a pint under the main stand at the break only to get caught up in a skirmish between a handful of blokes throwing bar stools at each other. It was not pleasant, but some fans were prone to exaggeration afterwards – 'I thought it was going to be another Heysel!' cried one middle-aged bloke.

The second half was not particularly enjoyable either, with Saints fans wishing the seconds and minutes away. The second half remained scoreless, but Leigh midfield generals Derek Pyke and scrum-half Kerr were finding holes in Saints' defence. It took some desperate defence from man-of-the-match Phil Veivers at full-back to keep the rampant Leythers at bay. But it was Barry Ledger, superbly chasing back to haul down John Henderson with the try line begging, who saved the day. Ledger had his critics who say he never really used his talent to its full potential - and some fans even called him Barry *Lager* – but nobody else would have got back to make that match saving tackle that day.

We were on our way, the nine-year long wait was over and the Wigan popular side, packed with Saints fans, exploded with joy and we spilled onto the pitch. I hacked up a clump of Central Park turf and stuffed it in my pocket as a keepsake, and not even being called a daft scouse t..t by an irate Leyther, who wanted to punch my lights out, could dull the ecstasy. You feel a bit more bullet proof when you are 20!

After that victory, the league programme was put very much on the back burner as the club geared itself up for its biggest game in nine years. The entire focus became Wembley – and the league games in between were dismissively treated like friendlies, as key players suddenly developed 'injuries.'

Wigan quite rightly protested that Saints were devaluing the traditional Good Friday fixture when we fielded a virtual 'A' team including a couple of trialists, and young lads like Dave Large, Phil Price, Mark Lee, Phil Southward, Neil Gavin and Paul Hopkins. They all gave it a good go. For some like Mark Lee, it was only a taster for the future. For some of the others it was a one-off day in the professional limelight, but at least they have done what thousands of men and boys across the town would have given their eye-tooth for and played for Saints.

Halifax 19 St Helens 18, 2 May 1987
Challenge Cup Final, Wembley

Nearly 20 years on it is still hard to write about the Challenge Cup Final of 1987. It was supposed to be our time, but Halifax had not read the script.

Saints were supremely confident going to Wembley and those feelings were boosted after hammering Bradford the week before the final in the Premiership. After all Northern were a similar shaped side to Halifax, and we thought it would be the same against another set of fat, slow, old Yorkshiremen with bad haircuts.

The build up to Wembley was excellent, although a lot of people suddenly eased themselves out of the armchairs they'd been slumped in since 1978. That sounds moralistic doesn't it? It didn't matter in the grand scheme of things, as the whole town came together to get behind our team. It made a unique double for the borough as the Town football team had won the FA Vase beating Warrington at Wembley. St Helens, however, is a rugby town and the football side's win was just the hors d'oeuvre.

All the pubs on the eve of the game were full of people wearing the cheapo red and white flat caps that were being hawked by sellers who had spied a money making opportunity. There was already a lot of singing with anticipation and there were a few sore heads by the time the special trains started leaving Shaw Street at 7am. Transport police enforced a booze ban on the train so several fans, not just youngsters, had to swig their cans before departure. Those who did not have the stomach for it so early had to tip their booze down the grid.

Walking up Wembley Way for my first time with the Saints was a brilliant moment, much better than going up as a neutral basking in someone else's reflected glory. You want to take it all in and really soak it up. It became noticeable that Halifax had emptied their town – there were blue and white hoops everywhere. Even the Hull, Leeds, Bradford and Cas neutrals were wearing blue for the day.

Most of the Saints songs predictably revolved around the theme of 'Are you watching pie-eaters?' and banners declared Wembley a 'Pie free zone!'

The Halifax team had largely been cobbled together from other clubs cast-offs and Mick Scott, John Pendlebury, Colin Whitfield, Gary Stephens and Brian Juliff had all played for Wigan under Murphy. Most of them had shared in the bitter experience of Murphy's last Wembley appearance in 1984.

As soon as the game began, it became obvious that Halifax were really up for it. Their rock solid defence closed us down and although we clearly had more pace on the flanks, Saints tossed the ball about too much without settling it down first with a few hard solid drives. It led to some stupid handling errors, and allowed Halifax to take control and play the game in our quarter. They pinned us there and watched us panic even more.

They were as jammy as anything too and their first try by Wilf George should have been disallowed for a foot in touch. I watched the video once a week later – and once only – and screamed at the grey haired touch judge "Get your flag up you stupid bastard!" There was no disputing their second, with Irish hooker Seamus McCallion sneaking over for a soft try before the break.

Trailing 12-2, our end was a bit subdued at the break, but we were reluctantly coaxed into performing the Mexican Wave, which had been 'invented' at the previous year's football World Cup.

After the restart Saints hit back with a storming 80-yard try by Kiwi centre Mark Elia lifting our spirits. Just as we had fought our way back into it, came the pivotal moment in the outcome of the match - a substitution. Roy Haggerty was making errors because he was over-trying and was replaced by Paul Round. As we defended a scrum 20 yards out, rather than wait, the no-nonsense Arkwright packed down in Haggerty's second row spot and allowed the fresh man Round join the scrum at loose-forward. It was an accident waiting to happen and disastrously led to a chronic breakdown in communication with Round and Neil Holding going the same way from the scrum. Fax loose-forward John Pendlebury peeled off to send the barnstorming full-back Eadie on a direct run to the line.

It was a crushing blow, but we hit back with another corker with Paul Loughlin scoring a superb long-range try. Crucially Lockers missed the conversion, with Pendlebury slotting a snap drop-goal to make sure Saints needed to score twice. We did not think about it at the time, but when Round scored with 14 minutes to play, there was now just a single point separating us. Suddenly the momentum was with us and fast hands, moving the ball about, began finding more gaps in the once seemingly impregnable Halifax defence. Our players seemed so confident of scoring, that no one even attempted to snatch a levelling drop-goal.

Then came the moment that overtook Derek Noonan's 1978 mistake in the hall of shame. Mark Elia dashed over in the corner, and although the elated Saints fans around me were up in the air cheering the match winner, I could see referee Holdsworth at the far end of the ground signalling no try. As the Kiwi centre dived for the line, with the ball casually tucked under his arm, Pendlebury craftily knocked the ball from his grasp.

Minutes later Elia was over again, but this time recalled for a blatant forward pass. It was our last chance before the hooter wailed its sad, mournful sound to leave us all absolutely devastated.

I didn't think about it then, but in the post-mortem we talked about our failure to go for a drop-goal. If a certain Harry Pinner had been out on the park wearing the number 13 shirt he would have surely popped one over to give us a replay date at Old Trafford.

Instead of focusing on his side's tactical naivety Murphy blasted the ref for the disallowed tries and assistant coach Dave Chisnall had a set-to with Halifax substitute Brian Juliff.

Shell-shocked we gazed at the pitch to see players like Barrie Ledger and Andy Platt sobbing shamelessly on the Wembley turf, their heads bouncing up and down. There were plenty of blokes around me crying their eyes out too and I just sat on the cold stone steps, avoiding the trickles of piss emerging from the back of the terrace, unable to watch Chris Anderson collect that big silver cup.

You just want time to collect your thoughts, but you always get somebody who comes out with that stupid wisecrack, "never mind lads, it's only a game!" A young girl walked past and tried to comfort my mate with the soothing words of "You only lost by a point!" and promptly got told to f..k off.

It was *only* a game of rugby, but our lives were completely wrapped up in this *game.* The match took place in the run up to the 1987 General Election, and Labour leader Neil Kinnock used a clipping of his appearance at the event in his famous award winning party election broadcast the following month. It was only a brief glimpse, but you could see a load of red and white flat capped Saints fans surrounding him singing, "We hate Maggie and we hate Maggie!" The broadcast was part of Kinnock's presentation as a man of the people.

The players were vigorously applauded by the Leader of the Opposition from his seat in the Royal Box as they collected their medals. The best seats in the house invariably contained a collection of people who never set foot in a rugby league ground from one year to the next. These included the usual smattering of professional northerners, celebrities and politicians.

Saints got quite an impressive welcome back on the Sunday in Victoria Square. Although when we sang "We'll support you ever more", it was never more apparent that this was a loser's song. The players all promised to make amends in the next game against Warrington in the Premiership. But sadly yet again they failed to deliver and a season that had started so promisingly had fizzled out. It was the same for Kinnock's election campaign, with Maggie back in with another 100-plus seat majority.

Wembley 1987: Halifax versus St Helens.

Top: Tragedy for Saints! Mark Elia has the ball dislodged by a last gasp John Pendlebury lunge at the ball. Had he scored, Saints would have won the cup. (Ian Wilson)

Left: Saints skipper Chris Arkwright reflects on his team's narrow defeat. (Ian Wilson)

11. 1987-88 Sack the board

Widnes 26 St Helens 14, 23 August 1987
Charity Match

We lived with the disappointment of that bitter defeat – and hoped the board would use the cash windfall that a Wembley payday brings to strengthen the squad to challenge Wigan. Instead, on the eve of the season Saints' line-up actually looked weaker, with highly promising forward Paul Round leaving for Oldham.

A dozen of us decided to use the pre-season friendly at neighbours Widnes to stage a protest. My mam lent me an old blanket and I found an old tin of red paint under the stairs so got to work with the slogan *'Prescott and Co, splash out or get out!'*

There was no big plan, we had a few swift ones in the Cricketers Arms on the corner of the ground beforehand to loosen the vocal chords and then that was it. We were like town dogs let off the leash. Initially the 7 feet square banner was hoisted in front of the directors box and accompanied it with a few renditions of 'Sack the board!' just to let them know what the protest was about.

We then tied it to the barbed wire on top of the back fence at the shed end. Most people who came up to us at the end of the game actually agreed with our sentiments, but didn't really want to get involved with the shouting of abuse. Still, you can't make an omelette without breaking a few eggs and thought the ends would justify the means. Among the crowd of us - including Div, Andy, Big John, Kev, Mike, Neil, the two Daves, Tony and Ant - was Steve Ganson, who was always a confident lad able to get his point across succinctly.

Saints lost their first league game at Castleford and rumours that there was going to be a demonstration, a mass pitch invasion and a march to the ground against Hull KR snowballed.

The club was quite prepared both in terms of having a larger than normal police presence and in terms of launching a propaganda offensive in the programme. Protesters were treated like the 'enemy within', were denounced as 'thick' and told to go watching Doncaster or Keighley instead. We were also described as knockers who didn't have the best interests of the club at heart.

We had watched them through thick and thin and most of us would have carried on watching them in the Second Division had we ever been subjected to that fate. What we objected to was the apparent complacency that greeted Wigan's onward advancement. We weren't having a go at the players, but just felt the directors needed a rocket up their arses. A glimpse at the previous season's Wembley programme revealed a central weakness, Halifax had a photograph of a streamlined four-man board, yet ours still boasted 'the 12 apostles.'

It was one of those rare days though where I wanted Saints to lose, just to make a point, but we beat Hull KR, and other fans at that game told us rebels that we should "be loyal and get behind the team instead of moaning". I had smuggled my banner through the turnstile by stuffing it up my coat – and because we won it stayed bundled up all afternoon.

Away from the rugby suddenly St Helens borough had something else to be famous for apart from rugby league – in one of Stock, Aitken and Watermans's new prodigies. Newton-le-Willows' own Rick Astley topped the charts for five weeks with *Never Gonna*

Give You Up. Astley had a further seven top 10 hits in the late 1980s – and although his musical style and image was not every one's cup of tea, he did give the borough a bit of publicity. I say the borough because many Newtoners did not necessarily view themselves as St Heleners and some stubbornly resisted being tacked onto our town – preferring to be associated with Warrington.

Leigh 27 St Helens 21, 13 September 1987
Lancashire Cup Round 1

For good or ill Saints splashed the cash in the bulky shape of Welsh rugby union international Stuart Evans from Neath. The big prop bore all the hallmarks of a panic buy. Sure, Saints had boasted good contingent of Welsh forwards in the 1960s and 1970s, including John Warlow, John Mantle, Kel Coslett, Graham Rees and Mel James, but Evans looked every square inch like a specialist union prop.

Big Truck was thrown in at the deep end in the cup game at Leigh and unbelievably didn't even know how to play the ball correctly. In those days markers could strike for the ball as soon as it was placed on the ground – and opposing prop Derek Pyke had a field day. In a stroke of gamesmanship, the wily Pyke seemed to be telling the big Welshman where to put the ball and then whipping it away with his foot to leave Evans looking bemused. His loss of possession contributed to a costly debut and Leigh knocked us out of our first competition of the year.

People argued that Evans' money should have been spent on keeping a talented young local player like Paul Round at the club. It was a pity for Evans because he went from being the cornerstone of the Welsh union pack, playing a crucial role in a game where scrummaging has such central importance, to a game that needed a greater degree of mobility.

He aspired to be like Kiwi test prop Kurt Sorenson, but he was a long way short of that. Once he realised that he should have been able to hold his hands up, give the money back and go back to the sport he was good at – but instead Evans was trapped in a game to which he was quite simply not suited.

On a positive note, he did bring with him a coach load of followers from South Wales for the odd game who always added to the atmosphere, and must have returned home having learned a thing or two. His best game for Saints came in his try scoring performance in Saints' crushing victory over the touring Auckland side in November. However, rumours did the rounds that his best display came outside the Spicy Chicken one Saturday night when he allegedly flattened a famous local boxer, who had jumped the queue. Nobody has really testified as to the truth of that tale or whether it is an urban myth – but it is now firmly part of St Helens sporting folklore.

Wigan 8 Manly-Warringah 2, 7 October 1987
World Club Challenge

Rugby league is a small game on the global scene – so the title of World Club Challenge was probably a bit too over grandiose. It was billed as the 'Clash of the Titans' – a word a few Wiganers had trouble with, but it turned out into a terrific collision nonetheless. The match was also something different to add to the calendar as the teams played for a winner takes all prize of £20,000.

Like a lot of my Saints mates I viewed the arrival of Manly as like fetching over our long lost Australian cousin, who we believed would surely give our playground bully neighbours Wigan a bloody nose. We thought it would be quite funny to watch the Australian champs crush the cocky pie-eaters, who had won everything bar the Challenge Cup the previous season.

A huge 38,000 crowd was rammed in and we watched it from the clubhouse end, and could barely move come kick-off. Fireworks greeted the teams as they entered and they continued throughout the game with Wigan prop Shaun Wane really earning his spurs in the heat of the battle. It was nip and tuck but then Manly's fiery helmet wearing forward Ron Gibbs was dismissed for clobbering Joe Lydon late and high. It gave Wigan a crucial one man advantage in a game where no tries were scored and they edged it, which seemed unbelievable, as no British team had ever got within a whisker of beating the Australians on the last two tours. But watching Wigan humble the Australian champs was an ominous sign for the rest of the British league clubs.

St Helens 12 Widnes 10, 14 November 1987
John Player Trophy Round 1

'Chariots Offiah' had captured the imagination of the rugby league world with his scintillating performances on the wing since signing for Widnes in the close season. Widnes' coach Doug Laughton had spotted the flyer playing union for Rosslyn Park in the Middlesex Sevens and saw great potential in the well spoken Londoner. It proved to be an inspired signing, turning into the game's most prolific try scorer of the modern game. For all the skilful or powerful players on a rugby field, you cannot beat a speedy winger to really make the crowd roar.

Thankfully our match was already in the bag by the time Chariots got the chance to run at us. The ball worked left and then it was just *whoosh,* and Offiah was touching down, beating the Saints defence with his sheer pace.

Laughton had an eye for the off the beaten track signing and in subsequent years he raided rugby union, signing Emosi Koloto, Alan Tait, John Devereux, Jonathan Davies and Paul Moriarty from the XV-man code. It was a colourful and adventurous way to challenge Wigan's hegemony.

Saints chose a more traditional route signing established league players approaching their prime years like nippy hooker Paul Groves from Salford and big, pacy winger Les Quirk from Barrow.

Another crucial addition was the signing of New Zealand half-back Shane Cooper, who would become Saints' much needed playmaker. At least the board had broken with what we thought was their miserly ways.

On the field things were going well. In the John Player semi-final at Wigan our new-look team overcame an Oldham side, which was very well drilled by the school teacher type Eric Fitzsimons, to make it through to our first final in the history of that trophy. It turned into a real ding-dong battle before we eventually finished them off.

The fact that Wigan had been knocked out by Leeds in the previous week's semi maximised our enjoyment. Our boisterously vocal army of fans more or less marched back to Wigan North West station through the town centre singing 'Are you watching Pie-eaters?' at the bemused Christmas shoppers.

Wigan 22 St Helens 32, 27 December 1987
Division 1

The ill-feeling between Saints and Wigan had been festering for a couple of years, but it reached its lowest possible ebb at the start of the 1987 season after a controversial 'signing'. Saints' board claimed to have signed the massive Kiwi test prop Adrian Shelford, but so too did Wigan. In fact it emerged that Australian club Newcastle also claimed to have the big prop's signature. Newcastle soon dropped out, but Saints were so sure Shelford was their man that they took out a court order to prevent him from playing for their rivals.

Unfortunately the High Court found against Saints in December, which meant the club had not only lost the player to Wigan, but also a costly legal battle. The damaging saga left a bad taste in all of our mouths and most fans knew that defeat in court meant Saints would inevitably have to find a significant sum from somewhere to offset that loss. Our fears that we would have to lose a star player would soon be realised. A lot of supporters initially directed their venom towards Shelford, who had been frozen out of the game while the case was heard, calling him Judas.

Others blamed the board for bungling it. "What did they do – get him to scribble his name on the chairman's bloody autograph book?" said one fan.

Shelford had already fully played his role as the villain of the piece when in almost his first action he ploughed knees-first into the back of our first-half try scorer Kevin McCormack. Saints' healthy contingent of supporters, packed up in our customary spot in the clubhouse end, was in uproar.

As the front cover of the match programme declared in large 60 point lettering, Wigan were World Champions and predictably took a commanding 22-6 lead at half-time and some fans around us weighed up the prospects of leaving.

Unbelievably, it turned into one of those most talked about games of the past 30 years as Saints staged a magnificent comeback to win 32-22.

Phil Veivers had a commanding all-round game and bagged a brace of tries, with wingers Les Quirk and Dave Tanner grabbing the others as Saints really rubbed it in. Ten minutes from the end the 'Wigan walk' was in full flow with the dumfounded Pie-eaters streaming out to the jeers of those of us packed into the clubhouse end. It remains one of the all time classics, and probably went some way to let those culpable for the Shelford debacle off the hook.

That month the Nelson always seemed to have Belinda Carlisle's *Heaven is a Place on Earth* ringing out, I reckon a few of thought we had found it too that afternoon at Central Park.

Saints went on to complete a Christmas holiday double with a magnificent 20-0 win over Widnes.

Leeds 14 St Helens 15, 9 January 1988
John Player Trophy Final, Central Park

Although the cigarette-sponsored knockout had existed since 1971 we had never got our hands on the odd-looking trophy that consisted of a statue of a golden rugby player on a dark marble plinth. Although Leeds were probably favourites, having turned Wigan out in the semis, Saints were running hot.

There were considerable advantages to playing at Wigan, which was a place you could get to under your own steam, and the ground was a stone's throw from a dozen of half-decent centrally located pubs. Starting with the Swan and Railway opposite the station, you could take your pick trotting up to the ground - Crofters, Bricklayers, the White Horse and Billy Boston's pub the Griffin.

Leeds had led thanks to a David Creasser try that had been created by a tremendous surging break by Roy Powell. Paul Loughlin hit back when his momentum and a soggy surface helped him slide over to level the scores. Leeds fans in the Kop clearly felt it was a double movement and taunted referee Fred Lindop with a rendition of "Who's the bastard in the black?" All black was the traditional garb for referees in those days, unless of course one of the teams was decked out similarly. The modern switch to multicoloured, sponsored referee jerseys, which lack the same level of respect, has seen the demise of that particular chant.

Referees have always been the subject of abuse — that dreadful chant started by soccer fans in the late 1960s has now largely disappeared. To the tune of *My Darling Clementine*, abusive fans used to sing, "Who's your father referee?"

The Loiners brought quite a big, noisy following, and a lot of their songs had their origins at Leeds United, including the anthem *Marching all together!* and they had more to cheer at the break with a 14-9 lead.

Shortly after the restart Loughlin threaded his way over the line with a magnificent sidestepping run. He also converted to give Saints a one-point lead, which was defended superbly despite the relentless Leeds onslaught.

The men in the double red vee had the bounce of the ball for once with Leeds's Garry Schofield's drop-goal hitting the post seven minutes from time. After an utterly absorbing encounter, the hooter sounded to allow Kiwi Shane Cooper to become the first Saints captain to lift the trophy. Well, he would have been had the Beeb's pitch-side presenter Richard Duckenfield not intervened, bizarrely stopping our skipper before he collected his medal and the cup. As Cooper was telling the BBC viewers that "We tackled with our hearts for 40 minutes in that second half", the trophy was passed over to Andy Platt. It was fitting really, Saints won due to the side's defensive effort, with loose-forward Platt making a magnificent 43 tackles.

Platty held the trophy aloft to the delight of our posse of jubilant supporters who had spilled onto the muddy pitch in front of the Douglas Stand. Paul Groves clambered onto one of the other player's shoulders and swinging a scarf around his head he led the choristers in "Ole, ole, ole, ole! We are the Saints! We are the Saints!"

Jubilation suddenly, and quite irrationally, turned to fear when for some reason Saints fans started running away when the Leeds fans charged onto the pitch to see their side pick up their losers medals. There was no actual trouble as far as I could see, but it was like seeing one of a herd of antelopes start running on an Attenborough wildlife programme and other beasts following. The incident seemed to become one of those that gathered legs afterwards.

We were straight onto the train and into town for what turned into a loud session in the Nelson — which was then the town's busiest pub. Working on the door of the Bridge Street pub back then was St Helens middleweight boxer Ian Chantler, who had been good enough to get a crack at future World Champion Nigel Benn a couple of months previously. Unfortunately the 'Dark Destroyer' saw him off in one round — the fight being one of Benn's 22 consecutive knockouts between 1987 and 1989.

The *Sunday Mirror* felt our victory was good enough to have a special front page cover wrap around for the St Helens area declaring "Neil drops to victory". Lockers must have been wondering what he needed to do – 14 points out of 15 and Holding gets the big headline...

My BBC recording of the game was a tape to treasure until it bit the dust six years later when I was sharing a house with woman from West Bromwich who assumed that I "must have watched it by now as it looked so old" and taped *Home and Away* over it. The funniest bit on the tape was the look on Leeds second-rower Paul Medley's face after taking a tackle from Roy Haggerty. The Saints man had Medley pinned to the floor when he decided he needed to clear his throat. Suddenly a thread of thick, snotty spit dangled from Haggerty's mouth horrifically close to the Leeds man, who winced in horror and disgust.

We did not realise it then, but our season had peaked and so had this team under Murphy – it was downhill from there. It seemed there was trouble in the Saints playing camp, despite our run of success. Andy Platt gave voice to this in the *St Helens Star* accusing the board of "trying to get the best results with the minimum of outlay", and accused them of adopting "an amateur attitude". Platt, despite being unsettled, still did his level best for the club. The former West Park pupil was a terrifically dedicated player, who was just coming into his prime. Something told us that as soon as he started playing test rugby and rubbing shoulders with Wigan's internationals he would be joining the Central Parkers in the future – maybe the club drove him to it.

A further blow came in the loss of powerful prop Peter Souto, who had been a tower of strength in Saints' Christmas revival. The massive moustached former Cardiff rugby union forward only played six games in his two brief spells at the club, but he was never on the losing side and picked up a winners' medal. Not many players can say that - unfortunately the former Fulham forward was plagued by injury.

Leigh 12 St Helens 22, 31 January 1988
Challenge Cup Round 1

Saints were confident of heading back to Wembley when the cup campaign kicked off amid a flurry of fists in this bruising first round encounter. It was one of those "hey lads, hey" sort of games and as Les Quirk touched down he was kicked by Tony Cottrell. Leigh's abrasive packman was followed into the early bath by Saints' Andy Platt, who was first sin-binned, but received his marching orders once he returned following a clash with Phil Johnson. The dismissal earned Platt a four-match suspension, which was a massive blow as he was an integral part of our team.

Leigh led 10-2 after half an hour with former Saints skipper Harry Pinner, who had joined them from Widnes, playing a blinder in front of 9,500 crowd.

Saints hit back superbly, but with the game still in the balance Pinner's long pass was intercepted by Mark Elia, whose touchdown sealed the game. Saints fans with short memories sarcastically sang, "There's only one Harry Pinner."

Saints were again drawn away, this time against a tough Warrington side. Despite the television cameras a bumper 10,000 crowd rolled up at Wilderspool, including a large contingent of Saints fans.

Unfortunately a few of the beered-up Wires, from what was known as 'pond-life corner', steamed into the Railway End, scattering Saints fans in a menacing fashion bizarrely chanting "c'mon Scousers, c'mon Scousers" which was a bit rich given the Mersey runs through the middle of their town.

A few lads got a mild kicking – but no Saints stayed for a fight, there were no hooligans from St Helens there for a ruck, they just wanted to watch a rugby game.

The Wire took the lead with a great try scored by David Lyon on the wing following good work by Australian full-back Brian Johnson. Saints equalised with a try by Paul Forber, who was playing just 11 days after a cartilage operation. Tries from Billy McGinty and John Woods stretched the Wire's lead to 14-6 but Saints showed great hands to send Quirk in at the corner. Despite the pitch cutting up, which forced Warrington to appear in the second half in their previous year's jersey, the match was a corker. Crucially Warrington skipper Les Boyd did not return having broken his arm, and he watched the second half prowling the touchlines.

Saints sub John Fieldhouse, who along with Chris Arkwright, hadn't played through injury for three months, entered the fray. 'Foggy' had an immediate effect, latching onto a fine pass from Haggerty to edge Saints back in front.

But the Wire would not lie down with head-down Des Drummond's sheer strength and powerful fend leaving the dazed Saints full-back Phil Veivers in a crumpled heap on the floor.

With the clock ticking away both sides still created chances, but into the last minute Kit-Kat Paul Groves worked a run-around with Neil Holding, dummied and flicked the ball inside for Fieldhouse to plunge over for the winner.

It was a great victory, with skipper Shane Cooper the architect of many a move. Four days later, in a comfortable 64-2 win over Hull, Coops joined Tom van Vollenhoven, Alf Ellaby, Steve Llewellyn and Frank Myler in the list of Saints players who have bagged six tries in a match. It was landmark game in other ways too, although we did not really know it at the time, with long-serving hooker Graham Liptrot playing his last match in the red vee. Lippy had been a tremendous servant for the club – and it must have taken some coming back from those four broken jaw injuries he had sustained.

Salford 22 St Helens 18, 28 February 1988
Challenge Cup Quarter-Final

Salford's favourite sons The Smiths penned some great lines to encapsulate life for young blokes in particular, but *Heaven knows I'm miserable now* summed up how we felt when we had our bubble burst in unlikely circumstances.

Saints had looked like a side with Wembley written all over them, and that feeling gathered momentum when we came out of the hat with the struggling Red Devils. Victory seemed such a foregone conclusion against a team that was written off as "has beens and never wuzzers", and were languishing in the drop zone.

Salford had been the 'Quality Street' gang of the late 1960s and early 1970s, noted for signing top-drawer rugby union internationals like David Watkins and Keith Fielding, but now they had fallen on hard times. Their ground, which was once the most modern in the game, was tatty and decrepit with parts of the condemned, crumbling terrace fenced off.

Saints fans' only concern was getting hold of a ticket – there was a massive demand. Our supporters were given the majority share of the 8,000 available but when they went on sale, on a first-come, first-served basis the Sunday morning before the match a massive queue looped all the way round the training pitch. I disliked queuing – probably because as a kid back in 1972 my mam had taken me and my brother to Victoria Park to see the animal that played *Black Beauty* in the TV series. We queued for an hour until my mam decided the we were not moving quickly enough and took us home – telling us that it was not the real thing just an old nag from a farmer's field. I was gutted, stamping my feet and ripping my coat like a spoilt brat in protest.

A lot of people in the Salford ticket queue were to be disappointed, but alas not as dejected as those who got to see the game.

Saints turned in a diabolical display that was epitomised by a dreadful, overhead panic pass by Tony Burke, which was slung across his own try line allowing lanky forward Mick Worrall to seal it for the Red Devils.

Even when they were a man short after Darren Bloor had been sin-binned for elbowing Holding, Salford stayed in control. Robust, oversized scrum-half Bloor played his way into a contract with Saints that day thanks to the manner in which he had kept Holding in his pocket.

It was a typical performance from a Kevin Ashcroft team – the former Warrington coach seemed to know exactly how to rattle footballing sides like Saints. It wasn't just defeat that stung, but the fact that Saints weren't going back to Wembley so we had no chance to erase our awful memories of the previous season.

Widnes 16 St Helens 6, 14 April 1988
Division 1

After being so unceremoniously dumped out of the Cup, attention turned to the championship, which we had not won since 1975. The holiday fixtures held the key to the title's destiny and just before Easter's programme Murphy's men were two points adrift of the league leaders with two games in hand. Saints had a disastrous Easter, losing to Wigan on Good Friday by the odd point in 19 in front of a fervent 21,813. It was a double whammy - defeat meant the loss of Saints' 100 per cent home record and bang went any realistic chance of winning the league. Any faint hopes we harboured were shattered by a hat-trick from the irrepressible scoring machine Martin Offiah at Naughton Park.

The Widnes flyer's scoring knack and sheer pace was the critical difference. He was the fastest thing I had ever seen – give him a ball in space and it was pointless chasing him. He also had instinct, something you cannot coach, and his first try saw him just popping up in the right place to score. His second saw him finish off a fine movement with sheer pace. His hat-trick followed a superb break, kick and collection before grounding the ball and being mobbed by the scallies at the shed end. The young Widnes fans who smothered him were far more effective in bringing Offiah to a halt that any Saints defender.

You could understand their elation because Widnes had found a real hero in 'Chariots'. Those fans chaired him at shoulder height from the pitch at the end of the game. If only they had known then he would end up on television's *Come Dancing* and worse, playing for Wigan, perhaps they would had have dropped him off Runcorn Bridge and into the Mersey sludge below... Offiah's first season in league had been magnificent, scoring 44 tries and earning a place in the Great Britain tour squad heading down under.

The Easter Monday result left the Chemics with the formality of clinching the title at relegated Hunslet, which was a deserved reward for their attractive rugby and enterprising approach to recruitment that combined homespun talent with big money union converts.

Things could not be ending in a bleaker fashion at Saints, however, after such a promising season, with Andy Platt placed on the transfer list at £175,000. It was really bad news for Saints that one of the best forwards in the game wanted to leave the club. Saints needed more quality forwards, not less, especially not one we had nurtured from being a scrawny 18-year-old 12-stoner, too small to play in the pack, to one that was about to become one of the most formidable front-rowers in the game.

St Helens 14 Widnes 38, 15 May 1988
Premiership Final, Old Trafford

Rugby league's big idea of taking the Premiership Final to Old Trafford had proved to be a success in 1987. The brilliant backdrop brought a real sense of occasion to the last game of the season. Part of the attraction was the double-header and prior to our game, Oldham beat Featherstone in the Second Division curtain raiser.

We needed a good final to make amends for the Salford debacle and our passage to Old Trafford was relatively eventless, beating Castleford and Bradford. Widnes had a more controversial route with their semi-final against rivals Warrington being marred by a touchline brawl, which had spilled over into the crowd. Young fans sat on the low Naughton Park perimeter wall were caught up in the commotion and one kid needed stitches. Des Drummond, the Warrington winger, ended up getting caught in a fracas with an adult spectator and consequently lost his Australian tour place. An incident on the pitch following the Saints versus Wigan Good Friday game also cost Joe Lydon his place in the Lions squad, but that did not have the same widespread coverage.

The Widnes episode was very damaging for a sport that used "Man's game for all the family" as its slogan. Predictably, it made headline national news the following day, appearing above an item on USA President Ronald Reagan on both the BBC and ITV bulletins. Rugby league was only deemed worthy of headlines when something bad happened. You could count on the fingers of one hand the times that our game had actually made national television news.

The list included the depressing violence at the Black Friday Humberside derby from 1981, the Bradford players choosing to walk off the field during the game in 1982 and the brawl that had led to the abandonment of the match between Leigh and Oldham. When established union players turned professional, like Terry Holmes who had an ill-fated stint at Bradford and dislocated his shoulder in his first match, the game suddenly became newsworthy.

After the bad news headlines from the semi-final a David Hulme-inspired Widnes were keen to let their rugby do the talking, and they did so with style with a shirt-sleeved 35,252 crowd witnessing a 38-14 massacre.

Saints looked rudderless without Shane Cooper and were let down by terrible handling and pathetic, powder-puff tackling. Cooper was a bit of a magician – fans called him Merlin - and he made Saints play revolve around him. It effectively meant our skipper was indispensable, because when he did not play Saints invariably stunk. On those occasions everyone would say "We missed Coops today!" making it a win-win situation for the crafty Kiwi.

Well, that was almost another year over – but we still had the Ashes tour where remarkably Britain won the final test against Australia at the Sydney Cricket Ground. It was shown on television at the crack of dawn and we rubbed our eyes with disbelief at the triumph. Paul Loughlin had a storming game with his break setting up a pearling try for Henderson Gill. It was a massive boost for league, because it meant we had meaningful international competition once more after over a decade of whitewashes.

It was not the only thing on the up - the region's economy had also started to marginally improve with the south booming, and some of that prosperity at last beginning to percolate north. My labouring job was under the auspices of a government job start scheme, whereby if you were long term unemployed and took a low paid job, they'd top up your wage for six months with an extra £20 a week. A lot of lads I went to Saints with had left school in the early 1980s had gone through the whole raft of schemes through the YTS, Community programme and the £40-a-week Enterprise Allowance Scheme and still ended up back on the dole at the end of it all.

In the 1980s it seemed as though either you had a steady job and worked hard buying into the dream vision of owning your own home, or you were scrimping and saving, ducking between schemes, low-paid work and the dole.

Few of the people in the first category were like comedian Harry Enfield's Loadsamoney character, but some thought they were comfortable and the good times were here to stay. Many later got their fingers badly burnt, having to work all the hours God sent in overtime to see themselves through debt and avoid house repossession and the curse of negative equity.

The 1980s was a quite challenging, almost brutal decade, no wonder people sought solace in Saints. Even when things elsewhere were up and down, Saints were always there as a form of constant comfort or crutch. It did not matter that the team mostly performed dismally when it counted, because just by being there you could see your mates, have a laugh, a drink and a shout. Going to Saints was a safety valve where you could release all the bottled-up tension from the week.

12. 1988-89 Our darkest hour…and 20 minutes

Widnes 32 St Helens 24, 18 September 1988
Lancashire Cup, Round 1

Although there was a little bit more work knocking about in the north, I thought my future might be a bit rosier in the south west, where I headed for a three-month spell. Saints' send-off in my last game at Naughton Park was typical. We trailed 22-0 at half-time and despite our rally we were knocked out of the first cup of the year. Perhaps it was just the team's way of making sure I didn't get cold feet, with their performance grabbing me by the lapels and saying "Piss off – it's for your own good!"

It felt like I was walking out on the team but the first game I missed - at Headingley –made sure I didn't have any regrets. I lined up four 10ps and called home for the full round-up just after 6 o'clock. "They got bloody murdered. Rubbish they were."

Although it was always pleasing to hear familiar, northern voices - Leeds 32 Saints 0 - was not that cheerful. Nobody around me in my new settings was even vaguely interested in the score or rugby league for that matter. I might as well have been ringing up for the Homing News, checking the velocities of the racing pigeons flying back from northern France on the last weekend of the season.

Living away makes you even more loyal about your hometown team and an even more passionate advocate of 13-a-side rugby over the code with two too many players. Discussions usually got more animated after a few pints of Banks or Marstons. You do get homesick at first – and cling to any link home. Some nights I must have bored my new colleagues senseless by talking about the Ravenhead insignia at the bottom of another pint glass that I had drained, telling them that the number 478 etched into the glass meant it was made in my town.

My only glimpse of Saints down there was on a borrowed, fuzzy black and white portable telly when *Sportsnight* showed the British Coal Nines. After twiddling the aerial at right angles I was able to get my first look at our new winger Mike Carrington. The former Neath and Welsh 'A' union international looked big, but oddly shaped for a winger.

But the way he blasted through Widnes wing Martin Offiah's tackle to touch down meant I very briefly thought he could be nurtured into another Roy Mathias. It was just wishful thinking – Carrington never really developed and had an ungainly running style and dodgy moustache.

The other real talking point of the early winter were the rare back-page headlines in the *Daily Mirror* engineered by coach Murphy's invitation, via the press, to football bad boy Vinnie Jones, who was serving a suspension from his game at the time. Although it brought us publicity – loads of it - it also gave people the wrong idea of our game.

Up north people were saying "This fella reckons he's a hardcase, but he wouldn't last five minutes in our game." I was half expecting the *Daily Mirror* to invite Chris Arkwright, Roy Haggerty and Paul Forber to pose with their beckoning hands suggesting "Come and have a go if you think you're hard enough!" Down south it reinforced prejudices because it seemed we only wanted the Wimbledon player because of his reputation for thuggery. So as a PR stunt what did that say about our game?

St Helens 18 Widnes 20, 10 December 1988
John Player Semi-Final, Central Park

Saints' bid to retain the John Player Trophy was derailed by another Martin Offiah try. But the turning point for me came when Widnes's lanky centre Andy Currier gave Michael O'Connor a crack and while our star Aussie three-quarter's head was still spinning, the Chemics nipped in for a crucial score. Despite two good tries from Les Quirk, our own pacy winger, Widnes edged it 20-18 with Offiah's try contributing to our downfall.

Perhaps Widnes were a necessary evil to save us from ourselves and an embarrassing face-off with our Wigan rivals in the showpiece occasions. If only we had heeded that, we may have saved ourselves the indignity of what was to follow later in the season.

Shortly after the semi-final, Widnes coach Doug Laughton pulled off a masterstroke and the biggest publicity coup a cross-code signing has ever produced. He signed Welsh rugby union international skipper and British Lion Jonathan Davies shortly into the New Year, although the story was that our coach Alex Murphy was also supposed to have been after him.

Winter brought cold comfort for Saints, with our displays very inconsistent despite the presence of two Manly and Australia test superstars Paul Vautin and O'Connor. Both had arrived in the autumn and had brought mixed reactions from fans.

"That's never the same O'Connor. He's some bloody doppelganger!" was the theory of one bloke in the Popular Side. People expected a Meninga-like impact from the dual-code international - and we didn't get it. Big Mal had been due to return that year, but broke his arm in the Australia versus Rest of the World clash so could not make it. O'Connor, by popular consent, was not of the same calibre.

Saints 16 Widnes 14, 11 March 1989
Challenge Cup Semi-Final

It seemed that the entire rugby league world wanted the two 'Big Ws' to go head-to-head at Wembley as it would have been the showdown between the game's top clubs.

The trip to the once prestigious but now utterly dishevelled Station Road in the opening round was Saints' only away tie in our cup run, but it was a potential banana skin match against Frankie Barrow's workmanlike Lions.

Swinton's thickset forward Ian Connor was detailed by Frankie to follow Australian test star Paul Vautin wherever he went. And born-and-bred St Helener Connor gave his illustrious opponent a rough old ride, following his instructions to the letter. He probably even followed Vautin off the pitch for a drink of water. Connor was a handy lad and his robust display earned him a call from his hometown club six months later.

Saints were helped on their way by a fine performance from 17-year-old full-back Gary Connolly, playing in just his second game for the first team since signing from Blackbrook juniors. Coach Murphy was a believer in the adage that "if you are good enough you're old enough!" My mate Kev took a distinct but irrational dislike to Connolly, based on his bizarre view that the youngster's blond mane made him look like Princess Diana. Connolly gave an unbelievably committed and near faultless display in the semi-final against Widnes with one tackle on the danger man Martin Offiah proving crucial.

On paper a dream Widnes versus Wigan final seemed a safe bet and the Chemics were so confident they left new signing Jonathan Davies sitting in the stand and experienced Kiwi test prop Kurt Sorensen on the bench. Saints' largely homespun side, now missing the departed Australians Vautin and O'Connor, who were denied permission by their Australian clubs to return, really took the game to the team of all talents. Particularly impressive in the pack was John Harrison, the lanky second-rower signed from local amateurs Haresfinch.

You need luck in cup games and somebody was on Saints' side when Widnes's St Helens born loose-forward Richie Eyres was given his marching orders from referee John Holdsworth for a first-half trip on Neil Holding. In those days the man in the middle rarely ducked the issue on tripping – it was an automatic down-the-tunnel-job if you stuck your foot out. Despite their 12-man handicap Widnes fought back and looked to have clinched the match with tries from Darren Wright and David Hulme giving them a 14-12 lead with just three minutes remaining.

The Widnes followers were already mentally booking their tickets for their date at the Twin Towers, and we were resigning ourselves to falling at the final hurdle. Then Paul Groves threw an audacious dummy and raced through before his long pass sent Les Quirk plunging over in the corner for the winning try. It was the stuff dreams were made of – a proper grandstand finish with an unexpected twist. There were then a couple of minutes to hang on before that sweet sound of the hooter, followed by scenes of exuberant jubilation.

Que sera! Sera!
What ever will be, will be
We're going to Wem-ba-lee,
Que sera! Sera!

Wembley tickets went on sale to all-comers the following Sunday and by the time I shuffled up to Saints at 7am the queue from the front office already looped around the training pitch, up Dunriding Lane and then turned right up Willow Road, the street that backs onto the Popular Side. Queues are a very English way of doing things – and people are quite precious about their place in the line. There was talk that Wigan interlopers were after our tickets, because they had already sold their allocation, having qualified a week before us. There were frequent howls of protest - a few people - pushed into the middle of the queue and were hard-faced enough to brazen it out. Tickets were at a premium because Wembley's capacity had been slashed from just over 94,000 to 78,000 because the upper tiers behind the posts were now seated.

Wigan 2 St Helens 4, 23 April 1989
Premiership Round 1

Once our players had been measured for their Wembley suits our performances on the pitch went to pot. The worst of them all was briefly captured on camera at Halifax. Trailing 18-4 at the break Alex Murphy was filmed storming into the Thrum Hall dressing room to give his players a right royal rollicking. With the film crew present, he had clearly been told to watch his words after the shock of his last changing room appearance on the telly. This time all his potential 'f' words, were substituted by 'bloodies'. As his players looked at the floor trying to avoid eye contact, Murphy bawled:

"Is that what some of you call bloody playing? You should be bloody ashamed of yourselves?"

The pep talk did not do any good - we lost 40-8 to confirm our very patchy form. However, the following week, six days before the Wembley final, we beat Wigan in the Premiership which acted as a Cup Final dress rehearsal with two unlikely penalty goals from Paul Forber giving us a 4-2 victory. It certainly gave us hope, but there was a feeling that Wigan may just have been toying with us like a big cat playing with a puny little mouse before snapping its head off.

As the 17,542 crowd shuffled out there was even more consternation than usual about the younger fans pushing impatiently out the Wigan Kop end.

"Stop pushing! Have you lot got no bloody sense?" barked one red-faced 50-something. It may have seemed like an overreaction to a bit of impatient shoving. But he had one word burning into his brain - Hillsborough.

Eight days previously 95 Liverpool supporters had been crushed to death at the FA Cup semi-final at Sheffield Wednesday's ground. Hundreds more were injured as fans funnelled into an already over-packed Leppings Lane terrace at the start of the game. A lot of people from St Helens were at or had family members at Hillsborough. About half of all soccer fans in St Helens were Reds supporters so it was quite an emotive issue in the town. Coming only four years after the Bradford fire disaster sports fans generally were feeling a little bit more fragile, recalling the days too that they had been crammed onto shoddy, crumbling terraces or rickety old wooden stands. It was definitely a case of thinking, "There but for the grace of God go I".

The Sun newspaper's coverage of the Hillsborough disaster was disgusting, effectively blaming Liverpool fans for contributing to the tragedy. The newspaper apologised some years later, but not before it suffered from a dip in sales on Merseyside as people began boycotting it.

St Helens 0 Wigan 27, 29 April 1989
Challenge Cup Final, Wembley

The bitter taste of Wembley defeat had lingered on our palate for two years, but that was nothing compared to what we had to digest this time around. It was against 'them' for a start. But the fact that we did not score and were never really in the game made it a complete non-event. That was the biggest difference – we had talking points from 1987, but this 27-0 debacle was the blackest day in our history.

We had a laugh going down, scavenging bits and pieces off those who had taken a Pimblett's Wembley pack and winding up the occupants of Wigan coaches that frequently passed us on the M6. That banter continued on the car park of the Olympic Torch, where some Wigan and Saints fans scaled the drainpipe to tie their respective colours to the aerial. The laughing soon stopped inside the ground. Wembley Stadium itself was in transition, and the upper tier had been seated, leaving the lower sections behind the posts as the only standing areas. We were densely packed in and the view was awful – still, there was not that much to see.

Strategy-wise Saints bungled it, opting to fly winger Michael O'Connor and loose-forward Paul Vautin in from Australia just for the final. Fatty Vautin was made captain, which was a big call given that he was never going to wear the red vee again.

It was a kick in the teeth for lads like John Harrison and Dave Tanner, who had helped the side overcome the odds to make the final and subsequently did not even make it onto the subs bench.

Once the community singing, *Abide with me*, and the minute's silence for the Hillsborough victims was out of the way, the bandsmen left the turf and the mismatch commenced.

It was like seeing a daddy longlegs caught up in a spider's web. Within seconds the spider was out ruthlessly devouring the body of the hapless creature, leaving just the thin spindly legs as the remnants of the life that was once there.

Young Gary Connolly was the first victim, clobbered shortly after the kick off, knocking-on and forcing a drop-out, and Wigan were straight up and at us with Ellery Hanley brushing off Roy Haggerty's feeble tackle to send Kevin 'The Beast' Iro storming over after only three minutes. Hanley doubled that first-half lead with a rampaging, tackle-busting run to the line from halfway. It was a typical Hanley special – wrong-footing Paul Vautin to take him 20 yards from the line. Just as four Saints defenders closed in on him, Hanley found another gear and strode over to score.

Although Hanley lacked the refined passing qualities of a cultured loose-forward he had the raw power to make space by blasting through challengers. Even when carrying a knock he would make all his tackles, and offensively could come in and out of the game with a devastating impact. Hanley walked off with the Lance Todd trophy for his masterful display.

Another Iro try five minutes into the second half wrapped it up for Wigan, before Andy Gregory and Steve Hampson piled on further agony with touchdowns. Wigan's display was as clinical and as professional as we had ever seen, contrasting starkly with Saints' ramshackle effort. Saints lost the ball 27 times, missed countless tackles and lacked any form of game plan. The scale of the defeat induced a feeling of numbness. Saints suffered the indignity of becoming the first team to be nilled in a Wembley final since 1951, when Barrow lost 10-0 to Wigan. We were lucky to have got nil.

It was made worse by seeing Andy Platt, whom we had sold to Wigan earlier in the season for £140,000, with a winner's medal firmly in his hand. There was not much of a post-mortem on the coach coming back, and most of the grinning Wiganers passing us were met with half-hearted V-signs. It is the worst possible state to be in when your bitterest rival is the top dog. Life was easier in the early 1980s when the Hulls and Widnes were winning things and we were not even at the races, than this state of affairs. It was absolute hell – but some cruel bastards had plenty more coal to sling into the fiery furnace yet.

As bad as the day had been, nobody was crying into their beer when we piled into the Saints club before closing time. In one corner you could hear stalwart Audrey singing: "We'll come again, we'll come again, ee, aye, adio, but we don't know when!" Everyone thought she was just whistling in the dark to keep up spirits in our hour of need. Not many of the people in that room at the time could ever see a way that we could catch Wigan in the foreseeable future. Wigan looked, like Maggie Thatcher, set to go on and on and on.

When the Pie-Eaters had been in the doldrums in the early 1980s figures in the game constantly spoke in the *Rugby Leaguer* of how much "the game needed a strong Wigan?" But now we had it - Wigan had become like Frankenstein's monster. It was up to the other clubs to catch up, but it seemed impossible to close the gap when the best players in the league seem to be drawn to Wigan like a magnet by the immediate prospect of success.

It was like being at school when two captains picked sides during 'double games' and allowed the big kid to have first pick of all the best players. The other captain would be left to select a side from the massed ranks of obese lads, skinny kids, swots in glasses, smokers and those who had forgotten to bring a sick note. The results were similar.

For me the immediate aftermath was about keeping occupied – and the day after Wembley I headed up to Glasgow to watch Liverpool play Celtic in a Hillsborough charity game. After spending the post match necking pints of heavy beer I slept rough in a bank cashpoint lobby in the city centre, with my mate driving us back down at the crack of dawn the following morning. With it being May Day I went on a rally in Kirkby where trade unionists were protesting over the closure of the Bird's Eye plant in the already impoverished Knowsley town. There was no point just wallowing in my Saints misery.

There was still plenty to occupy folk under 30 and the Citadel Arts Centre had opened in the town centre. It was the place where St Helens comedian Johnny Vegas built up his local support base and 'refined' his act. It was also a good live music venue, and they put on a bit of alternative stuff as well. It was also the stage for the funniest thing I have ever witnessed - *The Gong Show*. It was a talent competition which let the crowd dictate how long the performers stayed on stage. If the crowd booed, a hook would drag them off. One bloke turned up dressed as a nun and immediately set fire to his habit and gloves. The organisers looked uneasy and then their worst fears were realised when the burning nun suddenly ripped off all his clothes and was wearing just a bandage around his privates, which he began twirling around before setting fire to it. The crowd cheered, but he could not be allowed to carry on in an audience that contained quite a few children. Unfortunately when the stewards tried to remove him, he dived into the crowd with his package still on fire. He was eventually bundled out through the doors, although the crowd were yelling for more.

A few years later I saw Wreckless Eric play there, but midway through his set a fish seller of the kind who used to frequent local pubs came in shouting, "Prawns, cockles, mussels, crabsticks". The veteran Cockney new wave singer had seen nothing like it and bawled in a mock northern accent, "F...kin 'ell, the pies have come!"

The cockle man was a regular feature of pubs and Labour clubs, but always had to run the gauntlet of the same jokes, such as "Have you got crabs, mate?"

Neil Holding celebrates scoring a try in the 15-3 win at Warrington on 29 October 1989.
He is celebrating with winger Dave Tanner. (Peers)

Les Quirk grabs the match winning try against Widnes in the Challenge Cup
Semi-Final in March 1989. (Peers)

Wembley 1989: Chairman Joe Pickavance, coach Alex Murphy and captain Paul Vautin lead out St Helens. (Peers)

Left: Dynamic scrum-half Paul Bishop. (Peers)
Above: Gary Connolly.

13. 1989-90 Neither fish nor fowl

Sheffield Eagles 20 St Helens 36, 3 September 1989
Division 1

Saints started the season under a dark, dirty cloud from the previous season's Wembley debacle. Coach Murphy and the board's response had been to stick 13 members of the squad on the transfer list. However, once the season got under way there had been no real clear out and it made you wonder whether it had been an empty gesture.

Scrum-half Darren Bloor moved to Swinton and was replaced by Welsh rugby union international Jonathan Griffiths. He may not have captured the same headlines as that certain other Jonathan from Llanelli, but Griffiths was a good signing for Saints. The jack-in-the-box half-back was a tenacious little player who would work like an extra forward. He did have his faults and one of his worst traits was his unhealthy habit of wanting to keep the ball for himself. But to give him his due, he liked to have a go and attack defences, and had pace to back himself.

Griffiths scored two crucial tries at newly promoted Sheffield Eagles on his debut on the opening day of the season. Unfortunately the Welshman otherwise had a disastrous first season, plagued with injuries, playing only 11 games that term. However, he went on to represent Wales, possibly becoming the first person to gain Welsh international caps at rugby union, league and cricket.

Also making his debut was former Barrow back Tony Kay, who slotted in at a variety of positions without really setting the world on fire.

The fledgling Eagles had enjoyed a slow but steady rise into the top flight since their formation five seasons previously. The Steel City side had made everyone sit up and take note the previous year when they hammered Swinton in the Second Division Premiership final at Old Trafford. They had their problems – on the eve of their first season in Division 1 they lost use of Owlerton Stadium due to ground safety issues. Their first game of the season, against Saints, took place at Hillsborough.

As the 6,200 crowd filed largely into one side of the famous old stadium, many of us could not help but gawp at the Leppings Lane end - site of the previous April's disaster. My Liverpool supporting mate, who had been there on the afternoon of 15 April, boycotted the Sheffield game on principle, saying he would not "set foot in that city again until the 96 fans got justice."

St Helens 78 Runcorn 10, 17 September, 1989
Lancashire Cup Round 1

Saints continued to recruit with scheming half-back Tommy Frodsham joining his hometown club from Swinton. More players would join later in the year, but it was all very piecemeal and there was no real high profile signing.

Not that I was taking much notice as I was already packing my bags and leave for Birmingham. I was going to have a farewell appearance on the Popular Side in the Lancashire Cup opening round.

Statistics show that 5,498 filed into Knowsley Road to watch Saints pile 78 points on Runcorn. But you can cross one off that number because I was there bodily, but spent virtually the entire game sat on the terraces with my head down between my knees, doubled-up after a Guinness and Jameson's bender that started on Thursday and finished in the early hours of Sunday morning. Although I was sober for the game, my head was cabbaged and I felt as though somebody was beating me in the kidneys with a pick-axe handle.

I looked up periodically at each roar – which invariably meant that Saints were scoring again against Dave Chisnall's Second Division strugglers, but it was a waste of time and money being there.

The weekend's heavy drinking bout was my way of saying goodbye to St Helens, having finished my job as a labourer that Friday to do a politics degree in Birmingham. For the previous six months I had been working with a gang of St Helens builders up in Preston and spending a fair chunk of my wages in the Rope and Anchor.

This red-tiled town centre boozer was a rough and ready, but welcoming haunt which was full of characters. It was an Irish pub in that most of its seasoned regulars were old Irishmen, not because they had pictures of leprechauns on the walls and bicycles and wheelbarrows hanging from the ceiling like the 'Plastic Paddy' chain pubs have.

One of the drinkers in there was a road worker from Dublin, with hands like shovels, who always had some pearls of wisdom and was mockingly dismissive of my own claims to be a labourer, claiming my hands were too soft.

He talked daft sometimes, once remarking, "I have worked out a theory that if you drink long enough, you can drink yourself sober." I saw him 48 hours later and he had his big, bearded face buried in crumpled piece of tin foil eating the remains of a piece of fish saying, "You can drink all you want, but you always need food!" Like a lot of 40 to 50-year-old Irish labourers I have met – from Sparkhill, Kilburn or St Helens - he said the same thing: "I'm going to have one more good summer on the roads and then I'm heading home." It seemed an aspiration rather than a realistic hope. It was like that line from Ralph McTell's *Clare to Here:* "I told her I'd be coming home with pockets full of green." This was, of course, before the rise of the Celtic Tiger and the Irish economy.

The stories of one bloke fascinated me more than most – I'll not name him – but he was a genuine, self-taught working class intellectual - not someone who got his good education before his first donkey jacket. He was a Marxist, although not one of these who you get into an argument with and their eyes glaze over while they trot out the party line or chapter and verse from the *Communist Manifesto*. But it seemed that the 1980s had just inflicted blow after blow on what he believed in. He still had his beliefs and had not switched sides or become a cynic, but was clearly demoralised by what he saw around him, which probably led to him pickling that wonderful brain of his to take the edge off this world.

The Runcorn game was my farewell appearance – although I always knew I'd be back 'picking my games'. Hats off to the loyal Saints fans who move away and yet still come home every week, rain, hail or shine, win or lose. But as disloyal as it sounds now, I had had enough of false dawns and having high hopes dashed and for the first time in my life I was looking forward to leaving town and not having Saints as the primary focus of everything I did.

St Helens 6 Oldham 36, 27 September 1989
Lancashire Cup Round 2

You only realise what a minority sport rugby league is when you move away from the M62 corridor and end up in a place like Brum. The tabloid papers barely carried a line, the radio stations were even worse – and all of a sudden you realise that even those snippets of rugby league you used to get on Granada and *Look North West* were like gold. Oh to pick up Radio Manchester for just a few minutes on a Sunday afternoon or for the *St Helens Star* to drop through my letterbox rather than the *Evening Mail* with page after page of Villa, Blues and Baggies. It is amazing the things you take for granted when you have rugby league on your doorstep. That said, I was not missing much - on my first weekend away we lost at Bradford and a few days later it got even worse.

During my first week in Brum I walked into the Ivy Bush Fish Bar in Edgbaston wearing my Saints sweater and the Greek bloke behind the counter summed it up. Looking at the town crest on my chest, he said, "St Helens. Do you play for them?"

There was a pause and then he followed up with, "They used to be good, didn't they?" I knew exactly what he meant. Used to be good – St Helens RLFC were now a laughing stock from Billinge to Brum. Still what did he know – he didn't even serve gravy and don't even bother asking for a split! It was also the first place I had eaten cod roe, thinking it would taste like a fish cake. Unfortunately it is fish eggs – and it went straight in the bin after one mouthful.

At least the bloke in the chippy expressed a mild interest. Perhaps he had read the small print in that day's newspaper results section. It did not jump out at you, but 6pt print type buried at the foot of an inside sports page read St Helens 6 Oldham 36.

Second Division Oldham had some half decent players, but that result was embarrassing. I rang my mate Dave up at some ridiculous hour in the morning and asked for the low down. He told me that former Saint John Fieldhouse, who had been discarded that summer, had run the show.

St Helens 27 New Zealand 26, 1 October 1989
Tour Match

Another week brought another debut, this time burly prop Andy Bateman who had signed from Hunslet for £60,000. He was a big, solid bloke who gave a good, but unspectacular stint in the pack that helped contain the Kiwis. We needed a morale-booster to pull us out of the slump and Saints pipped the tourists with a late try from Paul Forber. It gave the team a degree of self-belief and confidence, which sparked a 12-game unbeaten run with victories over Wakefield, Featherstone twice, Warrington, Salford, Barrow, Hull, Hull KR, Dewsbury after a replay and Oldham.

Slowly but surely our side was rebuilt; and in October another Kiwi landed at Knowsley Road from Shane Cooper's old club Mangere East. Chunky prop forward George Mann was like something I had never seen at the club before. Although built like a brick outhouse, he could motor like a threequarter. Mann had the most unorthodox running style, bouncing off the would-be tacklers like a pinball. His tackling technique, however, which saw him trying to body check opponents, was hit and miss.

Unusually for a prop, he became an idol of the fans who would chant "Oo-ah Georgie Mann, say oo-ah Georgie Mann!" It was a song the Popular Side had copied it off a song about Leeds and Manchester United's temperamental Frenchman Eric Cantona.

Another Kiwi signed on during their tour – Tea Ropati – but he was not fit, playing only one game before going home for an operation. He would return and would wear the red vee, or a configuration of it, with pride.

The touring Kiwis got off to the best possible start in the test series with a win at an Old Trafford ground completely devoid of atmosphere in stark contrast to the last time international rugby had been played there. With a disappointing crowd of 18,273, there was as much space on the Stretford End as there was in the British defence.

Great Britain rallied for the second test at Elland Road in a game I watched in the Big Bulls Head, a smoky old boozer in Digbeth - the Irish quarter of Brum. There I shared a table with a bloke called Eddie, an Irish republican from Strabane, County Tyrone. I did not get a minute's peace as motor-mouth Eddie spent the entire game shouting for the Kiwis just to wind me up. I could not believe somebody was shouting against a rugby league team on political grounds. Maybe I could have vaguely understood his stance against British Imperialism with more establishment sports like rugby union and cricket – but this, I thought bonkers. Eddie promised to show me the spent plastic bullets he had collected after they had been fired in his home town street to justify his stance for hating almost all things British.

Britain won the third test and the series, but five months later I was back in the Bull's Head on St Patrick's Day watching England lose to Scotland in rugby union's Five Nations. This time I was shouting for Scotland – it is a common rugby league thing to do. Eddie was again there – amazed that I was not supporting the English. "And you lot call the Irish thick!" he remarked. I was not particularly mixed up about my identity – but down in Brum I considered my nationality as 'northern'. Sad to say I wore my Saints badge or my sweater as much as I could to spread the gospel and make a statement. People did not really know where St Helens was - some thought it was near Leeds.

My political theory lecturer summed it up when chatting to me in a tutorial – "You are neither fish nor fowl", which was a reference to an accent that was neither Scouse nor broad, rounded Lancashire. It was strange seeing kids from posh parts of Cheshire like Macclesfield implying they were from Manchester, because that was the 'in' city. 'Madchester' was at its height with the Baggy scene prominent. Everybody who was into the Stone Roses or Happy Mondays walked around in really baggy jeans – which was comical given how much stick the 1970s flares wearers got.

St Helens 9 Halifax 10, 23 December 1989
Regal Trophy Semi-Final

"History repeats itself, first as tragedy, then as farce!" Karl Marx was no rugby league pundit, but it summed up our semi-final loss to Second Division Halifax. Just like they had done five years previously, 'Fax wrecked our Christmas by winning a dour game by a single point.

The match was deadlocked 2-2 at the break, with most of the 6,085 speccies wishing that they too had gone to buy tinsel and tin foil like the rest of the missing fans. The last shopping day before Christmas was a dumb date to hold a prestigious semi-final, but all the BBC was concerned with was keeping that awkward slot between the horse racing and football scores teleprinter occupied.

Despite a try from Andy Bateman, a couple of goals from Paul Loughlin and a Roy Haggerty drop-goal – something that was always greeted with such mirth – we lost. Defeat signalled the end of our unbeaten run and our chance to face Wigan in the final. Saints just did not do Christmas very well – there was always a different reason, but the facts are this defeat sparked a losing spree. Maybe they suffered from SAD - seasonal affective disorder. It really demonstrated that the side's victories over middle-ranking or poor opposition in the autumn was something of a false dawn. Beating all those sides that my dad called 'bum teams', inflated our very large but fragile bubble, one that the workmanlike Yorkshiremen took great pleasure in pricking.

We returned to Central Park three days later – this time the crowd was much bigger: 27,075, but so was the margin of defeat. We were utterly outclassed 38-6 and predictably failed to recover in time for New Year's Day when Widnes returned to the chemical town with both points.

The board had had enough and did probably what they wanted to do after the previous April's debacle at Wembley – they gave Murphy the bullet. Not literally, that treatment was reserved for Romanian dictator Nicolae Ceausescu and his wife who were shot on Christmas Day for their crimes against humanity. His demise was part of the revolutions that swept away the dictatorial Stalinist regimes behind the Iron Curtain, and led to the tearing down of the Berlin Wall.

Initial press reports suggested Saints and Murphy had reached an amicable settlement – but that is not how a blazing former coach saw it. He was outside the ground on the Thursday night of his departure where a handful of fans offered support and sang "Sack the board!" for the benefit of the cameras.

With a wooden spoon in hand, Murphy told the *St Helens Star*: "I hope the fans who have hurled flak at me in the past will now start to direct as much at the board – with the exception of Tony Ryan and Eric Latham."

You had to feel sorry for Murphy, who had been charged with the unenviable task of coaching Saints at the time when Wigan were just beginning to be the truly dominant force. He was, like Billy Benyon before him, the scapegoat for being unable to coach a side that, despite having a core of talented players, lacked the same sort of quality and strength in depth of Wigan and for that matter Widnes.

The only way to compete with Wigan was to splash the cash, but our signings for 1989-90 had an unspectacular feel to them. When you look at what happened to Widnes and even to Wigan, maybe with hindsight our board got it right by living within their means during that period.

On the other hand, whatever excuses you can make for Murphy, and whatever exceptions you make for him being one of the few legends to grace our game as a player, his Midas touch as a coach had left him in his latter years at Knowsley Road. Saints needed a fresh approach and some cobwebs needed sweeping out. Shane Cooper deputised very well as caretaker coach once he settled in, but the new broom was on order and was being sent over on a plane.

Saints were on the rocks again, and reached their nadir at Leigh. Losing at Hilton Park had become something of a habit for us – even when the Leythers were in the relegation zone.

This one – a 30-18 defeat – was truly shocking and made it four on the bounce. Assistant coach Frankie Barrow, who had resigned in protest at Murphy's sacking, took one look at the performance at Leigh and decided his club needed him in its hour of need and came back on board.

I was away from St Helens when other walls had been torn down that should have caused more anguish. Some bright spark decided to demolish Helena House, the big Co-op building which had been the centrepiece of town as long as I could remember. And what did they replace the old stores building with its history, ballroom, doorway blowers, old fashioned lifts and glorious facade with? On one of my infrequent returns the site was just a hole in the ground, and I felt like bawling out, like Charlton Heston viewing the Statue of Liberty at the end of *Planet of the Apes*, "What have they done?" There is a Wilkinson's store there now – but that took a while coming and not before the site was used to stage a funfair. I am sure our town's forefathers were spinning in their graves.

Hull 12 St Helens 24, 10 February 1990
Challenge Cup Round 2

This trip to the Boulevard for a Cup second round match was not without its tension on and off the field. Although Hull were no longer the force they used to be, under innovative Australian coach Brian Smith they were unbeaten at home in two months.

With the Threepenny Stand in full voice Hull took the lead with an Andy Dannatt try – although he appeared to drop the ball – and made a game of it until skipper Shane Cooper stepped up a gear. Merlin was supposed to be injured but he guided Saints to a 24-12 victory, with Kangaroo second-row Noel 'Crusher' Cleal kept utterly anonymous. That said, there were far more fearsome sights than the bearded Australian wild-pig hunter on the Boulevard terraces. In particular one shaven-headed Hull fan, with eyes bulging as if he needed his medication, decided to challenge our vocal section to a scrap. The bloke looked totally deranged as he snarled "Come on then you Scouse bastards."

All shuffled sideways, looking the other way or suddenly finding the contrasting shades of speckled concrete of the terrace utterly fascinating. Everyone hoped not to be the one to get their nose chewed off by the Humber Hulk. Eventually he was dragged away muttering in a demented fashion by a toothless old biddy – possibly his mother – and all of a sudden we were all brave again!

Bernard Dwyer, who had a shocking year for injuries, scored our first try in his first game back after a two-month layoff with a broken jaw. It was hard to believe that this same lad ran over my pathetic tackles when he played for Eddy Camp eight years previously. He was one of the toughest, hardest working blokes on the field. As a fan you progress and grow up, but you always still imagine the players being 10 years older because you tend to place them on pedestals.

Saints had a new coach in charge – relatively unknown Kiwi Mike McClennan had taken over the hot seat earlier that month and started with a home win over Leeds. He and Frankie Barrow formed a great coaching double act.

The coach may have been different but the fans' Wembley songs remained the same with "We're on the march with Macker's army..." ringing out. Macker always sounded a touch too Scouse to me because of that phlegmy ackk sound in the middle of the word. It is a name you expected to crop up in the Liverpudlian TV soap *Brookside,* as a mate of scallies Gizzmo, Damon and Ducksy. McClennan neither looked nor sounded like a Macker and you needed a dictionary to read the column he wrote for the *St Helens Star*. McClennan may have used unnecessarily elongated or bizarre words, but he was having an effect and performances had improved 100 per cent as the team began to gel together and believe in themselves. The dark cloud that had been over our club since Wembley was beginning to move and once again glimmers of blue sky were appearing above us.

The weather was perhaps a touchy point in St Helens at this time – later in February the game with Warrington was abandoned after only four minutes when a piece of the stand roof blew onto the playing area narrowly missing Warrington centre Gary Mercer.

St Helens 14 Wigan 20, 10 March 1990
Challenge Cup Semi-Final

After crushing Whitehaven our opponents in the semi were a more formidable and familiar foe - Wigan. On paper Saints stood no chance – not against Gregory and Edwards, Iro and Lydon, Mean Dean and Ellery, the very guys that had made us such a laughing stock at Wembley in 1989.

However, in an enthralling game worthy of the Old Trafford surroundings, a rejuvenated Saints stuck it to them, ensuring there was no walkover. Saints made full use of the open spaces with tries from teen scrum-half Sean Devine and Les Quirk giving us a 12-6 half-time lead. Quirk's try was a gem, a score worthy of booking a Cup Final passage. Taking the ball inside his own 20 metre line the deceptively quick Cumbrian scorched around speedster Joe Lydon and then his long strides ate up the yards to take him past Ged Byrne and Steve Hampson for a wonderful try. The noise from the Saints contingent in the 26,489 crowd reached a crescendo because suddenly there was a real belief there that we could do it.

Crucially Saints lost skipper Cooper through injury for a 10 minute spell – and while he was off the game turned and our lead became a two point deficit.

A Paul Loughlin penalty levelled scores 10 minutes from time and it became a game of 'next score wins'. Collectively our fans were all thinking, "It's now or never!" because we would never play so well in the replay.

There were half chances in the closing stages – and young Devine tore through the Wigan defence to roars of approval but the support was missing and he was dragged into touch. Saints' defence was also on its mettle epitomised by a tremendous try-saving tackle by teen full-back Gary Connolly on superstar Joe Lydon.

After throwing all bar the kitchen sink at Wigan, and soaking up all in return, Saints lost in the cruellest of fashion 90 seconds shy of a hooter that would have brought a replay. From 40 metres out Ellery Hanley blasted past four would-be defenders before popping a ball up for the supporting Andy Goodway. The final pass was a mile forward – but the protestations were in vain as the Great Britain second-row plonked the ball beneath the posts. The roars of "for-ward" were closely followed by the most horrible sound in rugby league from the other part of the ground, "Wi-gan, Wi-gan, Wi-gan!" The Pie-eaters in the crowd had spat out their Uncle Joe's mint balls and had suddenly found their voices again.

It was a genuine heartbreaker – even Saints fans hardened by miserable Wembley defeats left the ground ashen-faced, such was the manner of this loss. As a fan you felt for the lads – especially forwards like big Georgie Mann, Bernard Dwyer and Shane Cooper who had slogged their guts out. But it was that same old story – Saints had to be on our game for the full 80 minutes, not 78 minutes and 30 seconds, to beat Wigan, the team with unlimited resources.

All the focus was on the league now – but coach McClennan used his *St Helens Star* column to rally the fans into supporting the club. He stated, in his typically convoluted fashion, "The nucleus of the present team has proved beneficial in the resurgence of the much appreciated supporters of the club and spectators have witnessed consistently creditable performances. It is now important that every Saints supporter brings a friend, a neighbour, a wife or someone else's wife and let the roar at Knowsley Road be heard at Central Park!"

What was he on?

In the late 1980s the sporting world had bizarrely gone inflatable crazy. It all started at Manchester City FC with Imre Varadi inspiring one fan to take a plastic banana, stick a sky-blue shirt on it and call it 'Imre Banana'. It caught on with Harry the Haddock at Grimsby Town, and inflatable hammers at West Ham, even though the Cockney club's ICF hooligan crew were probably carrying the real things. Inflatables also emerged at Wigan in the form of blow up cherry-and-white light bulbs with sponsor's name Norweb across them. Others thought pies would have been more suitable, especially as football neighbours Bury had briefly waved inflatable black puddings.

Leeds 50 St Helens 14, 1 April, 1990
Division 1

The country was in open revolt ahead of the replacement of the council rates system with the community charge or poll tax. Even silver haired old ladies in horn rimmed spectacles were yelling "Can't pay, won't pay!" Every night on the news was a different protest outside another town hall. I was outside Victoria Square in Brum when the crowd beating their drums outside surged through the doors to occupy the council chamber singing, "We won't pay no poll tax, we won't pay no poll tax, na, na, nah, nah!" to the tune of "let's all do the conga".

Even the station archways in St Helens had been daubed with graffiti, with a sketch of Dennis the Menace declaring "Axe the poll tax". It stayed there for years after the poll tax and its main advocates and architects had been consigned to the dust heap of history.

On Saturday 31 March 1990 I faced two choices – join some of my student mates down in Trafalgar Square for the mass demonstration against the poll tax or get a train home for the big game at Leeds the following day. After dithering a bit, I opted for the latter; after all you always get a decent game at Headingley.

Boring history books claim that Margaret Thatcher was toppled later that year by disagreements in her own party over Europe, but the biggest nail driven into her political coffin was by the people who went on that 200,000 strong demonstration. I was still hearing stories from mates and colleagues who went on it years after, and none of them - surprise, surprise - were remotely interested in what happened at the Leeds game.

Like the demo the day before, it was a brutal affair with Leeds having their Australian scrum-half David Cruickshank sent off after only three minutes for flattening our hooker Paul Groves. Afterwards coach Mike McClennan claimed his players had been kneed in the back, bitten and gouged – we certainly came out of it with a lengthy casualty list.

The physical approach worked for Leeds, they knocked us off our game and despite their numerical disadvantage they overhauled a 14-6 deficit to rattle in 44 unanswered points. Leeds's veteran test wing Phil Ford grabbed three of their six second-half tries as Saints capitulated. Assistant coach Frankie Barrow didn't mince his words afterwards – does he ever – and called the display "pathetic".

Although it was a long shot anyway, defeat spelt the end of any slight hopes we had of chasing the title. Although we crushed Wigan 35-10 on Good Friday, it was simply the scraps from the master's table as our rivals were on their way to a comfortable League and Challenge Cup double. Our season finished in an opening round Premiership defeat at Odsal – but despite the ups, downs and heartache, there was a genuine feeling that under Mike McClennan, Saints were beginning to progress and slot things into place even if we appeared a long way off.

14. 1990-91 Put th' ead on it!

St Helens 56 Trafford Borough 24, 26 August 1990
Lancashire Cup, Round 1

It was a turbulent summer, with hard-line communists staging a coup against moderate President Gorbachev's perestroika. Although that coup failed, Boris Yeltsin seized his chance and it was the beginning of the end of Gorbachev and the USSR, which began to collapse, sending tremors across the world as we knew it.

Events at Knowsley Road were much less turbulent. Frowns were raised when veteran Castleford prop Kevin Ward was announced as our major signing of the summer. Many suggested Wardy was an old man, well over the hill with his prime years behind him. He had a tremendous pedigree and had been there, done that and got an XXL T-shirt to prove it.

Wardy had won the 'man-of-the-series' award in the Great Britain versus Australia Ashes series in 1986, which earned him a contract with Sydney giants Manly the following summer. While down under he helped the Sea Eagles to victory in the Australian Grand Final, earning the man-of-the-match award in the process. He had been an excellent footballer, but fans scratched their heads - surely he was past it at 33?

However, the robust and durable old warhorse was just what we needed – his name on the team sheet would put the fear of god into the opposition. Opposing teams would look at the list at 2.30 and think "We're going to have that big bastard coming at us for 80 minutes this afternoon."

At last we had someone to stand up and give it back to the Shelfords, Sorensons, Tamatis and Skerretts of this world. Not only that, Wardy also had an ability to get the ball away from the tackle. Our younger forwards would not only get protection from him, they would learn from this gruff, larger-than-life Tyke. Of those, he worked well with young utility forward and occasional hooker Bernard Dwyer and the pair were dubbed Fred Flintstone and Barney Rubble.

He eased his way into his new Knowsley Road surroundings with a comfortable win over Trafford Borough, scoring on his debut. Despite a comfortable winning debut for Wardy, Saints were going nowhere in the Lancashire Cup and fell to Trafford's more established neighbours Salford in the next round

St Helens 4 Australia 34, 7 October 1990
Tour Match

Saints' centenary game - the opening date of the Kangaroo tour - was marked by a parade of great players at Knowsley Road. Among them was wing legend Tom van Vollenhoven, who had jetted over from South Africa for the occasion.

You expect events like this to run like television's *This is Your Life*, without the big red book and Eamonn Andrews. All the younger fans wanted to do was cheer the people our parents had told us about, while older followers showed their appreciation and compared their waistlines and hairlines to those they once idolised. Unfortunately the parade turned into another Saints shambles with the PA system conking out, so only those with the keenest of eyes could tell who was waving at them from the middle of the field.

One Saints legend – however – was instantly recognisable and he had other things on his mind. Mal Meninga skippered the Kangaroos and was given a warm welcome by fans, even those who were only toddlers back in 1984. Big Mal led the Australians to a comfortable 34-4 win, with Les Quirk scoring our only try in front of 15,219 spectators.

Saints had hit bit of a slide, having lost the previous week at Leeds and then made it three losses on the bounce with a 29-16 home defeat by Castleford. The team needed something to pep them up really – and after a win over struggling Rochdale that tonic came in an unlikely form.

Trailing 10-4 at half time against Sheffield Eagles, Saints rallied after being helped by a 'headed' try that prompted a change in the international laws of the game. After first working out the move with assistant Frankie Barrow on the training pitch, coach Mike McClennan asked the referee before the game about whether their plans were legitimate. He got the nod – literally – with big John Harrison using his 6 feet 7 inches frame to head the ball over the Eagles defence for George Mann to touch down. Saints went on to win 34-17.

At the end of the season the move was barred, but in McClennan's eyes it had already done the trick. Speaking to Ron Barker, the late doyen of rugby league at the *St Helens Star*, McClennan said, "George's try resurrected Saints' confidence when we were on shaky ground – a confidence that must cause some people to question the wisdom of their words when their team had their backs against the wall." He went on to say, "Cowboys pull out the arrow and bite the bullet. In the face of adversity my team showed some grit."

In a bold move, the opening test against Australia was taken to Wembley, and the sensible decision to slash prices ensured a decent turn out of 54,569 fans. Saints fans in that crowd found the programme article about Meninga interesting, particularly the bit in which he said: "I'll see out my two-year contract with Canberra. After that, the plan is to finish my career in England, preferably with St Helens." Was he seriously thinking about it, or just taunting us? Or was he giving us hope for the future, a way of telling us to keep the faith in our darkest hour of Wigan domination.

The only Saints man on duty for Great Britain that day was veteran Kevin Ward, who was on the bench. Skippered by Hanley, two tries from Paul Eastwood and another by the other wing Martin Offiah secured a 19-12 British victory. It was the first time I had ever seen the Australians vanquished in the flesh. And was a massive shot in the arm for our game.

St Helens 22 Leeds 16, 20 January 1991
Division 1

When Leeds signed the rugby union All Blacks' World Cup winning full-back John Gallagher in a blaze of publicity, few in league had heard of him. One thing, however, that did him no favours whatsoever was the title of his biography *The World's Best Rugby Player?* Perhaps that question mark was there for a purpose and the answer to the question would be revealed once he had tested himself in the league arena. There were plenty of people thinking "cocky bastard" and waiting for him to fall flat on his face. That day ultimately, and quite literally, came at Knowsley Road.

Despite the title of his book, Gallagher was not a big-headed or arrogant bloke. Some years later, when Gallagher had moved on and was coaching rugby union outfit Blackheath I had to interview him for the *Birmingham Metro News* as part of my preview for their clash with Moseley. After discussing the prospects of the weekend's game and the problems faced by historic clubs like Blackheath struggling to break into union's top flight, I said I was from St Helens. There was a pause on the other end of the phone line and then all of a sudden he rattled off "January 20, 1991, thank you very much."

The incident had burned into him seemingly more than any other event in his packed career. It had done so much to damage his confidence just as he was making tentative steps in his new sport. Fielding a long Saints kick, Gallagher was collared by two defenders, turned upside down and driven into the ground. To add insult to injury the referee didn't penalise the spear tackle so when he spilled the ball, Saints scooped it up and scored what was a crucial try in a 22-16 victory.

He was never really the same player after that, although he did say that he enjoyed his spell playing with London Crusaders in subsequent years.

Gallagher was an unsuccessful convert at the top level because after playing behind a dominant and aggressive All Black pack that was used to trampling all before it, he was now the last line of defence behind a weak Leeds six. Still, it showed that Saints were not the only club to make recruits from union that didn't work out.

St Helens 19 Widnes 2, 30 March 1991
Challenge Cup Semi-Final

After all my whingeing about armchair glory hunting fans in the past, I felt like a hypocrite turning up at the semi-final having missed all the games on our cup run. There were excuses galore, but Halifax away was the one I really wanted to get to because you just knew it was going to be a 'proper' cup tie. The Second Division side now featured former Saint Mark Elia, but Fax' biggest strength was their hefty pack.

At the time I was living in a grotty house on the border of Smethwick, pronounced Smerr-ick by the locals, which had neither a phone nor a television. The first time I called home for a score check we trailed 12-4. I pictured the scene as I bit my nails from far away. The steam was billowing off big Brendan Hill's body as he rumbled down the slope with the mud caked to both sets of jerseys. The broad Yorkshire accents hollered abuse from underneath the sheds of the decrepit, but atmospheric old ground complete with picturesque old blue-tiled clubhouse in the corner. I could even taste the cigarette smoke, which must have been hanging even thicker that day with it being such a close game, prompting the 'chaineys' to go into overdrive. I envisaged Thrum Hall with 9,672 partisan fans packed into it and so wanted to be in that number rather than lining up 10 pence pieces in a phone box stinking of pee on Dudley Road.

It sounded like the sort of game that makes the Challenge Cup what it is. Despite a heavyweight bombardment by Big Brendan we came from behind to edge it 24-16 with tries from Paul Bishop, Les Quirk and two from Alan Hunte clinching it.

Our name went into the semi-final hat alongside the two big Ws, and Oldham. Typically those jammy swine from Central Park plucked the Roughyeds out. Saints were drawn with league leaders Widnes and nobody gave us a snowball in hell's chance of making it though to the final.

The semi took place on Easter Saturday, which meant Saints' traditional fixture with Wigan was put back to the following Thursday.

Widnes had a pack of big names and some considerable size - Kurt Sorensen, Emosi Koloto and Esene Faimalo - but it was Saints' six that got on top. Our tough-as-teak front row comprising the underrated Cumbrian Jonathan Neill, local lad Bernard Dwyer and Yorkshire warhorse Kevin Ward wore their illustrious opponents down. The pack, which also featured strong displays from big John Harrison and George Mann, was well marshalled by skipper Shane Cooper. The stars in the Widnes ranks – Jonathan Davies, who had been switched to centre, and Martin Offiah – never got a sniff of the line.

Neither side gave much away and the game was locked 2-2 at the break, but our pack's softening-up job paid dividends in the second half.

Three minutes after the break Mann collected Paul Bishop's smart kick to send Jonathan Griffiths scampering home for the first of his two tries. Sandwiched between those Alan Hunte collected Bish's spiralling kick to twist and turn his way over. Substitute hooker Paul Groves's cheeky drop-goal put the icing on the cake.

A 16,109 crowd filled three sides of Central Park because the old clubhouse end was being rebuilt to accommodate a new stand. The shell of the new structure was already in place – and a posse of Saints coaching staff and squad players stood there to get the best vantage point. You could see them jumping up and down as Saints took control.

Saints' 1991 team was of completely different character to the one that had gone down to Wembley defeat two years previously. At long last Saints had a hard-faced scrum half in Paul Bishop who could cockily strut and control the game despite looking only six stones wet through. We also had a pair of wingers in Alan Hunte and Les Quirk who could find their way over the whitewash. Their try tallies hit 26 apiece that year - it was short of the quantity and consistency of Les Jones and Roy Mathias 1970s partnership, but they were getting there and it was good to see.

Quirk scored some belting tries that year, and although I missed most of them I tried to belatedly catch up with the occasional Saints video that was lent to me. The highlights of those Saints videos were less about the match, and more about the commentary of bus driver Ron Hoofe who earned cult status after describing Quirk's score against Hull earlier that year as being "a try of orgasmic proportions!"

St Helens 8 Wigan 13, 27 April 1991
Challenge Cup Final at Wembley

I travelled to London on the train from Birmingham, so I was there quicker than all my mates but missed the collective banter you get going down on the motorway. You don't get that build up on the train, especially not on your own – the first moment you realise it is a Cup Final is when you poke your nose up at Euston Station and spot the northerners trying to work out the complexities of the tube map.

The square in front of Euston station was always a very bleak place – full of young people, many from the north, who thought the streets of London would be paved with gold. Instead they found themselves caught in a vicious circle, wrapped up in dirty blankets begging off passers-by. Not a single one of those lads and girls would have put their hands up 10 years previously and told a careers officer that "when I grow up I want to be a beggar, prostitute or rent boy.'

For all its bright lights, history and attractions, London always seems to have that harshness about it and people there seem too hyperactive and in a rush. Seeing everyone squash into the tube at Euston Square until the carriages become one heaving mass of bodies summed it up. I was glad to come up for air once our tube finally pulled in at Wembley.

The area around Wembley always seemed quite grimy, and not what one might expect around the country's national treasure. Wembley is just like any city suburb, full of chip shops, launderettes, off-licences and people trying to get on with their daily lives.

On the other hand, how must Brent's residents feel about having this regular invasion on their hands? It was not just for our so-called friendly final one Saturday in April or May, they had to put up with this countless times throughout the year – for England internationals, the League Cup Final, FA Cup Final, promotion play-offs and a string of big concerts. Every single one of those events brought tens of thousands of people to the area, filling the streets with beer cans, bottles and chip wrappers and then after it is all over they go home to complain about what a 'shit hole' Wembley is.

After being surrounded by strangers, it was comforting to get to the car park at the front of the Olympic Torch where all my mates had gathered. Prior to mobile phones, this pre-ordained meeting point was always essential to save wasting valuable drinking time or supping on your own.

Wembley had become an all-seater stadium, which meant tickets had experienced quite a price hike from our last appearance two years previously, now ranging from £15 to £32, which deterred some, meaning that this Final didn't sell out.

As for the action itself, Wigan had led us to believe that Elastoplast and painkilling injections were holding them together after a punishing run of fixtures on their way to another league title.

Influential skipper Ellery Hanley was only declared fit at the 11th hour but you don't know how much was kidology, sometimes you have to read between the lines.

It did not stop them taking a 12-point lead in as many minutes. Wigan's former All Black marksman Frano Botica slotted the opening penalty and two tries followed. The first came after full-back Phil Veivers lost the ball after being clobbered by a big hit from Shaun Edwards. Kevin Iro pounced to send Dave Myers in at the corner. Shortly afterwards Botica surged over, before converting magnificently from the touchline. There was that awful feeling of 'here we go again.' Perhaps Wigan knew they would be flagging at the end and were trying to stage an early blitzkrieg to finish us off. It was an all-out tactic to leave us dispirited and broken before they had chance to fall apart.

Just before half-time, with the hooter sounding, Dwyer broke 50 metres and was backed up by Connolly, who was on for the groggy Veivers. His kick to the line was perfect but the bounce favoured Botica who just beat Quirk to it. A crucial score then could have given Wigan the jitters, but it was not to be.

After the restart, a drop-goal from Andy Gregory nudged the score up to give Wigan a 13 point lead, although we showed signs of rallying.

Big John Harrison, who at 6 feet 7 inches became the tallest man in rugby league to gallop onto the Wembley turf, then put Paul Bishop through a hole. The terrier-like scrum-half was racing through only to be tripped by Wigan's last line of defence, Steve Hampson. Unfortunately, the former Vulcan full-back only got 10 minutes to cool his heels in the sin-bin rather than the sending off that such an offence immediately warranted. To compound our misery Bishop's penalty hit one of the uprights and bounced out.

Saints kept their heads up with Dwyer, who ended the game with 16 stitches in his ear, going close. And then we had something to really lift our spirits, with Harrison sparking the move that culminated in Hunte scoring in the corner. Bishop's conversion and a penalty nine minutes from time left us just a converted try short of glory.

Although Wigan were on the ropes, we could not find that killer blow and had to watch Ellery Hanley collect the Challenge Cup from cabinet minister Ken Clarke.

It had not been a classic – but the players had given their all and looked like Muhammad Ali and Smokin' Joe Frazier at the end of their famously draining 'Thriller in Manila' heavyweight title fight of 1975.

It was so close and our fans trooped out just thinking about what could have been. On my way back to Euston I bumped into a few lads I had gone to school with and so ended up having a few drinks with them around Baker Street. They then disappeared back to their coaches and I went to the off-licence for a couple of cans of Kestrel Super strength lager to drown my sorrows.

As I was sitting drinking in the bus shelter with my Saints cap tilted and scarf round my neck, a stretch limousine came to a halt in front of me. A young American bloke, who didn't look old enough to shave, popped his head out of the window and asked "How d' you guys get on?" He thought I was an Arsenal fan – how insulting. I exchanged a bit of banter with him and asked him to give me a drink out of what I suspected was a mini-bar in the back of his car. The electric tinted window very quickly wound back up and the car swiftly negotiated the London traffic and was gone. The little girl at the side of me was awestruck "That was New Kids on the Block". They weren't on my play list – thank God – and I am glad I didn't recognise the American teen pop heroes, especially if they couldn't tell the difference between Arsenal and Saints.

It was not a brilliant month for St Helens sport – local boxer Gary Stretch lost his WBO middleweight title tilt against Chris Eubank. It did not do Stretch much harm though, and he is now famous on the silver screen as an actor. Maybe Stuart Evans should have fought Eubank instead in a catch-weight contest. During the summer the big Welshman was placed on the list at £50,000 and with no takers effectively called it a day shortly after the start of the following season.

15. 1991-92 A speck of silver in a dark, dirty cloud

St Helens 104 Trafford Borough 12, 15 September 1991
Lancashire Cup, Round 1

There were a few changes again after Wembley, with Saints using their Cup Final windfall to splash out on Hull KR's flying winger Anthony Sullivan for £100,000. The son of former Great Britain legend Clive, who had sadly passed away at a desperately young age, Sully was definitely a chip off the old block and could really move and swerve. It did mean we had a choice of options on the wing with Les Quirk, Alan Hunte and youngster Mike Riley.

Three of those wingers – Hunte, Quirk and substitute Sullivan - scored hat-tricks in the 104-12 hammering of Trafford Borough in the opening round of the Lancashire Cup, so competition for those places was going to be intense.

Sullivan's signing was a good coup for Saints – although there was still the old chestnut of the one that got away – Mal Meninga. Apparently Big Mal, now the star man at Canberra Raiders, was offered a two-year, £250,000 deal to return to Knowsley Road. He never came back and still had history to make skippering the Kangaroos.

There were exits too with local hero Roy Haggerty put out to graze up at sleepy Barrow having been sold for £15,000. They liked him up there, and saw him as a character in the mould of their own folk hero Eddie Szymala.

In his place came strong, running Sheffield Eagles second-rower Sonny Nickle, who had been listed at £195,000, but joined Saints for £80,000 after an adjudication by the League's transfer-fee tribunal. The raw-boned former Hunslet junior was a good signing for Saints, giving our pack a bit more steel.

Coach McClennan was moulding his team and it was not just in terms of playing personnel, he was tweaking things off the park too by bringing in a different type of tackle bag and using unorthodox dietary supplements. He had heard that Peking Royal Jelly had positive qualities and started issuing sachets to the players. It raised a few puzzled eyebrows, even from some players, but in his question and answer session in the *St Helens Star* McClennan explained: "It is a tonic when poorly or suffering from a hangover. It also possesses certain aphrodisiac properties – as the 900 million population of China might confirm."

However, one of McClennan's initiatives was short-lived. He had a machine comprising a tackle bag, steel shaft and spring shipped over to assist with Saints' defensive technique. Unfortunately the much-heralded machine met its match – Kevin Ward, who struck it once in training leaving the kit in a crumpled heap fit only for the scrapyard.

McClennan also gave up the traditional coach's dugout and adopted what was then an unusual practice of sitting in the stand or in the clubhouse during the course of the game. From there he would phone - in the days before walkie-talkies and headsets become the trend – his instructions to his assistant Frank Barrow at pitch-side. Apparently Frank would get fed up after a few calls and used to let the phone dangle from the dugout and carry on watching the game.

Another change was nothing to do with the coach – it was the kit. With hindsight, it is hard to pick it out as a Saints strip and was missing a proper vee. There were red diagonal lines that hinted at one, but it could have been a Wigan or an Oldham kit. It was a trend the game was going through, with some club kits resembling a cross between pyjama jackets and leisure shirts. It was fair enough for the sponsor to call the shots, but in ditching certain aspects of a recognisable brand, the red vee in our case, and latterly the hoops in Wigan's shirt, was counter productive. Not only did it put two fingers up to tradition, it also damaged a key aspect of the club's persona.

St Helens 28 Wigan 16, 10 October 1991
Lancashire Cup Semi-Final

Wigan had it over us so much in the late 1980s and early 1990s, and that feeling grew each time they cut us down in a big game. But Saints fans going to the semi-final had a good vibe – if we were going to do them, a home cup tie was as good a place as any. The early signs were not good with 'daddy' Kevin Ward doubtful and on the treatment table before kick-off. Fortunately, the gruff Tyke came off the slab before the game and played like a man possessed to win the man-of-the-match. It was a typically robust display, which helped inspire the rest of the lads to victory. Saints licked them good and proper to book our place in the first final of the year. Tries from Paul Forber, Gary Connolly and Anthony Sullivan gave a healthy first-half lead.

It was going great and got better when Mike Riley cut inside Steve Hampson like a good 'un to waltz in at the corner. When Wigan's blockbusting centre Sam Panapa scored we worried briefly, but the night was ours, and there was no loss of nerve from our men in the front line. We roared them on, as loudly as we had ever done, with Bernard Dwyer's try and a drop goal from Paul Bishop followed by a bizarre one from a galloping Paul Forber putting the game beyond reach.

They should have handed Saints the cup there and then in front of that ecstatic, boisterous popular side that was bouncing all over the place. No disrespect to Rochdale Hornets, who gave a plucky display in the final, but beating Wigan was what it was all about. Saints reclaimed the cup last won in Big Mal's year.

It was 1-0 to us in the cup stakes, but the big games were all in front of us. In the John Player, now renamed Regal, Trophy, Saints downed Huddersfield, Oldham and Bradford before losing to Widnes in the semi-final. Of those the nail-biting clash at the Watersheddings was worth watching, particularly as young Oldham forward Chris Joynt caught the eye and very nearly inspired the Roughyeds to a shock win.

Leeds 12 St Helens 32, 8 February 1992
Challenge Cup, Round 2

Another thumping display from Kevin Ward helped Saints dump Regal Trophy winners Widnes out of the Challenge Cup in the opening round. It was the tie of the round and one we had not been so confident of winning. Although Widnes had lost Martin Offiah to Wigan for a world record transfer fee of £440,000 and inspirational coach Doug Laughton to Leeds, the Chemics were still a top outfit. And more than that they were desperate – the club had splashed out a lot during their post 1987 revival – and were determined to recoup some of that.

Although in that period they had won two back-to-back league titles, a World Club Challenge and three Premierships on the trot, the money-spinning Wembley appearances that had once been so frequent now slipped through their grasp.

It created tensions – Great Britain wing Martin Offiah 'stayed away' from the club with Widnes later claiming that he was after £600,000 for a three-and-a-half year deal. A move to Central Park was an inevitable conclusion, although there were a few twists along the way with Chariots threatening to pack in rugby league to play American Football. He was initially listed at a mammoth £700,000 before joining Wigan in the New Year. There had been a bit of a transfer merry go-round that year, with big bucks flying about and Ellery Hanley joining Leeds for £250,000.

Hanley's arrival at Headingley probably ruffled a few feathers, particularly as Garry Schofield was such a dominant personality. Crucially for Saints neither played in our crunch second round tie, with Hanley still recovering from the broken jaw that Hull prop Andy Dannatt had inflicted on him with a heavy challenge.

We had our injuries too, but did not make a meal of them as we rallied from a 7-4 deficit to run away with it in the second half to the tune of 32-12. Despite it being televised live on *Grandstand* a massive travelling contingent witnessed a cup cracker – the vocal support definitely acting like the 14th man, which contributed to us walloping the big spenders. It was great winning at Headingley – just watching all those dejected South Standers, who always seemed to be so cocky to start with, file out moaning. At least they could comfort themselves on the way home by calling into those two fantastic side-street chippies near to the ground which still fried their food in beef dripping and served up scraps.

St Helens 6 Wigan 13, 22 February 1992
Challenge Cup, Quarter-Final

Having disposed of Widnes and Leeds away – 'anybody at home' was on everyone's lips at the time of the draw. We didn't really mean it, we really meant 'anybody at home, bar Wigan'.

Typically, Saints came out paired with the pie-eaters, who were pretty buoyant after their recent World Rugby League Sevens triumph down under.

It was a difficult game – and it must have played on our minds that Wigan had ended our Cup dream every single year since 1989. And that story continued in a game that hinged on three incidents. First, Saints' opening 'try' by George Mann was ruled out. Then we temporarily went down to 12 men when Tea Ropati was sin-binned for retaliating against Wigan's big, niggling prop Kelvin Skerrett. And while Ropati was in the bin, Shaun Edwards went over for the try that gave the visitors a 10-point cushion despite 'double movement' howls from home fans after Alan Hunte had tackled the Wigan half-back short. We should have been used to not getting the rub of the green in these clashes, because it always seemed to be that the 50/50 calls went the way of the favourites. Sometimes you got the impression that match officials did not like shocks. If the underdog wins, perhaps people might point the finger at them and imply that they had a part in the favourites' downfall.

They were crucial turning points, but Saints were their own worst enemies in failing to retain the ball. Safety-first Wigan just gave the ball to their big men Ian Lucas and Kelvin Skerrett who ate up the hard yards and made our players tackle them. That gave them a solid platform and when they had half a chance, they took it. It was such a depressingly familiar state of affairs. Once more our Cup dreams had ended rendering our wonderful wins at Widnes and Headingley utterly worthless.

St Helens 16 Wigan 48, 17 May 1992
Premiership Final, Old Trafford

Saints' heads did not drop after that Challenge Cup defeat and we were neck-and-neck with Wigan as we approached the crunch Good Friday showdown at Knowsley Road. All we had to do was carry on winning – it was simple. Unbelievably the showdown was rendered meaningless by our slip up at Warrington in the first week of April. Fingers were pointed at McClennan's selection policy, after he omitted key man Tea Ropati, in order to "enable other players to shine ahead of the Australia tour selection." It was a big call – Paul Loughlin, Gary Connolly and belatedly Alan Hunte joined forward Sonny Nickle in the Lions squad. We blew the Good Friday game anyhow and finished second, eight points behind Wigan. Predictably, the Pie-Eaters accounted for a plucky Castleford side at Wembley, with Martin Offiah capping a turbulent year with the Lance Todd Trophy.

Wigan and Cas, unlike previous sides involved in the Challenge Cup, fought tooth and nail to progress in the Premiership. Usually that was a competition the teams who had qualified for Wembley contemptuously cast aside to focus on the big day ahead or the subsequent post-match festivities. Finishing second in the league gave us two home ties to get to the Old Trafford finale. We only saw off a dogged Castleford outfit, showing no ill-effects from Wembley eight days previously, in a late flurry with man-of-the-match Kevin Ward bagging the crucial try against his former club.

So it was Saints and Wigan once again at the Theatre of Dreams. Renovation work meant the capacity was slashed to 33,000. You always expect to get a ticket for the final, but Saints and Wigan were only given an allocation of 2,000 each. I suspected I could buy one at the stadium – even if it meant reluctantly paying a tout.

I was a skint student approaching the last month of my degree, but figured I could get a few extra quid together to buy a ticket. The plan was to use my landlord's tools to do a couple of straightforward strimming jobs on two overgrown gardens. I cleared one for a tenner and was expecting the same from a house a few doors down. It became a nightmare job as the long grass was littered with used nodders that had been nonchalantly tossed from the bedroom window above. It got worse because 10 minutes into the job the power went dead and the irate woman came out screaming that I had used the last of her electricity. She was agitated, claiming her freezer was defrosting, so the top and bottom of it was that I ended up running down to the shop to buy a tenner's worth of electric tokens before I could finish the job. Once I deducted my bus fare and price of bin bags I ended up with nothing to show for a day's work apart from plenty of earache and a realisation that I was going to miss another Saints final.

I settled for watching it on *Sunday Grandstand* with five housemates, who like me should have been swotting for final exams instead. Objective and impartial, they gave Saints little hope based on their observations of seeing me traipse up north for countless big days when "we were going to beat the pies" only for me to return with my tail between my legs. There was an added reason why they were tipping Wigan – the previous week Martin Offiah had grabbed an incredible 10 tries in Wigan's 74-point demolition of big-spending Leeds.

So Saints were given no chance, but by half-time I was bouncing up and down on the settee, although that was tempered with feelings that I should have got my arse into gear, cadged the money, taken a late train to Manchester and paid one of those dodgy looking touts you invariably get outside big games and gigs. Saints deservedly led 12-10 at the break, with Paul Loughlin scoring one, creating one for Anthony Sullivan and kicking two goals.

And then 10 minutes after the restart, our bubble was burst when Wigan's giant Australian test centre Gene Miles bust a big hole in our ranks and sent Offiah racing the final 50 metres. It broke our spirit and we conceded another five tries in a bitterly disappointing 25-minute spell. Victory for Wigan gave them a modern treble of League, Cup and Premiership.

Wembley 1991: St Helens versus Wigan. Saints skipper Shane Cooper switches the ball inside to Bernard Dwyer as Ellery Hanley closes in. (Peers)

Wembley 1991: Kevin Ward charges forward for Saints and is met by Kevin Iro. (Peers)

16. 1992-93 The agony and the agony

St Helens 4 Wigan 5, 18 October 1992
Lancashire Cup Final

The country was in turmoil following Black Wednesday and Britain's withdrawal from the European Union's Exchange Rate Mechanism, introduced to align the national currencies of EU members ahead of the introduction of the Euro. Interest rates were rocketing, home repossessions were up, as were redundancies. John Major's government was on the ropes barely six months after being re-elected with a slim majority. The problems hit the people who had scrimped together the deposits to buy houses and a lot of hard working people ended up trapped in negative equity.

Despite graduating in the summer, I stayed in Brum figuring that job prospects would be marginally better in a big city. It meant I was still picking my games – but there were some corkers to pick from.

Saints under McClennan were looking like real contenders again and they started the season with a 17-0 Charity Shield win over Wigan at Gateshead.

Chris Joynt, an up-and-coming second-rower, signed from Oldham and took his place in a workmanlike and effective pack unit. Our back line now oozed real pace and quality with Kiwi Jarrod McCracken joining for a guest spell from Canterbury-Bankstown. Not surprisingly Saints won their opening 10 league and cup games of the season, securing a place in the Lancashire Cup Final in that roll.

The last ever county final was a real blood-and-thunder occasion, with the 20,534 crowd roaring both sides on. Our front-row Kevin Ward, Bernard Dwyer and John Harrison stood toe-to-toe with their full-time Wigan counterparts and showed no deference at all. But the stand out player in the Saints' ranks was newcomer Joynt who introduced something different in attack. He had pace for a big man and his grubbers constantly caught out the Wigan full-back Joe Lydon only for the mine-sweeping of Shaun Edwards to neutralise the threat. That kicking aspect of his game was something that was coached out of Joynt as the years progressed.

We trailed 5-0 at the break, but two Dwyer goals closed that gap to a single point which ensured a gripping finale.

When the crowd is so densely packed and the game is so close, you can actually feel the fans moving with the players. It is particularly true up on the Scaff where you sway forward or sideways with each home charge and stand rigidly when the Saints line is under threat. All our swaying was in vain, and once more jubilant Wigan lifted another pot – taking the Lancashire Cup trophy home with them for the final time.

The county cups had a real place in rugby league's calendar – but they probably paid the price for sounding too parochial. Players moaned about too many games and these competitions were always likely candidates to go, but why did a cup tournament that was drawing in 20,000 have to go completely?

Great Britain 6 Australia 10, 24 October 1992
World Cup Final, Wembley

There was a general mood of dissatisfaction in the country, but the catalyst for mass protest that autumn was the government's president of the Board of Trade Michael

Heseltine's announcement on pit closures. Even in places like blue rinse Cheltenham where there were no mines, there were protests because people were concerned about the other issues.

One of the Tory-supporting papers at the time complained that a few years previously it would have been impossible to imagine a scenario where Arthur Scargill, leader of the National Union of Miners, would be more popular than the Prime Minister. But that was the situation, with "Sack Major, not the miners!" being the popular slogan.

St Helens' final two pits had already been closed, with Bold shutting in 1985 in the immediate aftermath of the year-long strike. Sutton Manor colliery followed suit in 1991, so neighbouring Parkside became the focus of some of the protests with Ann Scargill leading a 'Women against pit closures' demonstration underground. It was still shut the following year.

They were turbulent times and my leafleting sessions did overtime that autumn in Brum. Two massive 200,000 strong demonstrations snaked through Central London, one on Wednesday the other the following Sunday. Instead of listening to the speeches of Labour leader John Smith and NUM president Arthur Scargill in Hyde Park, I went to the pub instead and got into a big non-political discussion with a group of Featherstone miners about rugby. They were a cracking bunch of fellas who were not letting the struggle they now faced get them down, although one of them kept muttering to himself was "Everyone loves us now that it is too late."

These blokes were about to have their future employment prospects filled in with 6,000 cubic metres of concrete and instead we were talking about rugby. Specifically the discussion centred on March 1983 when Featherstone centre John Gilbert dashed our Wembley hopes. The Featherstone squad that day included 11 miners and they famously went on to beat Hull in the Challenge Cup Final. You always think, in a patronising way, about plucky little Fev. One of the blokes I was talking to was only about 10 years older than me and yet he had seen his side win the Challenge Cup twice and the League. What had I seen Saints win apart from a couple of piddling little pots?

The pits were closed down despite the wave of anger, though the government were forced to backtrack initially in order to take the steam out the national revolt. A lot of towns, like the mining triangle of Featherstone, Wakefield and Castleford, relied on mining for employment. Some rugby league fans showed their solidarity at the 1992 World Cup Final by covering the British Coal sponsors logos on their Lions jerseys with 'Coal not Dole' stickers.

The Final itself was a cracker and Great Britain, fielding Saints players Alan Hunte, Gary Connolly and Kevin Ward, were just 12 minutes away from being crowned World Champions for the first time in 20 years. It was an unbelievably intense game that had the international record 73,631 crowd on the edge of their seats, literally in our case. We had bought cheap tickets in those dreadful 'bus shelter' type benches in the lower tier behind the posts. Britain clung to a slender 6-4 lead until the 68th minute when Kevin Walters' smart ball sent helmet-wearing centre Steve Renouf blasting through Welshman John Devereux's tackle. Mal Meninga goaled and despite throwing everything at the Australians, Britain's World Cup dreams were dashed again.

As for our mining legacy – all that is left of it in St Helens are a few hundred bad chests belonging to former miners and a couple of monuments on roundabouts in and about the town.

St Helens 41 Wigan 6, 27 December 1992
Division 1

It is not healthy to hate your rivals. 'Hate' is a very strong word – probably one that should be reserved for that small number of people who should be genuinely reviled. But the fact that Wigan always seemed to get everything their own way seemed to magnify Saints fans' hostility towards them. For a start they were a full-time squad, playing, training and recovering together without the pressures and physical demands of 9 to 5 jobs such as laying bricks, plastering, digging ditches or driving trucks that the other teams' players had to endure.

Saints supporters' partisan view was that Wigan's players always got off lightly in disciplinary hearings and furthermore their players were always selected for representative honours before anyone else's. Players like talented back-rower Billy McGinty, who had been overlooked when he was at Warrington, suddenly became international class when he arrived at Central Park and became part of Great Britain's entirely Wigan pack that had taken on the Australians the previous summer.

In truth we just could not handle Wigan winning everything so convincingly that it was taking any sense of fun or unpredictability out of the game. There had always been a delicate equilibrium in the rugby league pond. Teams had dominated in the past, but the game would evolve and new teams would take over. Old men used to talk about what fantastic teams Oldham and Swinton had in the 1950s and 1960s respectively and where were they now? It was hard to see, bar a natural or man-made disaster befalling the Central Parkers, how this current period of dominance was going to end. They just seemed capable of regenerating themselves like a new Dr Who. So just as Jon Pertwee had morphed into Tom Baker, so Ellery Hanley became Andrew Farrell and Henderson Gill had become slippery wing Jason Robinson.

So, with that in mind, it was back home for Christmas and into the Black Bull for a prelude to our traditional stuffing. Well that is how it usually worked out, but this Saints side was made of sterner stuff. St Helens took to the field wearing a one-off kit, sponsored by Coors lager, but that seemed to be the only change to the festive routine as Wigan took a six-point lead through a converted Frano Botica try after only four minutes.

We should have had more faith in the new band of Saints warriors, who really gave it to the visitors over the next 76 minutes. It was a game that had everything for the purist and fair-weather fan alike – hard tackles, great tries and a victory. We had gone into the game without our 'daddy' Kevin Ward who was suspended – one of the occupational hazards of being an enforcer. But in his place our two unsung props of that period really came to the fore - tough as teak Cumbrian Jonathan Neill and big John Harrison. But our whole pack played a blinder that day and refused to bend the knee to their more illustrious opponents.

A break from Chris Joynt laid the platform for the first try from Alan Hunte. Saints were giving it to Wigan and received a further psychological boost when the prolific scorer Martin Offiah was carted off with a shoulder injury, to be replaced by a young Jason Robinson. Saints pressed home their territorial advantage by grabbing scores from blockbusting second-rower Sonny Nickle and a second from Hunte.

A converted try from Joynt plus a Paul Loughlin penalty goal gave us a commanding 24-6 lead at the break. A Dave Lyon try caused Wigan to be so rattled that they started to lose the plot and even Great Britain captain Phil Clarke was giving daft penalties away. Kelvin Skerrett clobbered our outstanding young Kiwi wing Jarrod McCracken with a high shot and deservedly got an early bath from referee Robin Whitfield. A subsequent melee saw former Saints Andy Platt and our fiery second-rower Nickle join him down the tunnel for a 10-minute spell.

Nickle grabbed his second score and on-song Kiwi Tea Ropati's deserved try helped push us to a 41-6 final score. It was incredible.

Saints were flying, and would have certainly maintained that momentum at Widnes on New Year's Day but for the intervention of the weather. Alas, when that game was finally replayed six weeks later the Chemics caught us on a midweek downer after our Challenge Cup exit at Wigan. It would prove a very costly blip that also included a defeat at Hull.

Wigan 8 St Helens 8, 9 April 1993
Division 1

The whole season had been about them and us – even more than any other year. Saints had been breathing down Wigan's neck all year and the title went all the way down to the wire. It was ultimately settled on Good Friday with 29,839 packing into Central Park to see the compelling decider. The crowd on the bridge over the River Douglas to the left of the Kop was packed too, with people three and four deep all enjoying the obscured view of the action. You can see a surprising amount of the action up there – I once watched a Wigan versus Leeds game from that spot, although the Douglas Stand obliterated a good chunk of one corner.

Saints needed a victory because despite being level on points, Wigan's points for and against tally was better.

It was just one of those desperate games that physically and emotionally drained all the travelling fans. The game was 8-8 at half-time with our points coming from tries by Gary Connolly and Alan Hunte. The second half remained scoreless and the match ended in a draw, which meant Wigan maintained their edge in the title race.

Although the cherry and white ribbons were not tied to the old pot just yet, it was hard to see the Pie-Eaters letting it slip away in their run in. Ultimately, there was nothing separating the teams when it was all totted up and we were left to rue those daft defeats that had foiled our title bid.

The one every fan and player pointed to was a dire night at Leigh in November when the basement side emerged from the mudbath with both points. Bad as it was, losing the title on points difference to our bitterest rivals was not the only thing that we had to contend with. Disaster had struck late in the game when our veteran warhorse Kevin Ward's leg crumpled beneath him in a hard, but fair Mick Cassidy tackle. It was a desperately bad double fracture which ended Wardy's career and at one stage there were even fears that he would not walk again.

It is quite a sobering experience when you see a tough bloke like Ward – a giant of a man, who had done so much in the game – agonisingly lying in a heap on the soggy Central Park turf. Of course all our fans still traipsed off feeling sorry for ourselves but none of us knew at the time how badly Wardy was injured. Had we it may have put our 'suffering' into some perspective.

St Helens 10 Wigan 4, 16 May 1993
Premiership Final, Old Trafford

Saints deserved something from the season that had promised so much and yet had been scuppered entirely by Wigan in the League, Challenge Cup and Lancashire Cup. We were now in last chance saloon but like an idiot I did not even go to the final. And it was not simply a case of being unable to cope with seeing us lose another game against this seemingly unbeatable Wigan side.

I have a dozen excuses for not keeping the faith for one more game – but the biggest one was cash. I was in the process of moving out of a grim, cold flat in a tower block in inner city Brum. I had lived there for just over a year and it was the worst, coldest place I have lived. It was great when I first moved in the previous May. Then it was warm, even though the lad whose flat it was told me that the concierge had been murdered with a hammer outside a nearby pub and not been replaced. Once summer ended the place became a fridge because there was no heating apart from one two-bar electric fire, which ate up all the credit on the meter. Someone four floors above me had had their water supply cut off and consequently used to crap into a newspaper and toss it out of the window making the daily walk up the path hazardous. The lift was always soaked with a pool of piss from someone who could never wait that extra two minutes to get into his flat. The place was a hovel and had my mam seen the state of it she would have drummed me back to St Helens. But I suppose I was being pig headed and looking at the bigger picture and keen to stick it out in Brum!

The recession meant work had dried up and I was strapped for cash. My mam had sent me my train fare so that I could come home for the final, but stupidly I spent it on other things.

It is exceptionally hard to feel part of this famous 10-4 victory, particularly as I did not even try to find a radio that might have carried it or a pub that was showing the game on television. Statistics show that the game was level pegging at the break with Gary Connolly grabbing our first-half try.

A couple of Gus O'Donnell drop-goals nudged us ahead and then Paul Loughlin went over for the clincher. Promising young second-rower Chris Joynt capped a fine maiden season at Saints with the Harry Sunderland man-of-the-match award granted for his tackling display.

When I found out the result I felt pig-sick instead of being overjoyed. It was such a stupid game to miss and one that affected me in subsequent years. It was like I needed to see us beat Wigan to heal some of those deep scars from previous battles or to give me a transfusion of faith to give me sustenance for the years ahead.

Dave Lyon scorches through in the incredible 41-6 league win over Wigan in December 1992. (Platt)

Sonny Nickle going forward in his first stint at Saints, Tea Ropati is in the background. (Platt)

17. 1993-94 Better things to do

St Helens 8 Warrington 16, 11 December 1993
Regal Trophy, Quarter-Final

Shamefully my halo was left gathering dust for the vast majority of the 1993-94 season. I won't go into the boring details here, but at the risk of committing heresy, I was just doing other things that seemed more important at the time. It seems I was not the only one giving Knowsley Road a wide berth, with our average crowds tumbling by more than 1,600 to 7,264.

It was a tough old season with Wardy gone for good and star centre Gary Connolly committing the cardinal sin of signing for Wigan. They were both top-drawer players who we struggled to replace as our results showed. It was not popular to sympathise with Connolly's dilemma, but you could not blame him for taking the better deal from the other side of Billinge. Here was a player who had been mixing with the cream of British rugby league on the test circuit – mostly Wigan players - but if reports are to be believed his contract at Saints was still relatively poor. The common view among Saints fans is that Connolly was just being greedy and he was and still is denounced as Judas for taking Wigan's pieces of silver. His then team-mate Chris Joynt gives his view in his autobiography *The Quiet Man*. Joynt wrote, "If Gary had been offered anywhere near the same deal at Saints as he got at Wigan I believe he would never have left because he loved it at Knowsley Road."

So just as Andy Platt had left as he was reaching his prime, so too went Connolly. Joining us was a young half-back from the Oldham club, Tommy Martyn, who had impressed in his team's Second Division Premiership Final win over Hull KR in 1990. He liked to play his rugby off the cuff and possessed bags of natural flair.

Saints' squad, unfortunately, was not the strongest so when the injuries accumulated the team's form suffered badly. They were inconsistent rather than dire, but as ever in these situations the coach was in the firing line. The lowest ebb was reached with a Regal Trophy knockout by Warrington and one of my mates had had enough. Mick, a supporter who had watched Saints through thick and thin, shouted up to coach McClennan, who was watching the game from the clubhouse behind the sticks.

There was an exchange of views and then the next minute the fiery coach picked up a pint, opened the window and tipped it all over his critic below.

It was effectively the end of the line for Mike. Maybe he had taken the side as far as he could. McClennan had been an innovative coach and had dragged us up to the second best team in the league, competing with but not overhauling Wigan.

But that incident, coupled with one or two flaky results, meant he was back home in New Zealand by Christmas and replaced by Academy coach Eric Hughes. It was not a case of trawling the world for a successor like last time around; more a case of what was available close to home. It was 'back to basics' for Saints – a policy the team had more joy with than John Major's government who had launched an initiative by that name at October's Conservative Party conference. The Tories immediately became mired in some sleazy scandals, and some translated 'back to basics' as 'back to my place'.

Despite hardly setting the world on fire, three relatively easy draws against Huddersfield, Whitehaven and Doncaster saw Saints make it into the Challenge Cup semi-final. We were 80 minutes from Wembley and the opportunity to play Wigan again.

It was not to be and an Ellery Hanley-inspired Leeds turfed us out at the final hurdle. The season was a write off and we lost eight of our last 10 games in miserable fashion.

Further gloom came in the bombshell that Beechams factory in Westfield Street was being axed, with the loss of 480 jobs, ending of the company's 150-year association with the town.

The fine building, containing a magnificent clock tower, still remains and now houses part of the college and a bar to mark our heritage – unfortunately you cannot spend heritage in the shops...

18. 1994-95 Curse the wind

St Helens 20 Doncaster 29, 21 August 1994
Division 1

In the early 1980s ITV showed a cracking documentary on struggling Doncaster entitled *Another Bloody Sunday*. A remarkable piece of work, the programme really showed how the other half lived in the non-glamorous lower echelons of rugby league. One of the larger than life characters of that show was a bloke called Tony Banham, who sadly died some years later. Banham was a big, fearsome looking prop whose 'day job' was working on the door of one of the city's nightclubs. He was shown breaking up fights, with the commentator's voice saying, "There is trouble on the dance floor... but not for long!" The documentary focused on Doncaster's dark, dismal season of 1979-80 when they went all year without a win until they met and beat Huyton.

Fast forward some 14 years and nobody would have ever dreamt that one day the South Yorkshire minnows would come to Knowsley Road and be victorious. The newly promoted side had not been expected to win a single match that year, but Saints trailed 18-4 at the break. Little known South African Jamie Bloem ran rings round us, and we were justifiably booed off. Despite two tries from Alan Hunte and one each from Paul Loughlin and Chris Joynt in the second half, Saints still lost 29-20.

Despite beating Saints and Widnes, the Dons slumped and that was hastened by the news that Bloem had been taking steroids and was banned for two years. One of Doncaster's scorers that afternoon was chunky Samoan centre Vila Matautia, who impressed so much that he joined Saints once the South Yorkshire side's bubble burst.

Our shocking start to season was made worse three days later when we were hammered by Warrington in a game that saw young Keiron Cunningham make his debut. Our tackling at Wilderspool was appalling and we again leaked tries left, right and centre. Fans were already calling for coach Eric Hughes's head to roll.

This time we couldn't point the finger at the board because they had strengthened in the off season with three new players – Bobbie Goulding, Scott Gibbs and Apollo Perelini - and they would need time to bed in.

Goulding, who joined from Widnes for £135,000, had already played for both big guns Wigan and Leeds. Saints moaned at the tribunal's valuation, expecting to pay only £60,000, but they got their money's worth. A quite remarkable footballer on his day and a marvellous tactical kicker, Goulding could control a game. He was a fiery little player, but in those golden years you always expected the shrewd number seven to have an ace card up his sleeve.

The other two recruits from union were gambles – but we need not have worried. Although Gibbs had been outstanding for Wales and the British Lions, when he arrived he was carrying a spare tyre and was lapped by our forwards in fitness sessions on the cinder track at Ruskin Drive. However, Gibbs was a fantastic competitor and he soon got himself up to speed to be a winner in the XIII-man code.

On the other hand Perelini, dubbed 'The Terminator' from his days in the Western Samoan rugby union squad, was as fit as a butcher's dog and once he settled in he took to the explosive nature of our game like a duck to water.

Unfortunately, if you come into league with a tag like 'The Terminator' you do have a bit of target on your head and somebody will try to knock it off. Leeds's dual-code international John Bentley tried to find out if he was all that tough when he ran directly at him and was knocked out for his troubles.

St Helens 14 Australia 32, 1 November 1994
Tour match

Saints had been demoted to a midweek tour match rather than playing one of the prestigious weekend games, which meant that Kangaroos skipper and honorary Saint Mal Meninga did not play, instead he remained tantalisingly rooted to the bench. It was probably a blessing in disguise, because two days previously against Wales Big Mal had blasted through John Devereux's mistimed tackle and left the Widnes centre with a broken jaw. We had three Welshmen who were gluttons for punishment and faced the Australians twice in three days – Anthony Sullivan, Scott Gibbs and Jonathan Griffiths. A crowd of 13,000 plus turned up, with the queues outside forcing a 10-minute delay to the kick off. Saints had a good go trailing only 12-8 at the break. Ultimately the absence of Great Britain stars Paul Loughlin, Alan Hunte, Bobbie Goulding and Chris Joynt took their toll and we lost 32-14 to an Australia side featuring a young forward by name of David Fairleigh.

The Australians had Paul Sironen sent off for putting the elbow in on Sonny Nickle, but their superior fitness made light work of being a man down.

Once more Great Britain's hopes were raised after an unbelievable first test at Wembley in front of more than 57,000 fans. The enduring image of that game is of former Welsh rugby union captain Jonathan Davies taking the ball from halfway, dummying and then sweeping around the Kangaroos' full-back Brett Mullins to touch down in the corner.

That moment was beamed around the world, but the victory itself was down to some steely determination after Britain played most of the game with 12 men. Captain and play-maker Shaun Edwards had been sent off following a high tackle on the Australian second-row Bradley Clyde after 25 minutes. Substitute Bobbie Goulding was thrown into the fray from the bench and helped guide Britain to victory.

Saints' stars played their parts – in unusual roles at that – with Alan Hunte at centre and Chris Joynt squaring up to 'the Chief' Paul Harrogan in the front-row.

Of course there were the cynics who argued that the Australians were off their game because they wanted to guarantee a more lucrative windfall from sell-out crowds at the subsequent two tests. No Australian wants to lose a game of tiddly-winks to the Poms, let alone the sport that is their national winter sport.

That said, such conspiracy theories gathered momentum when the expectations around British success went up like a rocket, but came down like a stick. The lame Lions were slaughtered at Old Trafford in front of an expectant sell-out 44,000 crowd.

It went to the decider at Elland Road, Leeds where another big crowd – 39,468 – saw the Kangaroos retain the Ashes with a clinical performance against the wounded Lions.

For some reason seeing Mal again made me dig out my video tape from 1984-85 season when I returned to Brum. After reliving the highlights of the Premiership and Lancashire Cup Final when Mal was one of us, I left the tape in the machine and went to the pub. Unfortunately that night someone smashed our back door in and burgled us, taking the video recorder and my one and only Big Mal tape.

I don't suppose the thieves saw the significance of that battered tape with Mal scrawled across it! On the bright side, at least they had the decency to rob the Play station and at least give me a break from *Sonic the Hedgehog*, which one of my housemates was addicted to and spent every hour of the day playing with his buddies. It meant the news, *Coronation Street* and *Sportsnight* could now get a look in, but it was scant consolation for losing Mal.

Batley 22 St Helens 22, 18 December 1994
Regal Trophy Round 3

Saints had clicked into gear and following our first two defeats we lost only two of our subsequent 14 games. In that victory roll was an impressive half-century drubbing of Bradford at Odsal. We were playing some decent football too with backs Steve Prescott, Anthony Sullivan and especially Alan Hunte having a beano in the try-scoring stakes. The 20-year-old Prescott was a revelation at full-back – he had a keen eye for the high ball and could defuse the bombs, but he was also a magnificent counter-attacker with real pace. Perhaps it was a sign that I was getting old because I remembered his dad, former Saint Eric, playing for Salford and Widnes in the 1970s and early 1980s.

For all our new stars, it was Bobbie Goulding who was pulling the strings with a series sparkling displays.

So with that in mind a trip to Mount Pleasant for a knock-out match should have held no fears. However, there was very little that was pleasant about going to the Heavy Woollen District in the bleak mid-winter. Batley's sloping, postage-stamp sized pitch was a sea of mud, which proved something of a leveller. Saints coach Eric Hughes did not want to play because the pitch was so bad, but it went ahead nonetheless and the players were soon indistinguishable from each other. The Gallant Youths were not there to make up the numbers and were leading 22-16 with only a minute left on the clock.

We were on the brink of another shock until David Lyon plunged over in the corner with Bobbie Goulding slotting the extras to force a replay.

Plucky Batley gave the rematch at Knowsley Road a good go, and even led at the hour mark before ultimately being swamped in the last quarter with the free scoring full-back Steve Prescott grabbing a hat-trick.

St Helens 25 Wigan 32, 26 December 1994
Division 1

Mad things tend to happen at Christmas. I bumped into a lad I knew outside the Black Bull and he had no teeth. He had gone out on Christmas Eve and got so blind drunk that he puked up, losing his false teeth down The Nelson's toilets in the process. He spent Christmas week looking like one of the gurners from the old Chewits TV adverts.

Saints' Boxing Day showdown with Wigan was just as mad. It was one of those thrilling, incident-packed derbies that had everything. Sadly it still left us feeling as though we had been kicked in the teeth by Shergar at the final whistle.

It seemed like the usual festive script, with Wigan sailing into a 20-2 lead in a stormy first half that had seen Wigan's Neil Cowie trading blows with our Adam Fogerty. It was not usually a smart move to have a punch-up with former heavyweight boxer Foggy.

Fogerty - the son of former Great Britain loose forward Terry - was an unusual character. He was possibly one of the most famous faces in rugby league from his acting days. However, there were no romantic leads, he was usually only seen clobbering someone and famously pole-axed Jack Duckworth in *Coronation Street*.

Both Foggy and Cowie were sin-binned. It was one of those days, with Kelvin Skerrett and Ian Pickavance knocking lumps off each other in a similar set-to and taking time in the cooler in the second half. Some hand-wringing commentators moan about "not wanting to see that sort of thing" in sport, but the crowd loves a punch-up. Just listen to the raised voices when it goes off. The only Christmas spirit there that day was in the hip flasks of the gents in the stand – and the pop bottles of the kids on the Scaff.

The colour of the cards being brandished changed from yellow to red when Henry Paul was sent off for a high tackle on Steve Prescott. It lifted us and after the break Chris Joynt sparked the move that sent centre Dave Lyon in. Two minutes later Bobbie Goulding's shrewd ball put Tommy Martyn in, with the stand-off doubling his tally to level the scores.

It was shades of the Boxing Day comeback of 1987 all over again, with Saints once again rallying from an impossible situation. The noise from the crowd raised the roof as first Goulding nudged us into the lead with a one-pointer and then Anthony Sullivan waltzed in for a try. Crucially Goulding's conversion attempt fell tantalisingly short.

But seven minutes from the end, the rollercoaster started to descend as we surrendered our five point lead with two lapses in concentration. The first saw Gary Connolly wriggle free to send Inga Tuigamala bashing his way over under the sticks. Then Martin Offiah, who had been anonymous all afternoon, stepped on the gas to deliver the coup de grâce. It was a cruel, utterly gut-wrenching defeat.

A fortnight later Wigan did it again in the Regal Trophy quarter-final at Central Park, pipping us by just two points in front of a 23,278 crowd. This was another fiery one with Skerrett and Sonny Nickle getting 10 minutes in the sin bin after a punch up. Skerrett scored their match-clinching try five minutes from time, but then could not resist another crack at Nickle in the closing stages and was given his marching orders for throwing a volley of punches. Star man for Wigan was fleet-footed Kiwi Henry Paul, who grabbed a brace of tries in their narrow win.

Wigan 16 St Helens 16, 11 February 1995
Challenge Cup, Round 4

Having shelled out £20 to make the trip from Brum, I was miffed by the early reports that the Central Park pitch was under water and game under threat. Undeterred I met my mates at 10am at Shaw Street and was soon getting soaked myself in the Bricklayers and then The Crofters in Wigan town centre. It turned into a good session and the craic was ninety, as we kept an eye on the pitch updates on *Grandstand*.

The pre-match was good, but the game was even better, with the on-off nature of the build-up failing to deter Saints fans from attending in their thousands. We packed the Kop end and our noise lifted our injury-hit side to a super human effort.

Wigan had not lost a Challenge Cup game since February 1987, but Saints were within the thickness of a few shavings of the goalpost of beating them on their own midden. We were in the driving seat for most of the game and had Wigan playing catch-up, with youngster Keiron Cunningham proving an absolute revelation at hooker.

Long-distance fans like me, who only came back for big games, always heard about the big signings whose names were up in lights and we looked out for them. But when you see a youngster quietly emerge onto the big stage without seeing the nurturing process it can really be a real 'Labour gain.' Prescott was one – but Cunningham was something else because of the position he played. He was a revelation - quick, strong, alert and great for sparking our side into life. Our patched-up team took an early lead when mobile prop Ian Pickavance touched down, but that drew a quick response from Inga Tuigamala.

It was nip-and-tuck with marksmen Bobbie Goulding and Frano Botica exchanging penalties. Cunningham then bustled through, the passage of play resulting in Alan Hunte flying in for a top try. Goulding missed the conversion and then a penalty leaving it at 12-6 at the break.

We knew Wigan would hit us with something after the break and it duly came with the explosive Denis Betts crossing to level it. It was nerve-wracking stuff as Goulding nudged us up by a penalty and then added a one-pointer.

On 63 minutes an unlikely drop-goal - and a first for Pickavance - gave us a crucial four point cushion. Unfortunately we just could not cling to it and nine minutes from time hooker Martin Hall went over. Botica's conversion went wide and as the game entered its desperate last stages Goulding's drop-goal attempt hit the posts. Finally, Steve Prescott pulled off a super try saving tackle on former Saint Gary Connolly to force a replay.

It had been an unbelievably tense game – and even though we had a psychological edge by bringing them to our place for the replay, at the back of our minds was the fact that these full timers had quality time to prepare and recover.

Rugby league had the rare luxury of top billing on mainstream BBC for the replay thanks to the antics of a crew of boneheaded football hooligans. *Sportsnight's* main scheduled item was due to be the Republic of Ireland versus England 'friendly' soccer match from Dublin. But that was abandoned when the bigoted English yobs decided that fighting with the Irish police and ripping up the Lansdowne Road seats was a statesmanlike response to the 'surrender to the IRA' they saw in the British and Irish government's Good Friday agreement, that sought to bring an end to the troubles that had raged for virtually as long as I had lived.

Knowsley Road had crowd trouble that night – but it was trouble fitting everyone in, with the 17,300 capacity reached 20 minutes before kick off, leading to 2,000 people being locked out.

After much anticipation the match did not go well for us with our already injury-hit side suffering a further blow when Scott Gibbs dislocated his elbow. It was a stormy game, with fired-up Wigan enforcer Kelvin Skerrett, Bobbie Goulding and Martin Hall being sin-binned after a brawl. Wigan had all the aces that night and had it wrapped up by the break, leading 32-8 with the irrepressible Martin Offiah scoring a hat-trick. After one of those tries Offiah and Shaun Edwards performed that smug, statuesque pose borrowed from former world middleweight boxing champion Chris Eubank. It was a look that said, "We are just so-oo good and we've done you again!" Although we made the scoreline respectable, it was still a hard defeat to take because we had gone so close and were left thinking that had the wind blown Goulding's drop-kick in by an inch we could have beaten them.

Wigan waltzed all the way to Wembley where they trounced Leeds in the showpiece for the second year running.

There was a strong feeling that our side was not a million miles away from being the finished article – but we had been here before and then gone into reverse.

Putting the game into perspective was the death of supporter Brian Dillon shortly after that drawn match at Central Park. He would have strained every emotion and made every tackle with the lads on the pitch. A dedicated man, who attended every week out of love and loyalty to his side, Brian is sorely missed by everyone who shared his company and quiet wit on the halfway line.

Wigan 34 St Helens 18, 14 April 1995
Division 1

Our game thrives on local rivalry and we have always relished our visits to Wigan, more than trips to Leeds or Bradford. And just to underline the importance of our derby, 26,314 filed into Central Park to watch Wigan wallop us and then be presented with the Championship trophy. It was awful to see 'them' lift another cup, but others had weightier matters to contemplate. The traditional derby for some was in danger because that dreadful word 'merger' slipped off the tongues of the suits at the RFL.

This was because the game had been rocked by the announcement that professional rugby league would be effectively under the direction of Rupert Murdoch's News Corporation and a Super League created. The British game was effectively just a pawn in the battle that had started down under between Kerry Packer, whose Channel Nine company had won the rights to cover the Australian competition, and Murdoch who was planning a rival league.

The revolutionary plan to merge clubs and switch to summer was a lot to take in for fans, players and especially club chairmen and indeed the bean counters who were bamboozled by the huge figures. If you supported a team that made the Super League cut there was going to be pots of cash and a brave new world opening up. The rest would face a much more uncertain future and some suspected they would just wither away or become feeder clubs.

The initial proposal to merge 15 clubs into six teams caused wailing and an understandable gnashing of teeth in proud, traditional and independent towns.

Rivals Featherstone, Castleford and Wakefield would form Calder; Widnes and Warrington would take the name of Cheshire, a county that the pair had only been shunted into some 20 years earlier. Sheffield and Doncaster would form South Yorkshire. Manchester sounded more grand and global than Salford and Oldham, who would also merge. A Cumbria team would be represented by a combination of the county's four professional clubs: Whitehaven, Workington, Barrow and Carlisle.

The proposal that summed up how illogical the mergers were, was the one to combine Hull with Hull KR – the bitterest of city rivals. Whoever envisaged such a team probably would have deemed a merger between Celtic and Rangers to be acceptable.

To add insult to injury of those left out of the brave new world, there would be no promotion or relegation for two years and the teams outside Super League would effectively be cut adrift.

Despite not finishing top, London automatically leapfrogged champions Keighley because a team from the capital made our European Super League sound bigger and better than a wet, windy town on the fringes of Bradford. It all really rankled with traditionalists and you got the impression that rather than being an ill-thought-out strategy, this was just the opening gambit.

Saints didn't have a game that weekend – and nobody was going to merge with us anyhow - but there were protests and chatter across the country. Questions were asked in the House of Commons and the All-party Parliamentary Group of MPs raised the view that the game was being sold "lock, stock and barrel to a private media interest".

A month of upheaval followed, with the Widnes and Warrington merger plan called off as both sides were initially allocated a Super League after a proposed venture from Toulouse pulled out, leaving Paris as the sole French representatives giving a thin continental veneer to what was being called the European Super League concept.

Castleford also pulled out of the merger to aim for their own place in the new competition. They had to really – after all a banner at Post Office Road declared, "Fev is Fev, Cas is Cas, stick your merger up your arse!" to sum up the level of hostility.

A lot of British players received loyalty payments to keep them in Super League and reject Kerry Packer's overtures. The other players, not signed up on loyalty lists, then demanded more money too.

By the end of the month the stick had been bent back into shape and all the mergers were dropped. A Super League of 12 clubs was finalised, comprising the top 10 in the league plus London and Paris. Bradford, Castleford, Halifax, Leeds, London, Oldham, Paris, Saints, Sheffield, Warrington, Wigan and Workington were all in. Former World Champions Widnes and both Humberside clubs were out in the cold.

News Corporation's offer was now £87 million – with clubs getting £900,000 per season for five years, money they could have only dreamed about a year earlier. I am sure Maurice Lindsay could have put it better when he declared "We want 12 Wigans!"

Leeds 30 St Helens 26, 14 May 1995
Premiership Semi-Final

The off-field shenanigans were enough to force me to make an effort to get up north again before the year was out. Saints had finished fourth, behind champions Wigan, Leeds and Castleford, but we were looking a reasonable bet for a good run in the Premiership, particularly as we played a Loiners team the week after their Wembley exertions and sorrows-drowning exercise. We had also beaten Leeds at Headingley a couple of months previously.

The Saints supporters' songbook had moved on from the simply chanting a player's name and to the tune of the Scaffold's *Lilly the Pink* Saints fans sang:

We'll drink, a drink, a drink
to Bobbie the King, the King, the King.
He's the captain of our rugby team...

Goulding had been voted First Division player of the year, was really making our side tick and was worthy of his coronation. At that stage he had the rugby league world at his feet – but we were yet to see his finest hour.

Things were going well and we seemed assured of a place at Old Trafford after leading 20-6 at half-time against a side that had skipper Garry Schofield sent off for verbally abusing referee Stuart Cummins. They also had former Widnes full-back Alan Tait sin-binned as we looked on course for the final. However, once things started going Leeds's way our depleted pack rolled over. Former Saint George Mann, playing in the unlikely position of stand-off, was the inspiration behind Leeds's rally scoring the first of their four tries in 19 minutes.

Although Alan Hunte came back with a try we lost 30-26, ending our season. It was utter humiliation, and one let-down too many for my mate Dave who had supported them home and away since the late 1970s. He packed in going for nearly two years and stuck to his guns too – at some cost! We missed Shane Cooper, who had played his last game for Saints after picking up a five-match ban for an incident in the previous round against Halifax. Coops joined Widnes on a free transfer later that summer. And we were further hampered in the creativity department by the loss of Tommy Martyn with a knee injury – something that would sadly become a feature in subsequent years.

Perhaps losing to Leeds was a blessing in disguise because Wigan really were running hot and completed a clean sweep of all domestic honours by putting a record 69 points past Leeds in the final.

19. 1995-96 Ex Terra Lucem

St Helens 55 Bradford Bulls 10, 20 August 1995
Centenary Championship

Our Bradford opponents showed us a taste of things to come by ditching their traditional and unfashionable appendage of Northern in favour of the Americanised moniker of 'The Bulls'. It was repeated across the league as clubs used the truncated winter Centenary season of 1995-96 to gear up for the arrival of summer rugby and the Super League. The irony was that Bulls seemed to be borrowing a lot of the techniques from neighbours Keighley who had become the Cougars three years previously.

Cougarmania had turned a struggling Keighley club into one that was averaging crowd figures of 3,787 – only 800 fewer than their big city neighbours. The Cougars were still excluded from a seat at the top table though.

With it being the game's centenary, clubs reverted to their original kits, with Saints taking on a blue and white striped jersey for the year. Stripes were usually reserved for football – hoops make rugby players look bigger and we didn't need tips off Trinny and Susannah to tell us that.

Changes that were more significant had come in the appointment of the shrewd and dynamic former RFL public relations officer David Howes as Saints' chief executive. Sometimes you need an outsider to weigh things up and present a good vision for the future. Howes laid some very important foundations for our onslaught into the new era.

It was tough to get your head around the truncated league season with 20 championship matches plus the Regal Trophy, crammed into five months. There was also the Centenary World Cup to take into account, which effectively took October out of the league programme.

Saints kicked off with a 55-10 win over the Bulls, and high scores would become a feature of the stop-start season. We piled 60-plus points on Workington and Sheffield with Wigan posting two half centuries past us, including our home game, which took place on the August Bank Holiday weekend. It was that sort of year.

It was a daft period in the game's history – and heaven only knows what must have been going through the players' minds with all the money and talk about who was getting what. It was almost like a 'freshers' period of celebration before the real work began. That said it was also a time for hatching plots and we cashed in Widnes's misfortune at being culled from the Super League by recruiting Karle Hammond. Moves were already afoot to slot in the final piece of the playing jigsaw.

The changes I was seeing on my infrequent visits home were not all for the better. I was now living in Balsall Heath, the red light district of Birmingham, and so was well used to seeing drug dealers and young girls staggering around off their faces on crack. At that stage vigilantes had started cleaning up the area, trying to get the brothels closed down, shaming the kerb crawlers and driving away the dealers. You associate drugs with inner cities, and perhaps absence had made the heart grow fonder, but I always viewed my home town as relatively free of such problems. Unfortunately, it either seemed to be changing or I had naively overlooked it. Approaching St Helens on the bus, after catching the coach up to Liverpool, graffiti now decorated the 'Welcome to St Helens' signpost with the words "A town called heroin". Our town did not have a massive problem, but you only need half a dozen addicts and you soon know about it. Suddenly you could recognise the pinched, thin faces of those addicted to smack and recognise the mannerisms as you went into town and saw them hanging around. It made me sad and angry – an anger that was directed four ways. At those gaunt users who rob, harass and beg off hard working people and vulnerable pensioners to feed their habit. At the "no such thing as society" brigade who robbed a generation of parents of work for a decade and then let their offspring slip through any welfare safety net. At the pop stars who glamorise the injecting and snorting of drugs and then casually spend a few grand getting detoxed at a private clinic. They can sell their stories to the press afterwards, in contrast to the more vulnerable addicts who simply flog their mam's video or granddad's war medals.

And of course there is anger at the big dealers, who enjoy lavish lottery winners' lifestyles paid for off the backs of the misery suffered by the drug users and their neighbours.

England 8 Australia 16, 28 October 1995
World Cup Final, Wembley

Despite months of uncertainty due to the shenanigans over the Super League war down under, the World Cup went ahead in England and was a rip-roaring success. For once our bosses, and Maurice Lindsay must take some of the credit, had managed to organise a tournament that pulled in the crowds and enhanced our profile.

Although the home nations were split into England and Wales, the Australians too were more significantly diluted because they did not pick any players who had signed up for the Super League competition. Their squad was selected only from players who had signed with the ARL.

England won the group opener against the Australians at Wembley, and the crowds flocked to the rest of the games with 26,263 and 14,041 turning up to see the hosts beat Fiji and South Africa respectively. There were other cracking encounters with New Zealand just edging out a tenacious Tongan side coached by Saints' former coaching duo Mike McClennan and Frankie Barrow.

I gave the group games a miss and saved up for the Final at Wembley – a game England lost 16-8. This was a massive anti-climax with Paul Newlove grabbing the hosts' only try just after the break. That said it was still a great tournament, and it really captured the imagination off rugby league's beaten track. One of the big success stories was in Wales, where former Saints full-back and now Welsh national coach Clive Griffiths did well in gelling his squad together into quite a unit. They beat Western Samoa in front of a passionate 15,000 Vetch Field crowd and they brought 8,000 spectators to Old Trafford for the semi-final. The result was a 25-10 defeat by England, but no disgrace.

It was an ideal time to forge ahead with a Welsh Super League franchise – but instead all those former union internationals returned to the XV-man code led by Jonathan Davies who signed for Cardiff. The wall that had divided our codes for a century had come tumbling down in August with union going 'open' and allowing professionalism. Saints' half-back Jonathan Griffiths also returned to his original sport, to Llanelli.

However, there were other more shocking departures in November when long-serving Paul Loughlin, Bernard Dwyer and Sonny Nickle were told that they were going to Bradford to make way for our major signing – Paul Newlove. The England centre was one of the most effective attacking players in the competition, but commanded a big transfer fee made up of £250,000 plus the three players.

It was a shame to see stalwarts like Bernard and Lockers go – both had played at Knowsley Road since the Hare & Hounds under-17s days and bled red and white. There was, however, excitement in the air with the capture of Newy – a player chief executive David Howes declared was "A calling card signing". As a publicity stunt, Newlove was delivered to the ground in the back of a Securicor van. Indeed, he was exactly the sort of player that would have gone straight to Wigan or Leeds a year before so the times, indeed, were a changin'.

St Helens 80 Warrington 0, 4 January 1996
Regal Trophy Semi-Final

Saints were focusing on their success in the Regal Trophy run and had sent a virtual reserve team to Central Park on Boxing Day. They were thrashed 58-4, but largely got away with it because chief executive Howes submitted detailed video evidence of how the absent players sustained those injuries. Their punishment was a £10,000 fine with half suspended for a year. I knew what was coming so for the first time I did not even bother coming home for Christmas – spending the festive period in Brum with my girlfriend and a couple of our mates seemingly listening to Oasis's *What's the Story Morning Glory* and *Different Class* by Pulp over and over again.

With my fridge and wallet empty I nipped home to see my folks and that extended family at Knowsley Road for New Year, staying to see the Warrington game.

A number of rule changes bizarrely came into effect in December, which was strange given that it was halfway through a season. It added to the sense that the Centenary season was there to merely refine the product before Super League kicked in. One of the changes was to make the scoring team restart play. It was supposed to stop one side getting a match-wining roll on after scoring, but against Warrington we made that look foolish. It was not a logical change, and had the opposite effect. Once a team scored all it had to do was put in a deep kick-off and tackle hard for a set and it would inevitably get the ball back on the half-way line. It made it easier to get a roll on – but not as easy as it was against Warrington in this match.

The game had been frozen off from the previous weekend and took place on a Thursday night, which was unusual for a semi-final. There was nothing frosty about Saints – they were on fire from the first whistle and led 36-0 at half-time. Unbelievably they upped the tempo after the break as the disinterested Warrington side just waved the white flag and crumpled. The point-a-minute scoring spree inflicted the heaviest ever defeat on the Wire and the disgrace prompted their coach Brian Johnson to fall on his sword the following day. To put the result into perspective Saints were missing three prolific members of their left hand side gang - Chris Joynt, Anthony Sullivan and Paul Newlove. With Johnson gone, former Saint Clive Griffiths took charge for the next game in the league between the sides three days later although Saints still won 54-14.

St Helens 16 Wigan 25, 13 January 1996
Regal Trophy Final, Huddersfield

Wigan had won the Centenary competition at a canter, but their skipper Shaun Edwards tried to use a bit of kidology, implying Saints were the favourites to win the last-ever

Regal Trophy on account of our butchering of Warrington. It was just Edwards's way of taking some of the pressure off his men and putting it onto our players' shoulders.

The match took place at the new all-seater McAlpine Stadium which had been built to house Huddersfield's football and rugby league teams at a cost of £16 million. It was a huge improvement on the crumbling Fartown and a good setting for the final.

When Inga Tuigamala blasted over from dummy half after 14 minutes we braced ourselves for another tonking, but then hit back in our inimitable way. Giving the ball plenty of air, it went through eight pairs of hands before Joey Hayes touched down. Centre Paul Newlove, playing his first game since mid-December, gave us an 8-6 lead at the break.

The game was in the balance but then came the first of Scott Gibbs's calamities six minutes after the restart. Bizarrely the chunky Welsh centre tried to release the ball after barely clearing his own line. Wigan's Kris Radlinski simply picked it up and walked in under the posts. It was a shame because Gibbs had a cracking match, but was later sent off for cleaning out Simon Haughton after carting the ball in with his elbow raised.

Wigan stretched their lead when sidestepping stand-off Henry Paul zipped in for a solo try, bamboozling the defence with a magical effort. Although Bobbie Goulding pegged a couple of points back, Edwards's drop-goal gave Wigan a 19-10 lead.

Still, dogged Saints were not done and Cunningham impersonated a wrecking ball to skittle four would-be tacklers to touch down and set up a thrilling finish.

The match hinged on a try-saving tackle from former Saint Gary Connolly who stopped powerhouse Samoan Vila Matautia's rampaging run to the line seven minutes from time. That try would have put us a point in front and we would have surely clung on from there.

Unfortunately Henry Paul had the last word to give the scoreline a flattering touch. Defeats against Wigan invariably left us feeling bitter, angry and with a really sour taste in our mouths. But we had to smile after this because most fans and players knew we were within touching distance. There was no longer a gulf between the sides. We had the personnel to match them and they were young players too, coming into their prime with their best years in front of them. To underline that, the man-of-the-match award went to young hooker Keiron Cunningham – that was only the second time it had gone to a player picking up a loser's medal.

Coach Hughes talked about finishing the job, but suddenly he was gone and in came Shaun McRae. Hughes seemed to be getting things right, but the directors wanted somebody to take it to another level and there was a large degree of impatient desperation.

Scott Gibbs scores against Wigan in the centenary season home defeat in August 1995. (Platt)

Apollo Perelini is stopped short in the Regal Trophy Final against Wigan in January 1996. (Platt)

Challenge Cup Semi-Final versus Widnes at Wigan, 9 March 1996.

Top: Phil Veivers in action. The likeable Australian played in every cup round in 1996, but was sold to Huddersfield before the Wembley Final. (Platt)

Left: Karle Hammond in action against his hometown team. (Platt)

20. 1996 Good things come to those who wait

Salford 26 St Helens 46, 24 February 1996
Challenge Cup Quarter-Final

Warning - you are entering the rugby league twilight zone! The league season had ended but the Challenge Cup kicked off our 1996 season ahead of Super League.

An away tie at Castleford did not seem like the easiest of fixtures, but we walloped them piling on 58 points with Newy getting three tries. We banged a similar score past Rochdale Hornets in the next round with Sully getting the hat-trick. I was not at Spotland – but my mates told me the loudest, most euphoric cheer of the day came with the announcement of the result from The Willows. Wigan had lost to First Division Salford – their first Challenge Cup defeat after 43 unbeaten matches stretching back to February 1987.

It was a very costly defeat for Wigan, who seemed to bank on getting to Wembley every year. There had been a bit of a furore over why it had happened, with some pointing the finger at their pre-season preparation in Spain.

Salford were coached by Wigan legend Andy Gregory and had two former Saints in Mark Lee and Paul Forber playing a crucial role in that shock triumph.

After nearly two weeks of gloating came the cold realisation that Salford could do a similar job on us. The atmosphere pre-match was quite boisterous and bizarre in some respects. Eleven days previously boy band Take That had split up and unbelievably our massed ranks of young fans standing up on the terrace behind the sticks sang along in mocking tones to the group's last single *Back for Good.* For a moment or two I felt old.

The lads on the pitch made sure the travelling fans carried on hitting the right notes as Apollo Perelini erupted into action – blasting through for a spectacular solo try from the halfway line. He created three more as Saints seemed to have killed the game off with a flurry of points either side of the break. After leading 34-6 we sat back, went to sleep and allowed the Reds to score four tries cutting the deficit to a mere 12 points.

We need not have worried and Matautia and Newlove put it well beyond doubt when they both bagged their second scores of the day to book our semi-final berth.

My visits home were sporadic, but I knew I had been away too long when I tried to direct a taxi driver home from Warrington that night, but reached a dead end where the system had been altered. I got out and walked home. On other visits I also had trouble at the big roundabout that had sprung up at the junction of North Road, Duke Street and Ormskirk Street. The area became known as the Landings, with a mining monument in the middle. That name was also adopted by my old haunt the Rope & Anchor.

St Helens 24 Widnes 14, 9 March 1996
Challenge Cup Semi-Final

The vagaries of the train ticketing policies meant that it was £7 cheaper to travel from Brum to Wigan via Liverpool than it was to go direct. I mention this mundane fact because had I paid the extra money I would have had a much more boring day and would have used this part of the book to talk simply about how we saw off a plucky Widnes side to confidently bounce through to Wembley.

First though, the rugby: The semi-final draw was kind in many ways because although Widnes had plenty to prove having been cut out of the inaugural Super League, we just had too much class for them.

On a muddy Central Park pitch, it was a no frills win with our defence tackling like Trojans. Chris Joynt topped the count with 41 and Apollo Perelini pitched in with 33 crunching hits.

Tries from Alan Hunte, Karle Hammond, Andy Northey and Anthony Sullivan saw us home 24-14, with our full-back Steve Prescott earning the man-of-the-match award for the way he defused the Widnes bombs. After the game our Widnes-born skipper Bobbie Goulding went over to applaud Widdy fans in the Kop. It is fair to say he got a mixed response — especially from the gang of lads who had turned up wearing full white chemical suits and communicated their feelings in sign language.

Getting to a Wembley that would be missing Wigan for the first time in eight years gave us all a sense that we could win it. Even though a victory over Second Division Widnes had been predictable, unlike our previous two conquests of the Chemics at this stage, there was a real outpouring of exuberance on the final whistle and that spilled over going back into Wigan town centre. The Swan and Railway pub was packed with men and women cheering at our success and that continued for a few hours — and then it all turned sour.

We got a heavy hint from somewhere — maybe someone had shouted inside the pub - that it would be preferable for Saints fans to start vacating the Wigan town centre before the evening. That sounded sensible.

However, when we were boarding the train to St Helens an incident developed seemingly out of nothing when a police dog handler felt threatened by what he thought was a gang of drunken louts surrounding him. He must have called for assistance — and we were then treated as if we were a football mob on our way back to Millwall. The situation quickly spiralled out of control with the police back-up team storming the train and dragging people off.

There were a few on board who had probably had a few run-ins with the boys in blue — and some of them had shouted abuse out of the window - but the vast majority were law-abiding citizens, including many women with kids who were petrified by what was going on. Children who 10 minutes previously had been beaming now had tears streaming down their faces. It left a bad taste in the mouths of people who always expected the police to be the good guys. I actually felt sorry for the van-load of St Helens coppers waiting at Shaw Street at the other end, because they were swamped by those with grievances when our train emptied.

My train traumas had not finished though as I was heading back to Brum that night — a journey made difficult because of the previous day's fatal rail crash between a mail sorter and a freight train which caused the line to be shut at Stafford. Coming up it had meant quite a lengthy detour — and a four-and-a-half-hour journey.

Returning my carriage contained a dozen or so 30-something Coventry City football hooligans coming back from Everton. In the next carriage a mob of young Birmingham City fans, who were heading back from Tranmere, kept peering through with menacing hard-knock faces. The two groups did not mix, but glared at each other frequently on the way to the toilets.

As we got off at Stafford to change trains, one of the Coventry lads lost patience with the constant stares from one wannabe member of the 'Zulu army' and cracked him in the nose, causing blood to spurt everywhere. Trouble did not 'go off' straight away with the two sides bizarrely agreeing to sort it out in Brum as we boarded the slowest train in the world to New Street.

The stand-off led to a very tense journey and a touch of black humour came when a lad got on at Sutton Coldfield wearing an Aston Villa hat, which immediately unified the other two groups of lads in their hatred. The poor lad stood petrified in that little section between the carriages, just waiting for someone to deck him.

Having had my fill of mither that day I legged it off the train and up the escalators as soon as the train stopped at New Street. This time around, unlike at Wigan some five hours previously, there was not a dog handler in sight.

St Helens 41 Wigan 26, 5 April 1996
Super League

It seemed strange qualifying for the Challenge Cup Final and yet having the full new season ahead of us. Usually sides getting to Wembley could take their foot off the gas ahead of the big day – Saints had no such luxury as every point in the Super League was going to be vital. Once again, despite their blip in the Cup, Wigan were going to be the team to beat and they took a 16-4 lead on Good Friday to underline that.

We should have had more faith – with Danny Arnold grabbing his and our side's second try and when hooker Keiron Cunningham powered his way over Saints were right back in it. A neatly struck penalty from Bobbie Goulding put us level within a minute of the restart and then the fun really began with Ian Pickavance and Arnold's third being matched by two scores from the visitors in a game of cat-and-mouse. But this was ours with Tommy Martyn and Andy Northey tries completing a resounding 41-26 victory.

The pick of our tries came when Derek McVey bustled through the middle, Keiron was on his shoulder and took the offload bang on the half way line. His weaving run wrong footed full back Kris Radlinski. Although caught on the line, Cunningham managed to flick the ball up for Arnold who simply collected the ball and fell over the line. For the first time the Wiganers leaving the ground that day could see we were the future... but we had won no silverware yet.

It was a strange Easter programme, with no Widnes in the top flight, meaning we ventured to Headingley on Easter Monday where we walloped Leeds 46-26 with the free-scoring Arnold bagging two of our seven tries.

The Wigan game was only our second of the Super League season. Although the big competition had been launched in a blaze of glory in Paris, our opening date had been in the less glitzy surroundings of West Cumbria where we hammered Workington 62-0. The talk before Super League had always been about how we needed a strong Cumbrian team, given that our game was such a part of the sporting fabric of that county. However, this was a far from powerful team which was butchered by our rampant backs, with Paul Newlove bagging a hat-trick and the prolific Danny Arnold sailing in for four.

One of those scores came from Phil Veivers - his last try in his last game for the club. He was soon sold to Huddersfield for £12,500 where he took on the job as player-coach. Veivers had played in every round of the Cup, and probably deserved a farewell at Wembley but it was not to be. He gave a lot to his adopted club in nearly 12 years, playing a multitude of roles, it would have been a fitting tribute to see him collect a couple more medals for his trouble.

There is no place for sentiment in top-level rugby league – and at full-back Saints already had another hero in the making in Steve Prescott. And nobody bats an eyelid when you get rid of old favourites as long as you are winning. That is just what we did as we kept up the momentum going into the Cup Final.

The fixtures did not fall too kindly, with a trip to Thrum Hall, where bruisers Karl Harrison and Paul Moriarty and that slope lay in wait. But we escaped with a two point win and headed to Wembley with an unblemished record.

Bradford Bulls 32 St Helens 40, 27 April 1996
Challenge Cup Final, Wembley

Arriving in Central London via a National Express coach from Brum it was immediately noticeable that Bullmania had taken off. There were already hundreds of loud people with horns on their heads shouting on their team and they outnumbered our followers. They were new people too – and you could tell a few of them had not set foot in Odsal during their dark, dismal days as Bradford Northern.

I met my mates on the Greyhound pub car park – which made a change from the Olympic Torch. They were all there - Div, Ant, Andy, Kev, Mike, Shawy, Rob, Colky and Martin. Well, all apart from Dave, who had stuck to his guns about boycotting Saints. Our spirits were high and we kept ourselves topped up from the off-licence next door – nobody there saw that glorious sun-baked day ending in anything other than a Saints victory. Many of our fans were cocky – and some sported banners linking the Bulls to the BSE Mad Cow disease crisis which was rocking British agriculture. But after 56 minutes it looked as though it was going to be us getting tipped into the Wembley knacker's cart again.

It had started so promisingly and it looked as though being given the lucky away dressing room was paying off.

We had barely – and admittedly shakily – taken our seats when Bobbie Goulding's bomb exposed hesitancy between former Saint Loughlin and Jon Scales. That allowed Danny Arnold and Scott Gibbs to send Steve Prescott over for a try.

Prescott bagged his second after Goulding's boot had again done the damage. Unfortunately the Saints skipper missed both conversions so when Bulls rallied with a try through Scales and a penalty, it was level. Goulding was having an off day with place kicks, and a Paul Newlove break led to a Danny Arnold try. We were comfortable with that but on the stroke of half-time Bulls did a Wigan trick, with Robbie Paul scuttling in to send them in 14-12 up.

For the first time the butterflies started, and they turned into fully fledged jitters when former Saints player Bernard Dwyer bustled through three defenders for a try. Then it became absolute despair with Paul's second shake of the hips and wriggle. We stared into the abyss as the scoreboard taunted us with the words Bradford 26 St Helens 12. The lads either side of me, who had been through this so many times before during our bittersweet lives as supporters, were white with shock. "They are going to let us down again!" Suddenly our new breed of innocent heroes were being visited by the ghosts of previous Wembley failures – Noonan, Elia, O'Connor. I actually had my head in my hands at that stage because I knew that teams never lost an advantage like that in a Cup Final. There was a realisation that perhaps this was our destiny – and we would never win the Challenge Cup again. I had had my chance in 1976 and turned my nose up at it, so this was my payback for showing such ingratitude.

They were a pretty desperate, desolate, agonising few minutes - and then it happened! As we approached the last quarter Goulding struck gold as his sweet bomb was stupidly left to bounce by Bulls full-back Nathan Graham. Every kid at school is told never to let a ball bounce and Graham paid the ultimate price. Keiron Cunningham sprung into action to collect it and touch down. Having found the chink in the Bulls armour, Goulding picked at it and it paid dividends again and again with Simon Booth and then Ian Pickavance following suit over the whitewash. Remarkably, we were in front – and were suddenly delirious, jumping up and down as if we had won the National Lottery jackpot. This time the Bulls were shell-shocked as Nathan Graham penned his name indelibly into the Cup Final hall of shame. We cashed in with Gibbs and Karle Hammond sending Arnold in at the corner for his second.

But nothing is ever straightforward with Saints and just as we were about to hit celebration mode – the rollercoaster shot down again with Robbie Paul's dazzling solo effort from the halfway line. The effort earned Paul the Lance Todd Trophy and a £10,000 for the first ever Wembley hat-trick, but King Bobbie had crafted this win and deserved the honour. He won the game out of nothing and he provided the last pass to launch Apollo Perelini on a mission to the line five minutes from time which settled it once and for all. Whatever his faults, nobody can ever take Goulding's final away from him or from the fans for that matter.

It has subsequently been called the 'Ultimate Comeback' final – and it was a classic, but we have never been as pleased to hear a final hooter. It was our first Challenge Cup win in 20 years and boy did the town celebrate. They were hanging off every vantage point when the famous old cup was paraded round Victoria Square the following day. Every ledge, lamp post and step was occupied, and some even tried to scale the statue of the portly monarch to get a better view of the team on the town hall steps.

There was a real feel-good atmosphere in town and Busby's, the Nelson, Market and Sefton were packed that Sunday night with Mark Morrison's number one *Return of the Mack* ringing out from most turntables, but some sang it as 'Return of the Saints'.

London Broncos 28 St Helens 32, Super League
27 July 1996

In all other years we could have wallowed in the glory of winning the Challenge Cup with a lazy summer of self-congratulation. But there was no honeymoon period, we had a Super League to win.

Normally we would been content, nay overjoyed, with 'just' the cup, but as we kept on winning it dawned on us that failure to win the inaugural Super League would be a massive anti-climax particularly as Wigan had clearly set their stall out to do it.

And we had it all to do – with plenty of big games in front of us. One of those crunch games took place at Wilderspool in May where with five minutes remaining, Saints trailed by five points. Then Derek McVey bust a hole through the middle and with the cover streaming across, Pickavance's superb angled run took him under the sticks from 20 metres without a Wolves player laying a finger on him.

It was the sort of game Saints sides under Benyon, Murphy, McClennan and Hughes would have lost - defeats that have ultimately cost us titles, but this side under Shaun McRae were a lot more switched on and had a steelier under-belly.

May had actually seen a very rare occurrence – Saints fans were shouting for Wigan. The walls separating the two rugby codes had come tumbling down in 1995 with rugby union officially allowing professionalism. Wigan entered the Middlesex Sevens at

Wembley 1996: Bradford Bulls versus St Helens: Bobbie Goulding kicking. (Platt)

Wembley 1996: Steve Prescott celebrates one of his two tries against Bradford Bulls, with Scott Gibbs and Danny Arnold. (Platt)

Wembley 1996: Celebrating the remarkable victory over Bradford Bulls. (Platt)

Left: Ian Pickavance scores the crucial match winning try against Warrington at Wilderspool in May 1996. (Platt)

Twickenham and won hands down. They also took on rugby union champions Bath at both codes, winning the league event at Maine Road 82-6, before losing the union encounter at Twickenham 44-19, scoring the best tries and taking a moral victory.

So despite not winning the Cup for the first time nine years, Wigan were flavour of the month again – and it was a two-horse race between us and them for the title. It was tight at the top with Saints losing to Wigan and Bradford in a three-week spell at the end of June and the beginning of July.

However, London's Terry Matterson did us a massive favour by taking a point off Wigan with a touchline conversion in their game. It meant that all we had to do was carry on winning, which is easier said than done.

London had copped some flak over their fast-track promotion to Super League ahead of more worthy 'northern' candidates. But, boosted by a handful of quality imports, the Broncos showed they meant business and finished the season in fourth spot. Having drawn with Wigan, they wanted to add our scalp to their belts, so it was a crunch game.

It was televised on Sky on Saturday evening and I tried seven or eight pubs in Birmingham with satellite dishes, and got some funny looks when I asked if they would be showing the rugby league. I suppose it was one of the punishments for my lifestyle choice of living in a soccer mad city like Brum. The game was 25 minutes old by the time I found one – a rough and ready Irish pub in Sparkbrook – there was no sound, just the jukebox blaring out the Dubliners, Christy Moore and Planxty. But at least the small writing in the corner of the screen told us that Saints were winning 14-2.

You feel daft when you are the only person in a busy boozer gawping at an alien game in the corner. One bloke thought I was a 'copper's nark' and kept loudly slagging me off to his mate as an 'ear-wigging c..t.' As the sounds of Patsy Cline's *Crazy* drifted across that smoky, noisy tap room I think I knew exactly how she felt. All seemed lost when we trailed 22-14 going into last quarter, but tries from Vila Matautia and a blockbuster from Scott Gibbs gave us a four-point lead. However there were more twists with first Steve Rosolen's try, converted by Greg Barwick, restoring the Broncos' two-point lead. Then Saints had a chance to snatch a draw with a late penalty, but they spurned it and went for gold. It paid off, with Karle Hammond dropping Apollo Perelini off and he blasted over. He started his scoring movement on his back and side before momentum took him over, which just about enabled him to ground the ball. It was one for the video referee, which had been hailed as the big development that was going to solve all the arguments. It was a decision that would have a massive say in the title race and fortunately Apollo got the nod.

It was Gibbs's last game for Saints and he returned to Wales – a much better player than when he arrived. He later went on to star on the rugby union British Lions tour to South Africa and destroyed England's Grand Slam hopes with a match-winning try for the Welsh at Wembley. However, for Saints there were already ominous signs that we had already spent too much, because there no talk of an external replacement.

St Helens 68 Sheffield 2, 18 August 1996
Super League

It had been the first year of summer rugby – and with the season starting on the last day of March and finishing on August Bank Holiday weekend it was sunshine all the way.

It had been an eventful year too with a trip to Paris giving the fixture card a more cosmopolitan feel. Saints fans, who journeyed to the French capital in August by trains, boats and planes, made up their own lyrics for the trip home and to the tune of *Y Viva Espana* they sang, 'We all went to gay Paris - with Vila Matautia'.

For me it was a season of missing out – and I felt a bit detached when I returned from Brum. Things had moved on, the nature of the game had changed and so had the 'song sheets' of the speccies around me.

St Bernard the mascot was now a permanent feature as were the short blasts of music after tries were scored. It was all such a contrast to the 1970s when I first set foot on the terraces and the only music was a crackly version of 'When the Saints go marching in' cranked up through the public address system as the players ran out.

Now we also had former Saints scrum half and groundsman Neil Holding whipping up the crowd – and the match day experience was much more of an event. By only coming up for a few big league games, the cup games and the last few matches of the season I felt like someone who had fast forwarded a cracking film to the good bits. There was plenty on the pitch to marvel at – not least our left-side strike force of Anthony Sullivan, Paul Newlove and Chris Joynt.

All rounder Joynt had quick feet and hands and was simply devastating in attack, but also did his share of tackling. When I was a kid I had always been told that a running second-rower could shirk on the defensive work, to keep him fresh for what he has to do in attack. That was not the case with Joynty - he did the lot. That triumvirate of Sully, Newy and Joynty deservedly went on to enjoy long glittering careers with Saints.

But there were other players who played key roles that season - like Karle Hammond, who was only 21 at the start of that double winning year yet displayed great maturity at stand off and loose forward. There was a heavy sprinkling of youngsters throughout the team - Andy Leathem, Keiron Cunningham and Danny Arnold were all teenagers.

Up front big Australian Derek McVey was a tower of strength, and explosive Samoan Apollo Perelini really did come into his own on the firmer grounds of summer rugby league. There was plenty of back up from the often under rated workhorses like Ian Pickavance and Adam Fogerty - this was their season more than anybody else's.

And at the back, of course, there was Steve Prescott – a player with immense flair, skill and courage. He grabbed four tries in our penultimate game of the season when we thrashed Sheffield Eagles. One of those tries in particular showed the young full back's timing, eye for the ball and speed from 30 metres out when he launched himself after Goulding's precision kick. He leapt and wrestled it from the Sheffield full-back and winger to touch down, showing tremendous strength.

Adding to the rout were Sully and Karle Hammond, who both grabbed hat-tricks. It was one of the nine occasions during that Super League season that we had racked up more than 50 points in a match. Suddenly our massive points tally was a big plus. We had lost titles on points difference – but not this year. All we had to do was avoid defeat by Warrington on the last day of the season.

St Helens 66 Warrington 14, 26 August 1996
Super League

Our first league title in 21 years was within touching distance – ironically Saints legend Alex Murphy was the team manager of the Warrington side that could stop us completing the double. Murphy, of course, had been skipper of the Saints side that had last pulled this off back in 1966 - six months before I was even born. We all thought he would have something up his sleeve, but we need not have worried. Warrington had some talented players, including a young starlet called Paul Sculthorpe, but surely we would not let it slip now.

It was a Bank Holiday Monday and the sun was cracking the flags, encouraging a massive 18,098 crowd to squeeze into every nook and cranny of Knowsley Road. I got up there early and by the 2pm kick off it was heaving on the Scaff. It was just like the Wigan days of the late 1980s. There was even a smattering of Wiganers present, wearing their colours and hoping to see if the Wire could upset the applecart and hand them the title once again.

The atmosphere was buzzing with Neil Holding leading the chants. It had been the summer of Euro 96 and the first time around for *Three Lions* and the crowd bellowed in anticipation, "It's coming home, Super League's coming home!" I always preferred 'Hand it over pie-eaters' - a song we had sung many years without it ever coming to fruition.

Despite all Murphy's talk we knew our day had come after only a couple of minutes when Tommy Martyn caught a high ball to go over for a try. We racked up a 22-6 lead and the sun was really shining on us, particularly when Sully tracked back to knock the ball out of Richard Henare's hands when he was going in for a would-be six-pointer.

By half-time the game was as good as all over – the second half being a case of how many. Winger Alan Hunte bagged a hat-trick but it was the score by unsung hero Adam Fogerty, who fell over the line for the last one, which raised the loudest cheer.

There were a few blokes stood around me – like Simon Edmondson – who recalled seeing the last time Saints won the Championship before a much lower crowd in 1975.

Sometimes, during our lean years, I wondered whether it was actually harder for those fans who had been brought up on success to cope with our perennial disappointment. Sure, I did not have those memories to cherish and keep me going, but there was also an element of what you've not had you don't miss.

After the final whistle there was the inevitable roar from the crowd, as lifting the Super League was like winning the Cup all over again. The players disappeared down the tunnel and then the 'four cups' legends from 1966 came out to give the new breed the guard of honour – including Warrington manager Alex. He had enjoyed a love-hate relationship with his home town club, but he was cheered to the echo that afternoon.

Bobbie Goulding led his players out again to a rousing reception and lap of honour, with speeches and both trophies being paraded along the popular side. How many times had we suffered bitter disappointment – in League and Cup – while stood on those terraces? Well this feeling more than made up for those dark, dismal days.

We milked it big time – a few of us, tempting as it was to get straight into the pub, did not want to leave. I am glad we won it there – the scene of all that heartache and false dawns of the past. I am glad too that my mate Dave gave up his self imposed exile to join us – it was a triumph for all of us who had endured those often desperate times in the 1980s and 1990s.

After the parade, we crawled it into town – with the Bull, Nags, Golden Lion, Cricketers and the Liverpool Arms all visited before we hit the town centre. Things were going well and it was a lively session until somewhere between the Nelson and the Forum my mate was assaulted by a stranger, who did not wish to share the day's celebration. It happened so quickly that none of us saw it, but a swiftly delivered head-butt to the face had left Ant with a broken nose. Although the blood was pumping through his nostrils, Ant still gamely managed to get down the stairs in the Bullion and order the next round before being bundled off in a taxi home.

It put a slight dampener on the day, but it did not do him any permanent damage. I saw him a few weeks later and at about three in the morning we were among the last to leave a 'private party' at a town centre pub. Ant refused to leave until the landlord put Oasis's Wonderwall on one more time. He just wanted one last song before 1996 – our glorious year – was consigned to the pages of the history books. The landlord had to go through all the rigmarole of turning the jukebox back on to allow Ant to adapt the words of the Gallagher Brothers with:

All the passes Bobbie throws are blinding,
All the runs that Newy makes are winding.
Concluding with,
And after all, Wigan won f..k all!

It was not strictly true because they had beaten us in the Premiership Final, but for once we could dismiss that competition as a mere detail in the season. The Saints had won the ones that counted and were top dogs once again.

Left: Celebrating the 1996 Super League triumph. (Platt)

Below: Ian Pickavance, Bobbie Goulding and Paul Newlove with the Challenge Cup and Super League trophy. (Platt)

Appendix: Statistics and records

1977-78
League: Third P:30 W:22 D:1 L:7 F:678 A:384 Pts:45
Lancashire Cup: Semi-Final lost to Workington (A)
BBC2 Floodlit Trophy: Final lost to Hull KR (A)
John Player Trophy: Round 2 lost to Featherstone (A)
Challenge Cup: Final lost to Leeds
Premiership: Semi-Final lost to Bradford (two legs)
Top try scorer: Eddie Cunningham 30

1978-79
League: Fifth P:30 W:16 D:2 L:12 F:485 A:379 Pts:34
Lancashire Cup: Round 2 lost to Leigh (A)
BBC2 Floodlit Trophy: Final lost to Widnes (H)
John Player Trophy: Round 2 lost to Widnes (A)
Challenge Cup: Semi-Final lost to Wakefield
Premiership: Round 1 lost to Leeds (A)
Top try scorer: Roy Mathias 22

1979-80
League: Eighth P:30 W:15 D:2 L:13 F:505 A:410 Pts:32
Lancashire Cup: Round 1 lost to Widnes (H)
BBC2 Floodlit Trophy: Semi-Final lost to Hull KR (A)
John Player Trophy: Round 2 lost to Widnes (A)
Challenge Cup: Round 2 lost to Bradford (H)
Premiership: Round 1 lost to Bradford (A)
Top try scorers: Roy Mathias & Peter Glynn 27

1980-81
League: Eighth P:30 W:15 D:1 L:14 F:465 A:370 Pts:31
Lancashire Cup: Round 2 lost to Widnes (A)
John Player Trophy: Round 1 Warrington (H)
Challenge Cup: Semi-Final lost to Hull KR
Premiership: Semi-Final lost to Hull KR (A)
Top try scorer: Chris Arkwright 15

1981-82
League: Seventh P:30 W:17 D:1 L:12 F:465 A:415 Pts:35
Lancashire Cup: Semi-Final: lost to Leigh (A)
John Player Trophy: Round 1 replay lost to Barrow (A)
Challenge Cup: Round 1 lost to Wigan (H)
Premiership: Round 1 lost to Hull (A)
Top try scorer: Chris Arkwright & Roy Haggerty 12

1982-83
League: Fourth P:30 W:19 D:1 L:10 F:516 A:395 Pts:39
Lancashire Cup: Final lost to Warrington
John Player Trophy: Round 2 lost to Wigan (A)
Challenge Cup: Round 3 lost to Featherstone (H)
Premiership: Round 1 lost to Widnes (H)
Top try scorer: Roy Haggerty 21

1983-84
League: Sixth P:30 W:18 D:1 L:11 F:649 A:507 Pts:37
Lancashire Cup: Round 2 lost to Warrington (H)
John Player Trophy: Semi-Final lost to Widnes
Challenge Cup: Round 3 lost to Wigan (H)
Premiership: Semi-Final lost to Hull KR (A)
Top try scorer: Neil Holding 20

1984-85
League: Second P:30 W:22 D:1 L:7 F:920 A:508 Pts:45
Lancashire Cup: Won versus Wigan (A)
John Player Trophy: Round 3 lost to Halifax (H)
Challenge Cup: Round 1 lost to Hull KR (H)
Premiership: Won versus Hull KR
Top try scorer: Barrie Ledger 33

1985-86
League: Third P:30 W:20 D:2 L:8 F:729 A:503 Pts:42
Lancashire Cup: Semi-Final lost to Wigan (A)
John Player Trophy: Semi-Final lost to Hull KR
Challenge Cup: Round 2 lost to Wigan (A)
Premiership: Round 1 lost to Leeds (H)
Top try scorer: Roy Haggerty 21

1986-87
League: Second P:30 W:20 D:1 L:9 F:835 A:465 Pts:41
Lancashire Cup: Semi-Final lost to Wigan (A)
John Player Trophy: Round 3 lost to Warrington (H)
Challenge Cup: Final lost to Halifax
Premiership: Semi-Final lost to Warrington (H)
Top try scorer: Barrie Ledger 24

1987-88
League: Second P:26 W:18 D:0 L:8 F:672 A:337 Pts:36
Lancashire Cup: Round 1 lost to Leigh (A)
John Player Trophy: Won versus Leeds
Challenge Cup: Round 3 lost to Salford (A)
Premiership: Final lost to Widnes
Top try scorer: Mark Elia 20

1988-89
League: Seventh P:26 W:12 D:1 L:13 F:513 A:529 Pts:25
Lancashire Cup: Round 1 lost to Widnes (A)
John Player Trophy: Semi-Final lost to Widnes
Challenge Cup: Final lost to Wigan
Premiership: Semi-Final lost to Widnes (A)
Top try scorer: Les Quirk 25

1989-90
League: Fifth P:26 W:17 D:0 L:9 F:714 A:544 Pts:34
Lancashire Cup: Round 2 lost to Oldham (H)
Regal Trophy: Semi-Final lost to Halifax

Challenge Cup: Semi-Final lost to Wigan
Premiership: Round 1 lost to Bradford (A)
Top try scorer: Alan Hunte 24

1990-91
League: Sixth P:26 W:14 D:1 L:11 F:628 A:533 Pts:29
Lancashire Cup: Round 2 lost to Salford (A)
Regal Trophy: Round 3 lost to Warrington (A)
Challenge Cup: Final lost to Wigan
Premiership: Round 1 lost to Hull (A)
Top try scorer: Alan Hunte & Les Quirk 26

1991-92
League: Second P:26 W:17 D:2 L:7 F:550 A: 388 Pts:36
Lancashire Cup: Won versus Rochdale
Regal Trophy: Semi-Final lost to Widnes
Challenge Cup: Round 3 lost to Wigan (H)
Premiership: Final lost to Wigan
Top try scorer: Alan Hunte 25

1992-93
League: Second P:26 W:20 D:1 L:5 F:632 A: 345 Pts:41
Lancashire Cup: Final lost to Wigan (H)
Regal Trophy: Round 3 lost to Castleford (H)
Challenge Cup: Round 2 lost to Wigan (A)
Premiership: Won versus Wigan
Top try scorer: Alan Hunte 31

1993-94
League: Eighth P:30 W:15 D:1 L:14 F:704 A: 537 Pts:31
Regal Trophy: Round 3 lost to Warrington (H)
Challenge Cup: Semi-Final lost to Leeds
Premiership: Round 1 lost to Wigan (A)
Top try scorer: Anthony Sullivan 24

1994-95
League: Fourth P:30 W:20 D:1 L:9 F:893 A:640 Pts:41
Regal Trophy: Round 4 lost to Wigan (A)
Challenge Cup: Round 4, replay lost to Wigan (H)
Premiership: Semi-Final lost to Leeds (A)
Top try scorer: Alan Hunte 30

1995-96
League: Fourth P:20 W:12 D:0 L:8 F:732 A:508 Pts:24
Regal Trophy: Final lost to Wigan
Top try scorer: Anthony Sullivan 23

1996
League: Champions P:22 W:20 D:0 L:2 F:950 A:455 Pts:40
Challenge Cup: Won versus Bradford
Premiership: Final lost to Wigan
Top try scorer: Paul Newlove 36